T0214859

# Communications in Computer and Information Science 972

*Commenced Publication in 2007*
Founding and Former Series Editors:
Phoebe Chen, Alfredo Cuzzocrea, Xiaoyong Du, Orhun Kara, Ting Liu,
Dominik Ślęzak, and Xiaokang Yang

## Editorial Board

More information about this series at http://www.springer.com/series/7899

Quan Yu (Ed.)

# Space Information Networks

Third International Conference, SINC 2018
Changchun, China, August 9–10, 2018
Revised Selected Papers

 Springer

*Editor*
Quan Yu
PLA Academy of Military Science
Beijing, China

ISSN 1865-0929          ISSN 1865-0937   (electronic)
Communications in Computer and Information Science
ISBN 978-981-13-5936-1        ISBN 978-981-13-5937-8   (eBook)
https://doi.org/10.1007/978-981-13-5937-8

Library of Congress Control Number: 2018967959

This Springer imprint is published by the registered company Springer Nature Singapore Pte Ltd.
The registered company address is: 152 Beach Road, #21-01/04 Gateway East, Singapore 189721, Singapore

# Preface

The Space Information Network Conference is the annual conference of the Department of Information Science, National Natural Science Foundation of China. SINC is supported by the key research project on the basic theory and key technology of space information networks of the National Natural Science Foundation of China, and organized by the "Space Information Network" major research program guidance group, in order to explore the progress and development tendency of the space information network and related fields, to show the latest technology and academic achievements in the space information network, to build a platform for the academic exchange of researchers at home and abroad in the space information network and industry sectors, to share the achievements and experiences in research and application, and to discuss the new theory and new technology of the space information network. There are three sections in the proceedings of SINC 2018, including "Architecture and Efficient Networking Mechanisms," "Theories and Methods of High-Speed Transmission," and "Sparse Characterization and Fusion Processing."

This year, SINC received 140 submissions, including 98 English papers and 42 Chinese papers. After a thorough reviewing process, 24 outstanding English papers were selected for this volume (retrieved by EI), accounting for 29.6% of the total number of English papers. 23 of the 24 English papers are included in this volume.

The high-quality program would not have been possible without the authors who chose SINC 2018 as a venue for their publications. We are also very grateful to the Academic Committee members and Organizing Committee members, who put a tremendous amount of effort into soliciting and selecting research papers with a balance of high quality and new ideas and new applications.

We hope that you enjoy reading and benefit from the proceedings of SINC 2018.

November 2018

Quan Yu

# Organization

SINC 2018 was organized by the Department of Information Science, National Natural Science Foundation of China, Changchun University of Science and Technology, Jilin University, and PTPress.

## Organizing Committee

### General Chairs

| | |
|---|---|
| Quan Yu | PLA Academy of Military Science, China |
| Jianya Gong | Wuhan University, China |
| Jianhua Lu | Tsinghua University, China |

### Steering Committee

| | |
|---|---|
| Zhixin Zhou | Beijing Institute of Remote Sensing Information, China |
| Hsiao-Hwa Chen | National Cheng Kung University, Taiwan, China |
| George K. Karagiannidis | Aristotle University of Thessaloniki, Greece |
| Xiaohu You | Southeast University, China |
| Dongjin Wang | University of Science and Technology of China, China |
| Jun Zhang | Beihang University, China |
| Haitao Wu | Chinese Academy of Sciences, China |
| Jianwei Liu | Beihang University, China |
| Zhaotian Zhang | National Natural Science Foundation of China, China |
| Xiaoyun Xiong | National Natural Science Foundation of China, China |
| Zhaohui Song | National Natural Science Foundation of China, China |
| Ning Ge | Tsinghua University, China |
| Feng Liu | Beihang University, China |
| Mi Wang | Wuhan University, China |
| Changwen Chen | The State University of New York at Buffalo, USA |
| Ronghong Jin | Shanghai Jiao Tong University, China |

## Technical Program Committee

| | |
|---|---|
| Jian Yan | Tsinghua University, China |
| Min Sheng | Xidian University, China |
| Junfeng Wang | Sichuan University, China |
| Depeng Jin | Tsinghua University, China |
| Hongyan Li | Xidian University, China |
| Qinyu Zhang | Harbin Institute of Technology, China |

| | |
|---|---|
| Qingyang Song | Northeastern University, China |
| Lixiang Liu | Chinese Academy of Sciences, China |
| Weidong Wang | Beijing University of Posts and Telecommunications, China |
| Chundong She | Beijing University of Posts and Telecommunications, China |
| Zhihua Yang | Harbin Institute of Technology, Shenzhen, China |
| Minjian Zhao | Zhejiang University, China |
| Yong Ren | Tsinghua University, China |
| Yingkui Gong | University of Chinese Academy of Sciences, China |
| Xianbin Cao | Beihang University, China |
| Chengsheng Pan | Dalian University, China |
| Shuyuan Yang | Xidian University, China |
| Xiaoming Tao | Tsinghua University, China |

## Organizing Committee

| | |
|---|---|
| Chunhong Pan | Chinese Academy of Sciences, China |
| Yafeng Zhan | Tsinghua University, China |
| Liuguo Yin | Tsinghua University, China |
| Jinho Choi | Gwangju Institute of Science and Technology, South Korea |
| Yuguang Fang | University of Florida, USA |
| Lajos Hanzo | University of Southampton, UK |
| Jianhua He | Aston University, UK |
| Y. Thomas Hou | Virginia Polytechnic Institute and State University, USA |
| Ahmed Kamal | Iowa State University, USA |
| Nei Kato | Tohoku University, Japan |
| Geoffrey Ye Li | Georgia Institute of Technology, USA |
| Jiandong Li | Xidian University, China |
| Shaoqian Li | University of Electronic Science and Technology of China, China |
| Jianfeng Ma | Xidian University, China |
| Xiao Ma | Sun Yat-sen University, China |
| Shiwen Mao | Auburn University, USA |
| Luoming Meng | Beijing University of Posts and Telecommunications, China |
| Joseph Mitola | Stevens Institute of Technology, USA |
| Sherman Shen | University of Waterloo, Canada |
| Zhongxiang Shen | Nanyang Technological University, Singapore |
| William Shieh | University of Melbourne, Australia |
| Meixia Tao | Shanghai Jiao Tong University, China |
| Xinbing Wang | Shanghai Jiao Tong University, China |
| Feng Wu | University of Science and Technology of China, China |
| Jianping Wu | Tsinghua University, China |
| Xianggen Xia | University of Delaware, USA |

| | |
|---|---|
| Hongke Zhang | Beijing Jiaotong University, China |
| Youping Zhao | Beijing Jiaotong University, China |
| Hongbo Zhu | Nanjing University of Posts and Telecommunications, China |
| Weiping Zhu | Concordia University, Canada |
| Lin Bai | Beihang University, China |
| Shaohua Yu | FiberHome Technologies Group, China |
| Honggang Zhang | Zhejiang University, China |
| Shaoqiu Xiao | University of Electronic Science and Technology of China, China |

# Contents

# Architecture and Efficient Networking Mechanism

# Blockchain Application in Space Information Network Security

Shaochi Cheng[1(⊠)], Yuan Gao[1,3], Xiangyang Li[1], Yanchang Du[1],
Yang Du[1], and Su Hu[2]

[1] PLA Academy of Military Science, Beijing 100091, China
csc04@tsinghua.org.cn
[2] University of Electrical Science and Technology of China,
Chengdu 610054, Sichuan, China
[3] State Key Laboratory on Microwave and Digital Communications,
National Laboratory for Information Science and Technology,
Tsinghua University, Beijing 100084, China

**Abstract.** With the rapid growth of satellite communications, space information network based on various aerospace equipment and corresponding ground equipment, is considered to have broad application prospects. However, since nodes of space information network are susceptible to a variety of cyber & physical attacks, security in space information network gives rise to a great concern. This paper proposes blockchain application in space information network security and some problems that might arise.

**Keywords:** Blockchain · Space information network · Security

## 1 Introduction

With the rapid growth of satellite communications, space information network which is based on communication satellite constellation and includes various aerospace equipment and corresponding ground equipment, is considered to have broad application prospects. However, since nodes of space information network are susceptible to a variety of cyber & physical attacks, security in space information network gives rise to a great concern.

Kang analyzed cyberspace threat to space information network and proposed a new situation awareness and information defense strategy by combining multi-domain approaches [1]. In [2], a secure and reliable big data communication scheme which selects multipaths and transmits data in parallel according to the requirements of network reliability was proposed. Dawei Li proposed a new cryptosystem in which private keys can be generated from PKG or corresponding superior in the upper layer for cluster organized space information network [3]. Weiwei Zhao put forward an authentication protocol for space information network [4]. Yuchen Liu proposed an anonymous distributed key management system for space information network [5]. Wang K presented a basic framework for the key distribution in the space network [6].

From the above we can see that previous studies on security in the space network paid attention to key exchange, authentication and routing protocols, which rely

© Springer Nature Singapore Pte Ltd. 2019
Q. Yu (Ed.): SINC 2018, CCIS 972, pp. 3–9, 2019.
https://doi.org/10.1007/978-981-13-5937-8_1

heavily on centralized cloud. Centralized nodes of the space information network are vulnerable to cyber & physical attacks, we need additional methods to strengthen the security of the space information network. In this paper, we propose blockchain application in space information network security, including areas, advantages and challenges of application.

The rest of this paper is organized as follows: In Sect. 2 we review the development of blockchain. Section 3 gives a discussion of blockchain in space. The proposed blockchain applications in space information network security are given in Sect. 4. Section 5 analyzes the challenges of blockchain application in space information network security. Finally, we conclude the paper in Sect. 6.

## 2   Development of Blockchain

Blockchain is a decentralized and distributed database which was invented by Satoshi Nakamoto in 2008 [7]. It is composed of a list of records called blocks which are linked using cryptography and in chronological order. Once recorded, the data in any given block are impossible or extremely difficult to change or remove. The development of blockchain could be divided into three phases. In the first phase which is known as blockchain 1.0, blockchain is the decentralized transparent ledger with the transaction records of the digital currency, which could achieve the avoidance of being spent twice by the same person without requiring a trusted authority such as banks. Blockchain 2.0 refers to the decentralization of market, by smart contracts which are based on programs that function on predetermined conditions between the supplier and the client, escrow transactions, bonded contracts, third party arbitration, multiparty signatures and smart property exchange are supported in real time at near zero marginal cost. Blockchain 3.0 is not clearly defined, but it must include coordination applications beyond currency, economics, and markets, such as government, health, science and education.

## 3   Blockchain in Space

Blockchain has begun to apply in space and made some progress [8]. On August 15, Blockstream, a blockchain technology company, leased bandwidth on satellites to broadcast real-time Bitcoin blockchain data from space. The Blockstream Satellite network currently consists of three geosynchronous satellites: Galaxy 18 at longitude 123 W, Eutelsat 113 at longitude 113 W and Telstar 11 N satellite at longitude 37.5 W. It could cover across two-thirds of the Earth's landmass and enable Bitcoin users in Africa, Europe, South America and North America to download Bitcoin blockchain data. Blockstream Satellites allow for one-way communication and give users a way to receive new blocks. In the future, Blockstream plan to lease a fourth satellite to cover Asia, and 99.999996% of the world's population could receive blockchain data from Blockstream Satellites [9]. In addition, Nexus Earth, an innovative open source blockchain technology company, plans to deploy its own low Earth orbit satellite network to support the distribution and use of its NXS cryptocurrency in

2019. The low Earth orbit satellite network would consist of two layers: a relay layer and an outer processing and storage layer. It is estimated that 300 cubesats could achieve global coverage. Nexus envisions thousands of cubesats by 2025 [10]. Nexus satellites would act as nodes of the Nexus blockchain. Third-party applications could be hosted on satellites, and customers could pay for these third-party services using NXS cryptocurrency (Fig. 1).

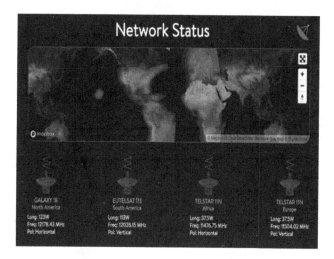

**Fig. 1.** Blockstream satellites network status [11]

# 4 Blockchain Application in Space Information Network Security

## 4.1 Identification

Generally, nodes of space information network could be divided into different mission areas, and in terms of positions, some nodes could be clustered. For example, some satellites are GEO satellites, and others orbit in LEO or MEO circles around earth. As a result, there are various inner-satellite links, inner-orbital links and user data links. Plus, aerospace equipment could irregularly participate in communications in cluster organized space information network (Fig. 2).

Members in this system need authenticated key exchange to resist cyber attacks from Man-in-the middle [12]. Nodes of space information network could use asymmetric key encryption to create identities on a blockchain, and only those with the private key can decrypt data encrypted with the public key [13]. Plus, every block on a blockchain has a timestamp, and hash values are used to connect blocks. When asymmetric key encryption is used to validate identities, any alternations to records will change the blockchain as a whole, which is almost impossible.

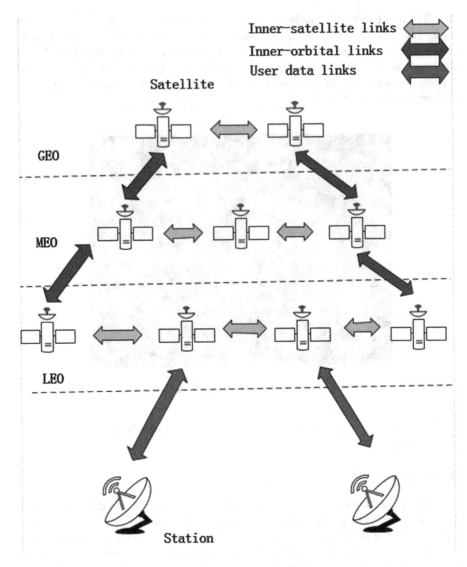

**Fig. 2.** Communications in space information network

## 4.2   Self-reconfiguration

Typically, the relative positions of communication satellite constellation and various aerospace equipment in the space information network are constantly changing, which could result in the failure of communication links. Plus, if some satellites are hit by cyber & physical attacks, some communication links connecting among these satellites could not work. In this case, we might spend a large amount of time detecting and solving the problem, which could cause a long interruption in communications in certain areas. If nodes of space information network are self-configurable, when some nodes are disabled, the neighboring nodes could automatically take the place of the failure node, the resilience of the space information network would definitely improve [14]. Blockchain could use smart contracts which is a software program that is capable of self-executing to improve the resilience of space information network. The orbits of satellites are determined before their launch, at any given moment, the relative positions of satellites could be predicted. By smart contracts, we could allow some satellites which are likely to approach each other at some time to cluster automatically at given time. In this way, even if the ground station which is responsible to control the satellites is hit by cyber attack, satellites could still create communication links by themselves using the program of smart contracts. Plus, smart contracts on a blockchain is hard to tamper, attackers who are trying to tamper the control instructions of satellites from ground stations could not change organization schemes of satellites written in smart contracts. When some satellites failed due to attack, the neighboring satellites could take the place of the failure node automatically by smart contracts and achieve self-reconfiguration of space information network in a very short time, which is conducive to maintaining the stability of space information network.

### 4.3 Decentralization

Nodes of space information network are distributed everywhere, and the weight of nodes varies greatly. For instance, GEO satellites are the backbone of space information network, large data transmission relies heavily these satellites. However, the positions of GEO satellites are almost fixed, they are vulnerable to intentional cyber & physical attacks. Plus, some MEO satellites are important routing nodes of space information network that receive and transmit more data than ordinary nodes, attackers could eavesdrop and detect these nodes, and then use cyber attacks to jam the communication of network at a small cost. Blockchain is based on P2P network and could achieve decentralized data storage and transmission. Nodes of space information network could be divided into different clusters according to their abilities of data storage and transmission, and nodes at the same level could form a blockchain according to spatio-temporal correlation. This would achieve decentralization to some extent, reducing the bad influences of Single-point Fault.

## 5  Challenges

### 5.1  Storage

Generally, blockchain requires every node store the whole blockchain. However, the major of nodes of space information network have a limited storage capacity. As new data is written on the blockchain, some nodes could not store the whole blockchain. As a result, there is a need for a new method of storing the whole blockchain. For example, we could deploy some space & aerospace equipment and corresponding ground equipment to store the whole blockchain specifically. This method needs a detailed research on dynamic change of the topological structure of space information network, thus optimizing the deployment of the storage node.

## 5.2   Consensus

Blockchain is based on consensus algorithms which determine nodes that have rights to create new blocks. Currently, Proof-of-Work, Proof-of-Stake, Delegated Proof of Stake and Practical Byzantine Fault Tolerance are the most common consensus algorithms. Proof-of-Work needs all nodes to compete in the computing power, which would cause huge waste of computing resources. Proof-of-Stake and Delegated Proof of Stake could save some computing power by assigning some nodes to compete for creating new blocks, but they would still waste the computing resources of network. Furthermore, as for Proof-of-Work, Proof-of-Stake, Delegated Proof of Stake, the more computing power nodes have, the greater possibility they create new blocks. It is unsuitable for space information network because different nodes have different computing power naturally, in the end, the rights of creating new blocks would definitely centralize on nodes that have more computing power, which is contrary to decentralization. Practical Byzantine Fault Tolerance could avoid the competition of computing power, but if $(N-1)/3$ nodes are attacked, a blockchain would not work. From the above, we can see that consensus algorithms that are suitable for space information network need further research [15].

## 5.3   Transmission Delay

Space information network generally includes GEO, MEO and LEO satellites. Data transmission delay between GEO satellites and users on earth approximates 250 ms–280 ms, MEO satellites and users 100 ms, LEO satellites and users 10 ms–40 ms. Transmission delay could create a situation in which a node that should have got the right to create new blocks is not validated by other nodes. In addition, current blockchain technology requires spending about 10 min creating a new block, but the visible time between nodes of space information network such as two LEO satellites is probably less than 10 min, which cause losing the possibility of creating blocks. For this reason, applying blockchain in space information network requires solving the problems that data transmission delay and limited visible time between nodes make.

## 6   Conclusion

In this paper, we discuss the development of blockchain and its characteristics in every phase. Furthermore, we detailed current blockchain in space, and found that existing blockchain application focused on broadcasting cryptocurrency data. Then we analyzed several potential blockchain applications in space information network security, including identification, self-reconfiguration and decentralization. On this basis, we listed a variety of challenges that result from blockchain application in space information network security and proposed further research areas.

**Acknowledge.** This work is funded by National Natural Science Foundation of China (61701503). The work of Su Hu was jointly supported by the MOST Program of International S&T Cooperation (Grant No. 2016YFE0123200), National Natural Science Foundation of China (Grant No. 61471100/61101090/61571082), Science and Technology on Electronic Information

Control Laboratory (Grant No. 6142105040103) and Fundamental Research Funds for the Central Universities (Grant No. ZYGX2015J012/ZYGX2014Z005). We would like to thank all the reviewers for their kind suggestions to this work.

# References

1. Kang, S., et al.: Space information security and cyberspace defense technology. In: 2013 IEEE International Conference on Green Computing and Communications and IEEE Internet of Things and IEEE Cyber, Physical and Social Computing, pp. 1509–1511 (2013)
2. Geng, R., et al.: A reliable big data transmission algorithm for space information network. In: 2016 IEEE International Conference on Internet of Things (iThings) and IEEE Green Computing and Communications (GreenCom) and IEEE Cyber, Physical and Social Computing (CPSCom) and IEEE Smart Data (SmartData), pp. 888–893 (2016)
3. Li, D., et al.: Secure and anonymous data transmission system for cluster organised space information network. In: 2016 IEEE International Conference on Smart Cloud (Smart-Cloud), pp. 228–233 (2016)
4. Zhao, W., et al.: Analysis and design of an authentication protocol for space information network. In: 2016 IEEE Military Communications Conference, MILCOM 2016, pp. 43–48 (2016)
5. Liu, Y., et al.: An anonymous distributed key management system based on CL-PKC for space information network. In: 2016 IEEE International Conference on Communications (ICC), pp. 1–7 (2016)
6. Wang, K., et al.: An agile reconfigurable key distribution scheme in space information network. In: 2007 2nd IEEE Conference on Industrial Electronics and Applications, pp. 2742–2747 (2007)
7. WIKIPEDIA. Blockchain [EB/OL]. https://en.wikipedia.org/wiki/Blockchain
8. Doug Mohney. Blockchain in Space [EB/OL]. http://www.techzone360.com/topics/techzone/articles/2018/04/10/437785-blockcha-space.htm
9. Blockstream. Blockstream Satellite FAQ [EB/OL]. https://blockstream.com/satellite/faq/
10. Nexusearth. SATELLITE NETWORK [EB/OL]. https://nexusearth.com/nexus-satellite-network
11. Blockstream. Network Status [EB/OL]. https://www.blockstream.com/satellite/satellite/
12. Yantao, Z.: Research on Key Issues of Security in Space Information Networks. Xidian University, Xi'an (2011)
13. Jaikaran, C.: Blockchain: Background and Policy Issues [EB/OL]. https://fas.org/sgp/crs/misc/R45116.pdf
14. Xipeng, Z.: Design and implementation of space information network topology reconstruction scheme. Northeastern University, Shenyang (2009)
15. Castro, M., Liskov, B.: Practical byzantine fault tolerance and proactive recovery. ACM Trans. Comput. Syst. 20(4), 398–461 (2002). Association for Computing Machinery

# Blockchain Based Distributed Network Architecture

Yanchang Du[✉], Xiangyang Li, Shaochi Cheng, and Yang Guo

PLA Academy of Military Science, Beijing 100091, China
duyanchang198@163.com

**Abstract.** Blockchain, as an emerging information technology, can transmits trusted data in untrusted networks. As a overlay network, blockchain based network can be used to construct low-cost distributed networks. It has the characteristics of non-destructive and transparent transmission. Blockchain based network architecture can be divided into: infrastructure layer, network layer, transport layer and application layer, and it has the potential changing the network security paradigm and the existing Internet operating mode. But as an immature technology, the blockchain network still faces great challenge in information security, privacy protection and communication bandwidth.

**Keywords:** Blockchain · Distributed network · Architecture · Network security · Privacy protection

## 1 Introduction

At present, computer networking has penetrated into all aspects of human society. Especially with the development of Internet of Things (IoT), we are gradually living in an era of interconnectedness. However, it is unrealistic to high-effectively deal with data management and communication in a single-central complex, large-scale computer network system. All these need a decentralized distributed peer to peer network system which should be dynamically scalable, self-adaptive, flat, and can deal with a large number of data interaction, information distributing and collaborative computing.

The blockchain was first proposed by Nakamoto in the "Bitcoin: A Peer-to-Peer Electronic Cash System" in 2009 [1], and was successfully applied in Bitcoin for the first time. As a distributed ledger, blockchain ensures that the ledger can't be practically controlled by any one entity or node, eliminates the possibility of failure of single-node, and allows for the verification of transactions without the need for a trusted third-party intervention. Since each interaction is public, blockchain technology offers a reliable, incorruptible transaction-based infrastructure and the value it provides isn't just limited to cryptocurrency.

The blockchain creatively implements reliable information exchange in unreliable networks, support low-cost decentralized distributed network which featuring tamper resistance, high availability, and transparency, and can be seen a breakthrough technology that will lead to the next generation of information and communication technology (ICT) [2].

© Springer Nature Singapore Pte Ltd. 2019
Q. Yu (Ed.): SINC 2018, CCIS 972, pp. 10–14, 2019.
https://doi.org/10.1007/978-981-13-5937-8_2

# 2 Blockchain Based Distributed Network Architecture

Blockchain network is an overlay network architecture, relies on peer-to-peer connections between nodes, including validators that produce information blocks and store the entire blockchain list [3]. According to computer networks architecture, blockchain network can be roughly divided into the following four layers.

## 2.1 Infrastructure Layer

It mainly includes a large amount of existing Internet infrastructure, especially PCs, which can be seen as nodes in the network. For blockchain network, it does not require the deployment of a large number of expensive centralized storage facilities and network facilities. As nodes, Masses of sensors can access the blockchain network to form a decentralized, trusted distributed network, forming a self-organizing, self-adaptive network system.

## 2.2 Network Layer

The network layer is a peer-to-peer network architecture, includes networking mechanism, data propagation mechanism, and data verification mechanism, which build the network channel. The blockchain network is not a layered network architecture, but a plat organizational structure, and have a scalable feature. Any node can access or exit the network at any time. Any node can verifies the received data and transmits only the verified data.

## 2.3 Transport Layer

The transport layer contains consensus mechanisms and incentive mechanisms (not necessary), and transact defined data structure. Blockchain network use a joint verification mechanism to realize consensus mechanism, which can quickly, efficiently, and securely verify blockchain data, ensuring information consistency and tamper-proof. The data structure contains asymmetric encryption, timestamp, hash algorithm, and Markel tree, providing the block sourcing address and targeting address.

## 2.4 Application Layer

The blockchain is initially applied to Digital Currency and is currently entering into the blockchain 2.0 era represented by Ethereum [4]. The applications area of blockchain network include digital finance, knowledge management, and anonymous security communications [5]. the blockchain is expanding into other areas such as intelligent transportation systems (ITS) [6], autonomous unmanned systems, Supply chain management, internet of things (IoT) [7].

# 3   The Feature of Blockchain Based Network

The problems that distributed systems usually require to solve are consistency, availability, and partition fault tolerance. These issues have become major challenges for large-scale distributed systems. Blockchains network features decentralization, flexible networking, tamper proof, anonymity, trust translation, which represent the development direction of large-scale Internet.

## 3.1   Change the Network Security Paradigm

Traditional data storage and network-controlling often rely on trusted central entities. Management defects or attacks on the central node may lead to terribly network security problem. Blockchain network have a more robust security. First, the blockchain network does not use a centralized defense strategy. It uses consensus mechanism to ensure reliable transmission of data in an unreliable network environment. Second, it uses asymmetric encryption mechanisms and digital signatures to ensure data credibility. In a blockchain network, each node must be able to perform data authentication & verification, and through a consensus mechanism and Hash algorithm to ensure that the data can't be tampered. Any attempt to tamper with any part of the blockchain is apparent immediately—because the new hash will not match the old ones [8]. Third, the blockchain has strong fault tolerance. With the consensus of most trusted nodes, a few malicious nodes can't destroy or degrade the network. The blockchain network security strategy will change data management, IoT device permissions and communication management, and other aspects, change the network security paradigm [9].

## 3.2   Change the Current Internet Mode

At present, the existing Internet mainly adopts the Client/Servers(C/S) architecture. This makes it easy for attackers to lock the terminals or servers, and conduct targeted fraud. Blockchain technology migrate the core network functions of the network, such as routing, data storage, and network computing, to the edge of the network. More independent network edge nodes will change the collaborative mode of the entire network, improve the flexibility of the network and the stability of communications, and reduce the cost of network access.

Blockchain based network has the characteristics of decentralization and dynamic configuration, which can improve network flexibility and redundancy and simplify network management functions. Although the blockchain P2P network topology will increase the routing overhead in the entire network, but the network overhead is sparse in both time and space.

# 4   The Challenges

## 4.1   Information Security Issues

The security of blockchain networks needs to build security systems around physics, data, applications, and encryption. Affecting the blockchain security includes four aspects [10]: cryptographic algorithm security, network protocol security, usage security, and system security. Password security is affected by high-performance computing and quantum computing; protocol security involves the design of consensus algorithms; the application security mainly comes from user key management; system security issues mainly come from system security vulnerabilities.

## 4.2  Privacy Protection

Blockchain technology is also faced with issues such as privacy leakage problem. In the traditional centralized IT architecture, privacy protection is mainly through data encryption and ensuring that data is not leaked. In the blockchain, privacy protection includes identity privacy and transaction privacy, which corresponds to address information and data information in the network [11]. The data is transparent to all nodes in blockchain network, and any node can verify the data. In other words, the data stored in blockchain is accessible to all nodes in the network. The attacker can monitor the communication of the entire network, obtain the data of the network layer and the application layer, and steal the privacy information of the user through various analysis methods.

## 4.3  Network Applicability

Currently, blockchain is now built around specific applications. The blockchain must develop the underlying network transport protocols to form a Protocol-agnostic network solution that solves the blockchain scalability problem, without having to consider the existing blockchain application model.

If blockchain protocols become a common basic network protocol for the Internet, there is still require extensive research in domain name management and network protocols [12].

Blockchain networks also lack adequate tiers of authority management. In some application scenarios, such as military communications, trade secret transmissions, and citizen healthcare data storage, it is necessary to transfer encrypted data in layers. Without affecting the consensus mechanism, how to reduce data transparency and ensure data confidentiality has become an important issue in the development of blockchain technology.

As time passes, blockchain data will grow rapidly, which may result in some nodes failing to accommodate whole data, resulting in fewer and fewer stable operating nodes, blockchain networks tending to be centralized, and triggering a blockchain crisis.

## 4.4  Communication Bandwidth

Consensus mechanism, block size, block fork and other factors, make the capability of network interaction and data throughput is relatively low in blockchain network. A blockchain transaction always takes more time to process than a conventional transaction. With the increase of the number of nodes, a large number of data are frequently interacted, which imposes higher requirements on network bandwidth. it is a challenge to decrease the latency and improve processing speed in the blockchain network.

# References

1. Nakamoto, S.: Bitcoin: a peer-to-peer electronic cash system. [EB/OL], [2018-06-25] (2008). https://bitcoin.rg/bitcoin.pdf. Accessed 22 Jan 2018
2. Kogure, J., Kamakura, K., Shima, T., Kubo, T.: Blockchain Technology for Next Generation ICT [EB/OL], 25 June 2018. https://www.fujitsu.com/global/documents/about/resources/publications/fstj/archives/vol53-5/paper09.pdf
3. Danzi, P., Kalør, A.E., Stefanovic, C., Popovski, P.: Analysis of the Communication Traffic for Blockchain Synchronization of IoT Devices [EB/OL], 25 June 2018. https://arxiv.org/pdf/1711.00540.pdf
4. Buterin, V.: Ethereum White Paper, A next generation smart contract & decentralized application platform [EB/OL]. https://www.ethereum.org/pdfs/EthereumWhitePaper.pdf
5. Skrumble Network: Decentralized Communication Powered by Blockchain WHITEPAPER [EB/OL], 25 June 2018. http://skrumble.network/wp-content/uploads/2018/02/WhitePaper_0207_v2-min-1.pdf
6. Yuan, Y., Wang, F.-Y.: Towards blockchain-based intelligent transportation systems. In: de Janeiro, R. (ed.) 2016 IEEE 19th International Conference on Intelligent Transportation Systems (ITSC), pp. 2663–2668. IEEE (2016)
7. European Parliamentary Research Service: How blockchain technology could change our lives [EB/OL], 25 June 2018. http://www.europarl.europa.eu/RegData/etudes/IDAN/2017/581948/EPRS_IDA(2017)581948_EN.pdf
8. Economis. The promise of the blockchain: The trust machine [ED/OL], 26 June 2018. https://www.economist.com/leaders/2015/10/31/the-trust-machine
9. Chen, Y., Xu, D., Xiao, L.: Survey on network security based on blockchain. Telecommun. Sci. **3**, 10–16 (2018). (陈烨, 许多瑾, 肖亮. 基于区块链的网络安全技术综述.电信科学)
10. Baimaohui security institute: Blockchain industry security analysis report [EB/OL], 26 June 2018. http://baijiahao.baidu.com/s?id=1601256956398779805&wfr=spider&for=pc
11. Liehuang, Z., et al.: Survey on privacy techniques for blockchain technology. J. Comput. Res. Dev. **54**(10), 2170–2186 (2017). (祝烈煌, 高峰, 沈蒙, 李艳东, 郑宝昆, 毛洪亮, 吴震. 区块链隐私保护研究综述. 计算机研究与发展)
12. Wang, J., Gao, L., Dong, A., Guo, S.Y., Chen, H., Wei, X.: Block chain based data security sharing network architecture research. J. Comput. Res. Dev. **54**(4), 742–749 (2017). (基于区块链的数据安全共享网络体系研究. 王继业, 高灵超, 董爱强, 郭少勇, 陈晖, 魏欣. 计算机研究与发展)

# Situational Awareness in Space Based Blockchain Wireless Networks

Yuan Gao[1,2,3(✉)], Su Hu[3(✉)], Wanbin Tang[3], Dan Huang[3],
Yunchuan Sun[4], Xiangyang Li[1], and Shaochi Cheng[1]

[1] Academy of Military Science of the PLA, Beijing 100142, China
[2] State Key Laboratory on Microwave and Digital Communications,
National Laboratory for Information Science and Technology,
Tsinghua University, Beijing 100084, China
yuangao08@tsinghua.edu.cn
[3] University of Electronic Science and Technology of China,
Chengdu 611731, Sichuan, China
husu@uestc.edu.cn
[4] Business School, Beijing Normal University, Beijing 100875, China

**Abstract.** Blockchain is a new type of cryptographic distributed network transaction accounting system. Blockchain adopts some new security ideas, methods and technologies in its design to meet the real-world security requirements of various types of large-scale network transactions worldwide. In this paper, we discuss the state of art in space based blockchain wireless networks, and provide the future challenges in such scenario, which lead to the future researches in this area.

**Keywords:** Situational awareness · Blockchain · Wireless network ·
Space information network

## 1 Introduction

Blockchain technology also has broad application prospects in the military field. For example, in recent years, the US military has taken a fancy to the anonymity of blockchain in recording transactions, and has begun to expand to the field of intelligence gathering to achieve covert targeted payments for incentive personnel.

Traditional weapons and equipment life management uses paper or electronic media as a storage medium, which has defects such as difficulty in ensuring security and difficulty in transfer and handover. Bringing equipment files into the blockchain technology and allowing multiple departments to participate in the maintenance and update of equipment status can effectively improve safety and convenience. Blockchain technology can also solve the problems of network communications [1], data preservation, and system maintenance facing the current military logistics. So, the technological innovation of the blockchain also has great significance in the military field.

In this paper, we discuss the state of art in space based blockchain wireless networks and then provide the challenges in the upcoming future. The rest of the paper is organized as follows, in Sect. 2, we provide the status of situational awareness in space

© Springer Nature Singapore Pte Ltd. 2019
Q. Yu (Ed.): SINC 2018, CCIS 972, pp. 15–20, 2019.
https://doi.org/10.1007/978-981-13-5937-8_3

based blockchain wireless networks, and in Sect. 3, we discuss the challenges in such area by presenting some open problems. Finally, we give the conclusion in Sect. 4.

## 2 Situational Awareness in Space Based Information Networks

The military has a high level of information requirements and requires control over a wide range. Therefore, the blockchain is in the working mechanism (such as consensus mechanism, password mechanism, data dissemination mechanism [2], etc.), situational awareness such as key nodes, communication relations, business problems, vulnerability and its utilization methods are particularly prominent. There are many fragility in the characteristics of the blockchain, so we must take certain measures to solve [3] the security problems of the blockchain to prevent it from being compromised and compromised, and we must make full use of its existing vulnerability to inspect and monitor it. And behaviors such as prevention and control, so that the blockchain can play a better role.

### 2.1 Distributed Ledger

Distributed Ledger Technologies (DLTs) [4] is a technology that is different from traditional billing methods in blockchain systems. In essence, it can be shared across multiple sites, different physical addresses, or multiple organizations. The asset database. Compared with the traditional centralized database tables, the accounts exist in multiple copies on the P2P network [5]. Each node in the network keeps accounting and maintains the same database information, maintains the consistency of the account information of each node, and makes the information of the database. The changes can be quickly identified by a mathematical algorithm to effectively prevent tampering with the data information. The distributed account book of blockchain has four characteristics: decentralized innovation [6], highly transparent data, no dependence on trust, and information backtrackability.

At present, distributed ledger technology is widely used in the financial industry. Many market players consider the use of distributed ledger technology based on computer algorithms so that various financial [7] institutions can collaboratively maintain and share information in the same database, achieve "transactions that are settled", and eliminate costs incurred by banks for independent billing and communications verification, simplify redundant intermediaries' processes.

### 2.2 Consensus Mechanism

The consensus mechanism is the soul of the blockchain. Blockchain uses distributed ledger [8] technology to achieve the advantages of decentralization. At the same time, it also brings certain problems: how to orderly build a chained storage structure, how to ensure its credibility and security [9], and how to ensure distribution Storage consistency of the book, and so on. The solution to these problems depends on the consensus mechanism. In a blockchain distributed system, all nodes need to present a consistent state externally, and the consensus mechanism is to use a consensus algorithm to allow everyone to agree on a proposal negotiation. The goal of the negotiation is to enable the entire network node to quickly form a consistent blockchain structure, the following attributes must be satisfied: 1. Consistency: All honesty nodes save the blockchain with exactly the same prefix part; 2. Validity: Information published by an honest node will eventually be recorded by all other nodes in its own blockchain (Table 1).

**Table 1.** Status of consensus algorithm

| Algorithm | Application |
|---|---|
| PoW | Bitcoin, Litecoin, Ethereum (Frontier, Homestead, Metropolis) |
| PoS | PeerCoin, NXT |
| DPoS | BitShare |
| Paxos | Google Chubby, ZooKeeper |
| PBFT | Hyperledger Fabric |
| Raft | etcd, Corda |
| BFT-Raft/Raft | TrustSQL |
| RPCA | Ripple, ChainSQL |
| Quorum Voting | BitChainDB |

Currently recognized consensus mechanisms include Paxos algorithm, Raft algorithm, PBFT (Practical Byzantine Fault Tolerance) algorithm, PoW (workload proof) mechanism, PoS (equity rights certification) mechanism, and DPoS (trusted rights holder certification) mechanism. The first two (Paxos, Raft) solve the problem of the non-Byzantine general, that is, only for the problem of consensus in the presence of inconsistent fault nodes in the distributed system, but no malicious nodes, where the Paxos algorithm is applied to Google In Chubby and ZooKeeper, the Raft algorithm is used in etcd and Corda. The latter four algorithm mechanisms (PBFT, PoW, PoS, and DPoS) are used to solve the Byzantine general problem of distributed systems to avoid malicious nodes defrauding betrayal and achieve The consensus is that the PBFT algorithm is used in Hyperledger Fabric [10]. The PoW mechanism is widely used in Bitcoin, Litecoin, and Ethereum's first three stages (frontier, home, and metropolitan). The PoS mechanism is applied to PeerCoin, NXT, and Ethereum's Phase 4 (quietness), while the DPoS mechanism was applied in BitShare.

In addition, in some block chain system is also designed protocol or algorithm system for their own use as a consensus mechanism, for example: BitChainDB use Quorum Voting (registered voters) mechanism to reach a consensus; Ripple payment network applications are built-in RPCA algorithm, and China's ChainSQL platform is built based on Ripple network, and RPCA algorithm is also used as a consensus mechanism. The TrustSQL issued by the Tencent team uses the BFT-Raft [11] algorithm and the improved Raft algorithm improved by independent intellectual property rights. The application of various consensus algorithms is summarized in the above table.

## 2.3    Data Dissemination and Verification Mechanisms

The blockchain data dissemination [12] and authentication mechanism is actually a P2P protocol based on a blockchain-based P2P network structure. The data dissemination and authentication mechanisms also provide a network foundation for distributed ledger technology and consensus mechanisms, respectively.

The P2P network adopts a flat topology structure. Therefore, each node has the same status. There is no centralized server. Each node has the same functions as the routing, verification, and broadcast in the blockchain system. Data dissemination in the blockchain is divided into two ways, active sending and asking for data. When a node receives a transaction or a generated block, it broadcasts messages to other nodes of the entire network. Since the P2P network architecture is used, it is not guaranteed that all nodes receive the message when broadcasting the message. At this time, the node can send a data request to the neighboring node, and the neighboring node sends the data for synchronization. At the same time, the network layer also includes a data check mechanism. When a node receives information from a neighboring node, it verifies the validity of the data. For effective information, this information is broadcasted to neighboring nodes to implement the entire network. The message is synchronized, and for invalid information, the node does not perform data forwarding operation to prevent malicious attacks in the blockchain network, and at the same time, the node that transmits the invalid information is disconnected within a period of time. The network layer of the blockchain uses distributed network technology and uses the P2P network protocol to achieve decentralization. The entire network has high availability.

## 2.4    Password

In a blockchain system, due to its decentralized distributed architecture and peer-to-peer trading in P2P networks, a strict cryptographic mechanism is needed to meet security requirements and ownership verification requirements. Hash algorithm and asymmetric encryption technology are used in the blockchain to ensure the security and privacy of the system. The use of the nature of the hash function to encrypt information, mainly used in the blockchain for data integrity verification, data encryption, workload verification of consensus calculation, link between blocks, and so on.

Asymmetric encryption usually uses two asymmetric ciphers in the process of encryption and decryption, which are called public and private keys. Asymmetric key pair has two characteristics. First, after encrypting information with one key (public or private key), only the other key can be unlocked. Secondly, the public key can be public and private to other people. The key is confidential, and other people cannot extrapolate the corresponding private key through the public key. The private key is the most important in the blockchain system. Once lost, the property that represents the corresponding public key address is also lost. By using digital signatures, blockchain system transactions ensure message integrity and non-repudiation. The application scenario of asymmetric encryption technology in blockchain mainly includes information encryption, digital signature and login authentication.

In the blockchain, the commonly used hash functions are SHA256 and RIPEMD160. The commonly used asymmetric encryption techniques are RSA and

ECC (Elliptic Curve Cryptography). In the Bitcoin system, the SHA256 algorithm is used to hash the transaction information to form a block, use the RIPEMD160 algorithm to generate a bitcoin address, and then use the secp256k1 elliptic curve cryptography algorithm and the Base58 cryptographic algorithm for digital signature.

## 3 Challenges in Space Based Blockchain Information Networks

1. Study the main working mechanism of the typical blockchain system, focusing on clarifying the main working principles of the consensus mechanism, password mechanism, data dissemination and authentication mechanism. Through the contrast analysis and fusion to improve the existing consensus mechanism, a self-adaptive DPoS-Raft consensus mechanism is proposed to optimize the consistency and security of the system.
2. Study and build a simulation system for a typical blockchain system, and integrate the mechanisms of the data layer, network layer, consensus layer, excitation layer, contract layer, and application layer into each functional module of the blockchain simulation system.
3. Research on Situational Awareness Techniques for Blockchain Systems: Based on the perception of key nodes in the blockchain system, design key node identification algorithms based on flow control and key node awareness algorithms based on Page Rank; for blockchain system service types The perception is based on the business type sensing algorithm that combines deep packet inspection and deep flow detection; and based on the perception of the block-chain system connection relationship, the TOPSIS-based relational awareness algorithm is designed.
4. Study the fragility of the blockchain system in implementing the four aspects of the framework, data generation, identity verification and business security, and then design the above four methods of vulnerability utilization: the method based on the vulnerability of the framework; based on data Generating methods for exploiting vulnerabilities; methods for exploiting identity vulnerabilities; methods for exploiting vulnerabilities to business security.

## 4 Conclusion

In this paper, we discuss the space based blockchain information wireless networks, the state of art and the outlook in this system.

**Acknowledgement.** This work is funded by National Natural Science Foundation of China (61701503), the work of Su Hu was jointly supported by the MOST Program of International S&T Cooperation (Grant No. 2016YFE0123200), National Natural Science Foundation of China (Grant No. 61471100/61101090/61571082), Science and Technology on Electronic Information Control Laboratory (Grant No. 6142105040103) and Fundamental Research Funds for the Central Universities (Grant No. ZYGX2015J012/ZYGX2014Z005). We would like to thank all the reviewers for their kind suggestions to this work.

# References

1. Buterin, V.: Ethereum: a next generation smart contract and decentralized application platform (2013). https://github.com/ethereum/wiki/wiki/White-Paper
2. Hyperledger. About the hyperledger project [EB/OL]. https://www.hyperledger.org/about
3. Cachin, C.: Architecture of the hyperledger blockchain fabric. In: Proceedings of the Workshop on Distributed Cryptocurrencies and Consensus Ledgers (DCCL), Chicago, USA (2016)
4. Brown, R.G., Carlyle, J., Grigg, I., et al.: Corda: An Introduction. White Paper (2016)
5. Corda, H.M.: A distributed ledgers. White Paper (2016)
6. McCinaghy, T., Marques, R., Müller, A., et al.: BigchainDB: a scalable blockchain database. White Paper (2016)
7. Lazarsfeil, P.F., Elihu, K.: Personal Influence. Free Press, New York (1957)
8. Darus, N.M., Yasin, A., Omar, M., et al.: Team formation model of selecting team leader. An Analytic Hierarchy Process (AHP) approach. ARPN J. Eng. Appl. Sci. **10**(3), 1060–1067 (2015)
9. Lam, H.W., Wu, C.: Finding influential eBay buyers for viral marketing – a conceptual model of BuyerRank. In: Proceedings of IEEE Conference on Commerce and Enterprise Computing, pp. 778–785. IEEE (2009)
10. Zhang, J., Ackerman, M., Adamic, L.: Expertise networks in online communities: structure and algorithms. In: Proceeding of the 16th Conference on World Wide Web, pp. 221–230 (2007)
11. Stutz, B.D., Rejaie, R.: Characterizing today's Gnutella topology, CIS-TR-04-02 [R], [S.I.]: University of Oregon (2004)
12. Ongaro, D.: In search of an understandable consensus algorithm. In: Proceedings of USENIX Conf on USENIX Technical Conference, pp. 305–320. USENIX Association, Berkeley (2014)

# Research on Internet of Things Vulnerability Based on Complex Network Attack Model

Chengxiang Liu[1(✉)] and Wei Xiong[2]

[1] Company of Postgraduate Management,
Space Engineering University, Beijing, China
billgates_ea@163.com
[2] Science and Technology on Complex Electronic System Simulation
Laboratory, Space Engineering University, Beijing, China
13331094335@163.com

**Abstract.** The Internet of Things brings convenience to people's lives and it is also vulnerable to external attacks due to its own vulnerability. For this reason, analyzing the vulnerability of the Internet of Things is very necessary and meaningful. The paper starts with the characteristics of the Internet of Things and firstly constructs its network attack model. And then we simulate the attack on the model according to the attack rules. Furthermore, an experimental analysis of the nodes vulnerability is conducted by the theory of complex networks, and indicators of network characteristics are quantified based on the removal of vulnerable nodes. The experimental results show that the vulnerability of the system will show different patterns of attenuation as the proportion of node deletion increases.

**Keywords:** Internet of Things · Complex network · Vulnerability ·
Attack model

## 1 Introduction

With the upgrading of the industrial revolution and the rapid development of global network information, the Internet of Things (IoT), a new product, emerged from the beginning of the 21st century. Information sensing devices such as radio frequency identification (RFID) technology, infrared sensors, global positioning systems, and laser scanners were adopted. According to the agreement, a network that connects any item with the Internet, carries out communication and information exchange, and realizes intelligent identification, positioning, tracking, monitoring and management [1]. However, while various types of network nodes and related communication technologies ensure the interconnection and interoperability of IoT and complete functions, its internal reliance on informatization and network technology excessively brings IoT itself as well as system acquisition, transmission and application security issues, which exposes new security threats and presents certain vulnerabilities. Specifically embodied in:

(1) There are a large number of low-cost remote control nodes such as sensor nodes and RFID tags in IoT. These nodes have the characteristics of large number, wide

© Springer Nature Singapore Pte Ltd. 2019
Q. Yu (Ed.): SINC 2018, CCIS 972, pp. 21–29, 2019.
https://doi.org/10.1007/978-981-13-5937-8_4

distribution, limited function and long life cycle, which bring new challenges such as management of nodes and key distribution [2]. (2) Because of the access of multiple heterogeneous network in IoT, it is easier for attackers to find system weaknesses and carry out attacks in the process of connection between networks based on different protocols [3]. (3) IoT communication generally uses wireless channels for information transmission. Therefore, the wireless channel can be intercepted and stolen [4]. (4) The operation of IoT communication connection is inseparable from the excellent control host and IPC. Based on this, attackers can inject the malicious code or virus through the radio frequency wireless injection technology, so that the IoT can achieve the purpose of resource occupation, denial of service, identity or address deception, etc. Furthermore, attackers intrude into host computers and IPCs to obtain management and control rights of terminal nodes, which makes the entire IoT system and application tasks can't be implemented [5, 6].

For these reasons, it is very urgent and meaningful to analyze the vulnerability of IoT by finding out the key issues that affect the perception, transmission and application of the normal work [7, 8].

## 2  Attack Model Construction Based on Complex Network

### 2.1  Model Construction of the IoT

At present, the IoT architecture is divided into three layers: the sensing layer, the transport layer, and the application layer. The sensory layer responds to the environmental monitoring of the material world or the required information for object interaction by applying a large number of sensing technologies. It transmits information to the Internet through a transmission layer composed of a plurality of networks, and uses cloud computing, pattern recognition, and other intelligent technologies for mass data analysis and processing, so that it can be used for various applications of the application layer to satisfy the needs of different users.

From the Fig. 1, H1, H2, and H3 represent the sensing network, the transmission network, and the application network, respectively. The internal nodes have a complete topology connection relationship in the structural layer. Different nodes also have their own status attributes. This corresponds to the property layer.

### 2.2  State Attack Graph Model Construction

**Definition of Node Attribute Set**
For the entity nodes that make up IoT, the data transmission mode can be summarized as a set of attributes, and each attribute has a progressive relationship. The network abstraction based on node attacks is using the relationship between these attributes. In general, the attribute state vector of the network node in the confrontation mode can be expressed as:

$$V = (s_{P_1}, s_{P_2}, \cdots, s_{P_n}) \tag{1}$$

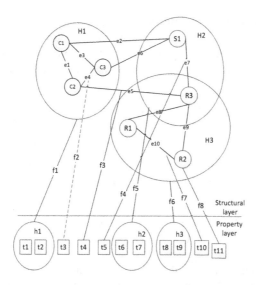

**Fig. 1.** Relationship between the structure and property layer of network nodes

Among them, V represents the state of IoT under confrontation mode A, and $s_{P_i}$ is the state value of the node attribute. Set $s_{P_i} \in \{0,1\}$, where '0' indicates that $P_i$ is destroyed, and '1' indicates that $P_i$ is in a normal state.

**State Attack Graph Model Construction**
The state attack graph is a visual description of the network property changes caused by network confrontation. It is a directed graph composed of nodes and directed edges. Its model is:

$$G = \{V_0, E, C, R\} \tag{2}$$

Among them, V0 is the initial state of the network. $E = \{A_1, A_2, \cdots, A_m\}$ is a collection of confrontations that the network may face. The attack edge Ai is a confrontational way to change the state of network attributes. $C = \{V_1, V_2, \cdots, V_n\}$ is the set of attribute states to which the network may transfer from V0 under the confrontation of A. $R = \{R_{A_1}, R_{A_2}, \cdots, R_{A_m}\}$ is the set of confrontation rules for A.

The confrontation rule is a specific description of the confrontation method and is the main basis for the generation of the state attack graph. It is expressed as follows:

$$R_{A_m} = \left\{ I_{A_m}, \left[ 0 \middle|_{P_{\text{pre}_1}}, \cdots, 0 \middle|_{P_{\text{pre}_{m'}}} \right], \left[ 0 \middle|_{P_{\text{seq}_1}}, \cdots, 0 \middle|_{P_{\text{seq}_{n'}}} \right], \eta_m \right\} \tag{3}$$

Among them, $I_{A_m}$ is the identification of confrontation route $A_m$. $\left[ 0 \middle|_{P_{\text{pre}_1}}, \cdots, 0 \middle|_{P_{\text{pre}_{m'}}} \right]$ is the status value of m' precondition attributes $\{P_{\text{pre}_1}, \cdots, P_{\text{pre}_{m'}}\}$ that was original '0' and not attacked by $I_{A_m}$. $\left[ 0 \middle|_{P_{\text{seq}_1}}, \cdots, 0 \middle|_{P_{\text{seq}_{n'}}} \right]$ is the state value of n' consequence attributes $\{P_{\text{seq}_1}, \cdots, P_{\text{seq}_n}\}$ that was attacked by $I_{A_m}$. $\eta_m$ is the probability of success by $I_{A_m}$ attack.

**Attack Path and Node Failure Analysis**

When attacking IoT nodes, if the normal state of attributes is more easily broken, it indicates the higher the vulnerability. Therefore, it is appropriate to use the probability that the attribute state is successfully destroyed to measure the vulnerability of the nodes and connections in IoT.

**Definition 1:** In the initial state V0, $\exists A_{t_i} \in A(i = 1, \cdots, k)$, which makes the state change 'k' times to reach the target state Vt. In that way, $L_{A_{t_1} \to \cdots \to A_{t_k}}|_{V_0 \to V_t}$ is called the attribute attack path of $A_{t_1} \to A_{t_2} \to \cdots \to A_{t_k}$. And $W_L = \prod_{i=1}^{k} \eta_{A_{t_i}}$ is used to measure the failure on the condition of $L_{A_{t_1} \to \cdots \to A_{t_k}}|_{V_0 \to V_t}$. $\eta_{A_{t_i}}$ is the success probability of the attacking method $A_{t_i}$.

**Definition 2:** If there are 'd' attack paths $\{L_1, L_2, \ldots, L_d\}$, and $W_{L_i} = \max(W_{L_1}, \cdots, W_{L_d}), (i \in 1, 2, \ldots, d)$. So, let Li be the maximum attack path $L_{max}$.

Available by Definition 1, if there are 'd' attack paths on the network on the condition of initial state V0 and attack method set A, the failure of the network will be

$$W_P = \sum_{i=1}^{d} W_{L_i}, (i \in 1, 2, \ldots, d).$$

### 2.3 State Attack Graph Generation Algorithm

The technical solution in this dissertation is a method for generating state of attack graphs for IoT. According to the state attack graph model and confrontation rules, the attack path and the convenience of property vulnerability calculation, the following attack graph generation algorithm is proposed. Including the following steps (Fig. 2):

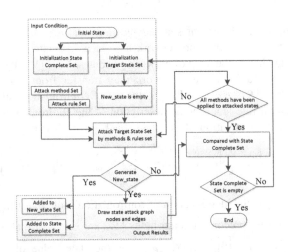

**Fig. 2.** State attack graph generation algorithm

Step 1: Initialize the network model. The initial state of the network is represented by the initial state complete set and the initial target set. Attack method sets and attack rule sets are also defined in the network initial model. Empty the new state set.

Step 2: Use the attack methods and attack rules to attack the target node and compare the results of the attack with the new state set.

Step 3: If the result of the determination is that a new state has been created, then the new state of the network is added to the new state set and the state complete set. The nodes and edges are drawn according to the attack graph generation methods and go to Step 5. If there is no new state generated, then loop to Step 4.

Step 4: Determine the affiliation relationship between the target nodes of no-generated new state and the state complete set. If the result of the determination is non-empty, Step 1 is returned to perform a recirculation attack. Otherwise, if the determination result is vacant, the cycle ends.

Step 5: Determine whether the state attacked graph in Step 3 is implemented by all methods. If the role is completed, go to Step 4 to determine whether it is compared with state complete set. Otherwise, return to Step 2 to continue the attack.

# 3 Vulnerability Analysis Indicators and Methods

The overall capability index of IoT refers to the indicators that measure the network capabilities from the entire network structure and information transmission of IoT.

## 3.1 Link Node Ratio

The link-node ratio index describes the integrity of information transmission in IoT that is consisted by various sub-networks during the confrontation process. The larger the value of index, the corresponding network has greater advantages in terms of information perception, information transmission, and command control. Its calculation method is:

$$C_\Gamma = \frac{\sum_{i=1}^{n} E_i}{V} \tag{4}$$

Among them, 'n' is the number of subnets that make up IoT. $E_i$ is the number of data transmission links in the subnet of 'i'. V is the number of the whole nodes in IoT.

## 3.2 Network Efficiency

Network efficiency reflects the degree of information communication between nodes in IoT. According to the measurement index of the complex network, denote

$d_{ij}(i, j = 1, 2, \ldots, V)$ as the shortest distance from node $v_i$ to $v_j$ in the connected network which is consisted by V nodes. Then, the average distance of the network is defined as:

$$D = \frac{2}{(V-1)(V-2)} \sum_{i>j}^{V} d_{ij} \tag{5}$$

If the network is a non-connected network, the average distance of the network will become infinite. At this time, the indicator cannot measure the connectivity of IoT. For this purpose, define the network efficiency $C_E$ as the average of the distance reciprocals between the nodes of the network.

$$C_E = \frac{2}{(V-1)(V-2)} \sum_{i>j}^{V} \frac{1}{d_{ij}} \tag{6}$$

### 3.3 Subnet Connectivity

Subnet connectivity represents the degree of connectivity between network nodes. Generally, the better the connectivity of the subnet, the smaller the number of subnets, and the smaller the average shortest path of each subnet is, the larger the connectivity coefficient $C_C$ and the higher the stability of the entire network exposes to be. The Subnet connectivity of the network is defined as:

$$C_C = \frac{1}{n \sum_{i=1}^{n} \frac{V_i}{V} D_i} \tag{7}$$

Among them, 'n' is the number of subnets that make up IoT. $V_i$ is the number of nodes in the subnet of 'i'. V is the number of the whole nodes in IoT. $D_i$ is the average distance of the subnet of 'i'.

## 4    Experiment

For a complex network that conforms to the BA model of IoT, this paper selects 450 nodes for its research.

The mapping of adjacency matrix is performed according to the connection relationship between each node and 450 nodes are modeled and simulated. To facilitate the display of the connection relationship, a 3% sampling simulation is performed, as shown in Fig. 3.

Based on the BA network, the node is attacked in accordance with the previous confrontational way. With a 2% increasing deletion ratio, the nodes in the entire network are removed from the highest to the lowest degree, and the connectivity of the entire network is analyzed.

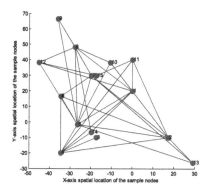

**Fig. 3.** Connection relationship between the non-deleted nodes

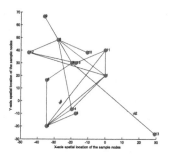

**Fig. 4.** Connection relationship between the deleted nodes

From the sampling model, we can see that when some nodes are deleted, their corresponding connection relationships have also changed. It can be shown in Fig. 4.

According to the network connectivity, the metrics that affect the entire network are normalized and analyzed as shown in Fig. 5 and Table 1.

**Table 1.** Normalized data for measure indicators

| Deletion ratio | Link node ratio | Network efficiency | Subnet connectivity |
| --- | --- | --- | --- |
| 0.02 | 0.9264 | 0.9892 | 0.7475 |
| 0.04 | 0.8634 | 0.9037 | 0.5985 |
| 0.06 | 0.8028 | 0.8927 | 0.5495 |
| 0.08 | 0.7527 | 0.9049 | 0.4787 |
| 0.10 | 0.7062 | 0.7873 | 0.4478 |
| 0.12 | 0.6740 | 0.4722 | 0.4287 |
| 0.14 | 0.6365 | 0.3978 | 0.4096 |
| 0.16 | 0.6044 | 0.3718 | 0.3833 |
| 0.18 | 0.5579 | 0.3185 | 0.3778 |
| 0.20 | 0.5124 | 0.2367 | 0.3306 |

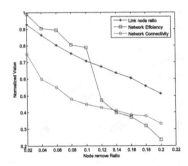

**Fig. 5.** Normalized simulation of measurement indicators

### (1) Link node ratio.

According to the network link node ratio formula, the pre-attack link node ratio is 44.386. The node deletion results in a continuous and linear decrease in the link node ratio of IoT. However, the number of removed nodes is 20%, the link node ratio has dropped to 22.796, which is about 50% of the original network.

### (2) Network efficiency.

It can be seen that when 10% of high-degree nodes are removed, network efficiency begins to drop dramatically. By removing 20% of high-degree nodes in the network, the network efficiency has dropped to about 35% of the original.

### (3) Subnet connectivity.

As can be seen from the figure, the more the number of high-degree node network nodes that are attacked, the smaller the connectivity of IoT. With the increasing in the number of attacks, the connectivity of the sub-network is rapidly declining. When the nodes with high degree have been deleted by 20%, the subnet connectivity has been declined about 33% compared with normal conditions.

## 5    Conclusion

This paper starts with the node attribute layer and the structure layer, analyzes the topological structure relationship of the Internet of Things, and builds the state attack graph model based on the complex network. The key nodes that affect the vulnerability of the network were found and then proportionally deleted on the basis to simulate the characteristics of the network. Experiments show that under different deletion ratios, the vulnerability of the network shows a larger decay.

# References

1. Kumar, S.D., Thapliyal, H., Mohammad, A.: FinSAL: FinFET based secure adiabatic logic for energy-efficient and DPA resistant IoT devices. IEEE Trans. Comput. Aided Des. Integr. Circuits Syst. **PP**(99), 1 (2017)
2. Zhang, J., Tian, G.Y., Zhao, A.B.: Passive RFID sensor systems for crack detection & characterization. NDT E Int. **86**, 89–99 (2016)
3. Li, F., Han, Y., Jin, C.: Certificateless online/offline signcryption for the Internet of Things. Wirel. Netw. **23**(1), 1–14 (2017)
4. Benaissa, S., Plets, D., Tanghe, E., et al.: Internet of animals: characterisation of LoRa sub-GHz off-body wireless channel in dairy barns. Electron. Lett. **53**(18), 1281–1283 (2017)
5. Sulyman, A.I., Oteafy, S.M.A., Hassanein, H.S.: Expanding the cellular-IoT umbrella: an architectural approach. IEEE Wirel. Commun. **24**(3), 66–71 (2017)
6. Quiers, M., Batiot-Guilhe, C., Bicalho, C.C., et al.: Characterisation of rapid infiltration flows and vulnerability in a karst aquifer using a decomposed fluorescence signal of dissolved organic matter. Environ. Earth Sci. **71**(2), 553–561 (2014)
7. Bertino, E., Islam, N.: Botnets and Internet of Things security. Computer **50**(2), 76–79 (2017)
8. Lv, H.Y., Wang, R.M.: Network real-time threat awareness and analysis based on attack state transition graph. In: ICT Energy Efficiency and Workshop on Information Theory and Security, pp. 198–203 (2012)

# Visualization Analysis About Cyber Physical Systems Research Based on CiteSpace

Chundong She[1], Xin Liu[1(✉)], Jingchao Wang[2], and Shaohua Liu[1,3]

[1] School of Electronic Engineering, Beijing University of Posts
and Telecommunications, Beijing 100876, China
1282182380@qq.com
[2] Institute of China Electronic System Engineering Company,
Beijing 100414, China
[3] Institute of Electronic and Information Engineering in Guangdong,
University of Electronic Science and Technology of China, Dongguan, China

**Abstract.** Cyber Physical Systems (CPS) is the next generation of intelligent systems in which computing, communication, and control technologies are tightly integrated. Since it focusing on the close integration and coordination of computing and physical resources, it has widely used in transportation, medical science, intelligent manufacturing, energy Internet systems and other fields. In order to further explore the future development trend of CPS, the paper visually analyzed the related literature about CPS research in Web of Science core database by means of bibliometrics and knowledge map analysis software CiteSpace to more fully clarify the development process, frontier hotspots of the key technologies and main applications about CPS research.

**Keywords:** Cyber Physical Systems · Visualization analysis · CiteSpace

## 1 Introduction

Cyber Physical Systems (CPS) implements the interaction between the computing process and physical entities through network sensors, embedded computing, network communication control, and feedback mechanisms. With its potential value of society, economy, and science, it has widely attracted academics, industry, and even governments. For example, space information network uses multiple spatial network nodes with the CPS as carriers to realize real-time information acquisition, transmission and processing. In July 2007, the US President's Science and Technology Advisory Committee (PCAST) ranked CPS as the first of eight key information technologies [1].

In the "Report of the 18th National Congress of the Communist Party of China" in 2012, the Chinese government highlighted the "intensified integration of information technology and industrialization, and accelerated the transformation and upgrading of traditional industries".

In the "Sino-German Cooperation Action Plan" published after the third round of Sino-German consultations held in October 2014 between China and Germany, it was announced that the two countries will carry out "Industry 4.0" cooperation, and one of the cores of "Industry 4.0" is to build CPS. He Jifeng, an academician of the Chinese

© Springer Nature Singapore Pte Ltd. 2019
Q. Yu (Ed.): SINC 2018, CCIS 972, pp. 30–41, 2019.
https://doi.org/10.1007/978-981-13-5937-8_5

Academy of Sciences, made an in-depth summary of CPS. He believes that the significance of CPS lies in the networking of physical devices, and in particular the connection to the Internet, which enables physical devices to have five functions: computation, communication, precise control, remote coordination, and autonomy. With the deepening of the concept of "Industry 4.0", its strategic core is realizing the real-time connectivity, mutual recognition, and effective communication of people, equipment and products through CPS networks, thereby building a highly flexible, personalized and digital smart manufacturing model. This article focuses on CPS related articles in the 2007–2017 Web of Science (WoS) database core set, using the Citespace visualization analysis tool to analyze the latest developments and hot application areas of CPS research.

## 2   Data Sources and Research Methods

- *Data Sources*

The data used in this paper comes from the core collection of the US Institute of Scientific Information Web of Science (WoS) index database, which contains the most important and up-to-date scientific research in science and technology. In this paper, "Cyber Physical System (CPS)" as "subject search" means that the retrieved vocabulary appears in "title" or "abstract" or "keywords". The search period is set to 2007–2017, a total of 1672 articles related to CPS research. The data is downloaded in plain text as "author, title, source publication, summary" and saved in a file named download_**.

- *Research Methods*

The main tool used in this study is the CiteSpace, a visual knowledge analysis software based on the Java platform developed by Prof. Chen Chaomei of the School of Computing and Information Science at Drexel University in Philadelphia, and Python as a data analysis tool. CiteSpace is used for the analysis of measurement and scientific literature with its multiple, time-dividing and dynamic characteristics. It macroscopically displays scientific knowledge in a specific subject area from all aspects including authors, keywords, cited documents, and cooperative organizations.

## 3   Analysis of Data Set

This paper used CiteSpace to draw corresponding maps of CPS research to conduct analysis of author cooperative, country cooperation, keyword co-occurrence, literature co-citation, etc. Then the paper revealed the development of CPS research by analyzing the frequency, Betweenness Centrality and other indicators in the map.

- *CPS Research Fund Distribution*

To learn more about the research support for CPS in countries, pre-process the downloaded data set through Python's Pandas data analysis package and extract the fund fields. In the Fig. 1, the abscissa represents the main countries that have support funds for the CPS study, and the ordinate represents the total number of articles supported by the national research fund for CPS.

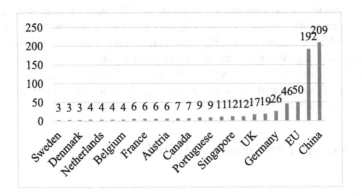

**Fig. 1.** Literature fund support distribution

Science funds play an important role in promoting the development of basic research, improving infrastructure construction, discovering and cultivating outstanding scientific and technological talents in CPS research. It can be seen from Fig. 1 that the number of CPS research articles has been ranked first in the world supported by Chinese fund, China provides strong support for CPS's development, innovation and application. For example, the "973 Program" and the "863 Program" all place emphasis on the research. The United States put forward the concept of CPS as the earliest, and its fund has supported 192 articles about CPS which have made significance in this field. As industrial power and organization, such as European Union (EU), South Korea, Spain, the United Kingdom and so on, they also contributed to the development and prosperity of the CPS.

- *Research Field of Cooperation In The Field of CPS*

The paper used the data set to generate the cooperation map of the countries in CPS study, as shown in Fig. 2, In the figure, the larger node, the more documents issued by the country, and the different colors of the node's annual ring represent corresponding time slices, the thicker rings means the more articles in the year. Each line between two nodes expresses cooperation relationship between two countries, and the thicker the line, the closer the cooperation. In order to more clearly reveal the development of the CPS, this paper conducted statistics on the volume of issued documents and Centrality for the top ten countries and institutions.

Centrality is a central indicator of the degree of resource control of the measure node in the network map. A node with high centrality is usually a key pivot connecting two different fields. The theory was proposed by Freeman in 1977 and its formula is as follows:

$$BC_i = \sum_{s \neq i \neq t} \frac{n_{st}^i}{g_{st}} \tag{1}$$

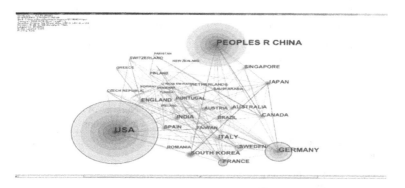

**Fig. 2.** National cooperation map of CPS (Color figure online)

In the above formula, $g_{st}$ is the shortest path number from node s to node t, $n_{st}^i$ is the shortest path number that passes node i in the $g_{st}$ shortest path from node s to node t. From the perspective of information transmission, the larger the Centrality is, the greater importance of nodes, and the greater the impact of removing these nodes on network transmission [12].

As we can see from Fig. 2 and Tables 1 and 2 the national cooperation map of CPS research, the cooperation between countries presents a non-network structure. Each node has lines to connect other nodes, and nodes with purple outer ring show its higher Centrality which indicate that the country cooperate with more countries and play a more important role in the research. For example, (1) The number of US documents is 560, ranking first in the world. The National Science Foundation (NSF) in US, which plays an important role in funding CPS research, believes that CPS will interconnect the world. China and Germany ranked 2–3, with 407,171 documents respectively. Countries such as Germany, Sweden, Italy, and South Korea started late in this field, but they have obtained more results in research. (2) In scientific research institutions, the top ten institutions in terms of the number of issued documents are well-known universities in science and engineering. These institutions rely on their rich research and the talent resources to play a crucial role in CPS research. Five of the top 10 scientific institutions are all from US, which also reflects the United States' absolute advantage in CPS research. There are four scientific institutions all from China, and both Guangdong University of Technology and Carnegie Mellon University in US are ranked first in frequency 36. Shanghai Jiaotong University, East China Normal

**Table 1.** CPS research top ten countries

| No | Country | Number of publications | First published | Centrality |
|----|---------|------------------------|-----------------|------------|
| 1 | USA | 560 | 2007 | 0.25 |
| 2 | China | 407 | 2008 | 0.03 |
| 3 | Germany | 171 | 2011 | 0.16 |
| 4 | Sweden | 75 | 2013 | 0.15 |
| 5 | Italy | 70 | 2011 | 0.03 |
| 6 | South Korea | 69 | 2011 | 0.11 |
| 7 | Canada | 59 | 2008 | 0.11 |
| 8 | France | 52 | 2011 | 0.23 |
| 9 | Japan | 52 | 2011 | 0.08 |
| 10 | England | 50 | 2009 | 0.11 |

**Table 2.** CPS research top ten institutions

| No | Institution | Country | Number of publications | Centrality |
|----|-------------|---------|------------------------|------------|
| 1 | Guangdong University of Technology | China | 36 | 0.03 |
| 2 | Carnegie Mellon University | USA | 36 | 0.13 |
| 3 | University of Illinois at Urbana-Champaign | USA | 30 | 0.09 |
| 4 | University of California, Berkeley | USA | 29 | 0.13 |
| 5 | Shanghai Jiao Tong University | China | 27 | 0.15 |
| 6 | Missouri University of Science and Technology | USA | 25 | 0.02 |
| 7 | Technische Universität München | Germany | 25 | 0.06 |
| 8 | East China Normal University | China | 23 | 0.01 |
| 9 | Tsinghua University | China | 23 | 0.10 |
| 10 | University of California, Irvine | USA | 22 | 0.04 |

University, and Tsinghua University have a certain influence in the international CPS research field, reflecting China's support and recognition for the development of this research.

From Centrality: (1) The centrality of USA is a maximum of 0.25 in the country's cooperation network. It has cooperation relationships with many countries including China, Germany, Sweden, Italy and so on. It also serves as a link and bridge for cooperation between different countries, which shows its core of the cooperation network. (2) Among the research institutes, Shanghai Jiaotong University has the highest centrality. It has cooperative relations with many institutions such as Aalto University and Luleå University of Technology. However, the centrality of some countries or organizations with high frequency of publication is relatively low. For example, Guangdong University of Technology, which has the largest number of documents issued, has a centrality of only 0.03. To sum up, it shows that in the current CPS research field, it is necessary to strengthen the exchanges to achieve complementarity of resources and provide more support for the development of CPS related technologies.

- *CPS Research Field Author Cooperation Distribution*

The thermalization and development of a research field is not only reflected in the rapid increase in the number of papers, but also in the growing size of relevant cooperation groups. Visualized cluster analysis of cooperative groups and representative figures from the perspective of authors can more specifically understand the power of research. Figure 3 is a collaborative clustering view of authors in the CPS. This map focuses on the structural features among clusters, highlights key author nodes and important connections between authors. Based on the clarity of the network structure, CiteSpace provides two indicators of the module value (Q value) and the average contour value (S value), which can be used as a basis for evaluating the mapping effect. The general Q value greater than 0.3 means that the community structure drawn is significant. When the S value is around 0.7, the clustering is highly efficient and convincing. If it is above 0.5, clustering is generally considered reasonable [2]. According to the parameters in the upper left corner of Fig. 3, the Q value of this clustering view is 0.9714, and the S value is 0.6106, indicating that the view reflected is reasonable and effective.

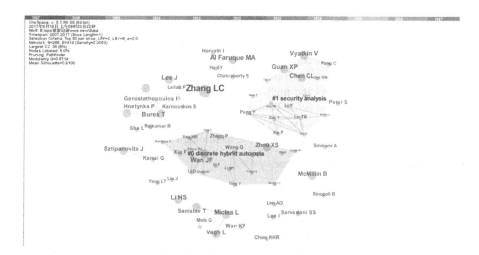

**Fig. 3.** CPS research author cooperative cluster view (Color figure online)

As can be seen from Fig. 3, the authors of the CPS research field are mainly divided into two large cooperative networks and some small cooperative groups. This paper mainly analyzes two large cooperative groups and their research directions. (1) The largest cooperative group (green network part in Fig. 3) is mainly based on Professor Wan JF of School of Mechanical and Automotive Engineering of South China University of Technology. There are 19 people such as Tang Y in the School of

Electrical Engineering of Southeast University, Prof. Zhou XS, Northwestern Polytechical University and so on. The main research contents of the cooperative group include Vehicular Cyber-Physical Systems (VCPS) and equipment control systems, CPS architecture and modeling, and grid CPS. For example, Wan J, Zhang D, et al. put forward the design, development and deployment of Vehicular Cyber-Physical Systems (VCPS) for some emerging applications with the advances in wireless communication technologies, vehicular networks and cloud computing. Based on the requirements, they designed a VCPS and Mobile Cloud Computing (MCC) Integration Architecture (VCMIA), which provides mobile services for potential users such as drivers and passengers to access mobile traffic cloud. Finally, the proposed VCMIA can provide the flexibility for enabling diverse applications after verification [4].

(2) The second largest cooperative group (Yellow Network in Fig. 3) is mainly based on the professor Chen CL from Shanghai Jiaotong University. It mainly includes Prof. Lu TB from the School of Software Engineering of Beijing University of Posts and Telecommunications, Pro Valeriy fVyatkin from Aalto University in Finland, Peng Y from China Information Security Evaluation Center, etc. The main research contents of this cooperative group include CPS risk assessment and security analysis, industrial CPS, wireless sensor implementation network, network and information security and so on. For example, Pro Chen C, Yan J, et al. pointed out that ubiquitous monitoring over wireless sensor networks (WSNs) is of increasing interest in industrial cyber-physical systems (CPSs). And they first adopted a Kalman filtering (KF) approach to estimate the unknown physical parameters. In order to facilitate the decentralized implementation of the KF algorithm in relay-assisted WSNs, a tree-based broadcasting strategy is provided for distributed sensor fusion. In the end, they improved the efficiency and accuracy of typical industrial CPS [5]. On the whole, there are scholars of scientific research from China in the two major research groups in CPS research, and they have inter- and multi-national cooperation to further reflect China's active research status in this field. Through discussion and exchange of cooperative groups, it is more conducive to the integration and sharing of resources to promote the continuous progress and development of the technological level.

- *The Evolution of Research Theme of CPS*

The keywords of academic papers are the conciseness of the problems studied by the authors and the academic viewpoints. They are the essence and the highly generalized content of the thesis. The high frequency occurrences of keywords are often regarded as research hotspots in this field [13]. The paper selected "Keyword" as node by using CiteSpace, the larger the node, the more times the word appears and the greater the degree of attention. The Timezone view was used to present the results of keyword clustering which can reveal CPS development trend in the time dimension.

Table 3 shows the time distribution of high frequency keywords. Figure 4 shows the increase of the year in the horizontal direction, and the vertical direction shows the high frequency keywords in the year. Through the combination of Fig. 4 and Table 2, we can understand the cutting-edge research and development trends in the CPS field. The CPS development process is roughly divided into the following three stages:

(1)  Initial exploration stage (2007–2010): Keywords such as modeling, design, simulation, hybrid system, communication, and wireless sensor network (WSN) appear frequently. It shows that in the early days, scholars in this field understood the hybrid system CPS consisting of computational processes and physical entities, and placed communication as equally important as control and computing, emphasizing physics' coordination between devices cannot be separated from communication in distributed applications. In order to further explore the structure of the system and discover its advantages and hidden values, researchers began to gradually design,

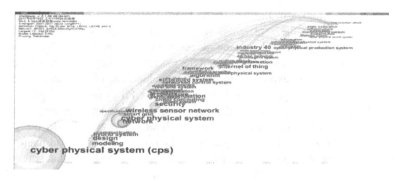

**Fig. 4.** Keywords co-occurrence timezone view

**Table 3.** High frequency keyword year distribution

| Keyword | Fre | First appearance | Keyword | Fre | First appearance |
|---|---|---|---|---|---|
| Cyber physical system (CPS) | 586 | 2007 | Internet of thing | 38 | 2013 |
| Embedded network | 2 | 2008 | Intrusion detection | 22 | 2013 |
| Design | 93 | 2009 | Cyber attack | 20 | 2013 |
| Modeling | 83 | 2009 | Industry 4.0 | 37 | 2014 |
| Hybrid system | 41 | 2009 | Big data | 20 | 2014 |
| Communication | 22 | 2009 | Ad hoc network | 14 | 2014 |
| Wireless sensor network | 127 | 2010 | Ontology | 16 | 2015 |
| Smart grid | 31 | 2010 | Cyber physical production | 15 | 2015 |
| Security | 109 | 2011 | Robustness | 10 | 2015 |
| Simulation | 58 | 2011 | Manufacturing system | 9 | 2016 |
| Architecture | 47 | 2011 | Infrastructure | 8 | 2016 |
| Cloud computing | 30 | 2011 | State estimation | 8 | 2016 |
| Algorithm | 48 | 2012 | Data injection attack | 5 | 2017 |
| Performance | 33 | 2012 | Particle swarm | 3 | 2017 |
| Vehicular cyber physical system | 20 | 2012 | Security of data | 2 | 2017 |

model and simulate CPS structures. The Wireless Sensor Network (WSN) is an important part of the CPS-aware physical world. Wu Fang-Jing of National Chiao Tung University in Taiwan stated that in the past two decades, a lot of research has been devoted to WSN. Some research activities in WSN include navigation, rescue, intelligent transportation, social networking and gaming applications. Through analysis of previous studies, it shows how CPS uses the physical information collected by WSN to connect the real world and information space, and points out the difficulties and challenges in applying WSN to CPS related fields [7].

(2) Application development stage (2010–2013): A series of keywords CPS-related application, such as smart grid, security, cloud computing, algorithm, performance analysis, vehicular cyber physical system, internet of thing (IOT), and intrusion detection, have emerged. After the initial exploration of the structure, the relevant technologies in the field have been continuously matured. In order to fully play its role, the researchers tried to integrate the CPS with the corresponding hot-spot technology and develop its unlimited potential. With the increasing demand for clean energy and the increasing level of automation, people have increased their expectations for the development of the smart grid. The electric CPS is the expansion and application of CPS in the power grid field. It will play a fundamental role in the deepening applications of energy networks, active power distribution networks, and traditional power grids. In the year of 2010, CPS and smart grids were jointly studied, and the power grid made use of information and network technology to build a new type of grid that was applied accurately and efficiently. In 2011, Wang J of Kyunghee University in Korea introduced CPS enhanced wireless sensor network architecture integrated with cloud computing and applied it to healthcare and decision support systems [8]. In 2012, Li X et al. of the State University of New York at Buffalo applied CPS to the vehicular cyber physical system (VCPS). VCPS uses the latest sensing, computing, communications, and networking technologies to improve the safety of transportation systems effectiveness. In 2013, Professor Wan Jiafu introduced the relevance between CPS and the IOT, and proposed that CPS is the evolution of M2 M (machine-to-machine) through the introduction of more intelligent and interactive operations under the Internet of Things architecture [9]. While CPS application field is expanding, its performance analysis, security detection and other aspects have gradually become a research hotspot.

(3) Entering the peak of CPS development after 2014: Keywords such as industry 4.0, big data, cyber physical production system, manufacturing system, and data injection attack have become hotspots in CPS research. The theory and technology of CPS is considered to be the technological foundation of Internet + application in the era of "Industry 4.0". The German Industry 4.0 strategy describes the concept of CPS in detail and hopes to adopt this system to create a new manufacturing method and realize a "smart factory". Taking the development of "Industry 4.0" as an opportunity, CPS will use the advanced computing capabilities of cyberspace in the real world to form a self-disciplined intelligent production system and gradually form a CPS manufacturing system.

- *Analysis of Cited Literature In CPS Research*

A high-cited paper in a research field reflects the high recognition of the paper's viewpoints by other scholars in the field and the significance of the paper's foundation. It can be seen from Table 4 that the high cited times list of documents, highly cited articles in the CPS research mainly appeared in the early stage of the development of the field around 2012. Most of the themes of these articles are the basic structure of CPS, the design and simulation of CPS model, and the specific application scenarios and challenges to achieve. In terms of infrastructure: The paper cited the most frequently cited paper is "Cyber Physical Systems: Design Challenges" by Prof. Edward A. Lee of the University of California, Berkeley, which summarizes the CPS composition and points out how to improve the embedded system to be applied to CPS and face the challenge during upgrade process. The most Centrality document is Professor Edward A. Lee's "Introduction to Embedded Systems", which introduces the concept of embedded systems and their application scenarios, modeling dynamic networks, software and physical processes and designing dynamic nodes. In the process of CPS design, a series of issues such as handling tense, thread understanding, message passing, and avoiding deadlock are discussed. From the specific application: Siddharth Sridhar of Iowa State University pointed out in paper that the development of a reliable smart grid requires a deeper understanding of the potential impact of successful cyber attacks and highlights the importance of the combination of network infrastructure security and power application security [11]. The paper specifies that to understand the security issues in the power grid, to prevent, mitigate, and tolerate cyber attacks, it is necessary to appropriately quantify the impact of attacks and evaluate the effectiveness of the countermeasures through the interaction of the CPS.

**Table 4.** The top ten literatures with highly cited frequency

| Cited frequency | Betweenness centrality | Literature name | Author | Year |
|---|---|---|---|---|
| 218 | 0.05 | Cyber physical systems: design challenges | Edward Lee | 2008 |
| 71 | 0.03 | Modeling cyber-physical systems | Patricia Derler | 2012 |
| 56 | 0.12 | Cyber-physical systems: the next computing revolution | R.R. Rajkumar | 2010 |
| 49 | 0.09 | Cyber-physical systems: a perspective at the centennial | Kyoung-Dae Kim | 2012 |
| 47 | 0.08 | Attack detection and identification in cyber-physical systems | Fabio Pasqualetti | 2013 |
| 43 | 0.14 | Introduction to embedded systems | Edward Lee | 2011 |
| 36 | 0.08 | Cyber–physical system security for the electric power grid | Siddharth Sridhar | 2012 |
| 35 | 0.03 | From wireless sensor networks towards cyber physical systems | Fang-Jing Wu | 2011 |
| 35 | 0.10 | Toward a science of cyber–physical system integration | Janos Sztipanovits | 2012 |
| 34 | 0.11 | Cyber-physical systems: close encounters between two parallel worlds | Radha Poovendran | 2010 |

## 4  Research Conclusions and Prospects

This paper analyzes the papers related to CPS in WOS core database through biblio-metrics and visualization analysis methods, and the CPS domain country cooperation map, the authors' cooperative clustering map, the keyword co-occurrence map drawn by literature analysis software CiteSpace which analyze CPS development status.

(1) As an infrastructure for the future development of information technology, space information network has important research significance. However, with the continuous development of space information networks, its security issues have also emerged, and has received more and more attention from researchers. Then as we know, the architecture of CPS is divided into three levels, the perceptual execution layer, the data transmission layer and the application control layer and different levels correspond to different security measures. The perceptual execution layer mainly involves the physical security of each node's infrastructure. The identity of the node is managed and protected. Better protection through technologies such as biometrics and near field communication to ensure the node data security. The security measures of the data transmission layer are mainly to protect the system communication data security, including data integrity, confidentiality consistency and so on. The application control layer is the core of the decision making of CPS. Security measures for the application layer of the information system include: Strengthen the access control strategy of the system and Strengthen the identity authentication mechanism and encryption mechanism for different application scenarios. In summary, the introduction of the CPS architecture security mechanism in the space information network nodes can effectively promote its security development.

(2) The development and popularization of CPS technology will promote the upgrading of industrial products and technologies, and greatly increase the competitiveness of major industrial sectors such as aerospace, defense, industrial automation, and health-care equipment, etc. [10]. As a result, it has gradually become an important strategic resource, and it is expected to continue to be a research hotspot for in-depth expansion in the academic and industrial sectors for some time to come.

(3) The combination of CPS's continuous research with cutting-edge technologies such as cloud computing, Internet of Things, big data, machine learning, fog computing and other information fields will accelerate its study, application and bring about tremendous changes in people's life, production, and management methods.

(4) CPS covers applications ranging from smart homes to industrial control systems to intelligent transportation systems, smart grids, and even national and even world-class applications. With the continuous increase of its application fields, its security problems such as network spoofing attacks, state estimation, control performance, and privacy protection are also becoming increasingly prominent. It is necessary to improve the CPS security performance through technologies such as intrusion detection, data monitoring, and user authentication.

(5) In order to strengthen theoretical research in the field of CPS, relevant countries, institutions, and scholars should increase their cooperation and exchanges. By complementing the advantages of resources in different research fields, CPS promotes the formation of a complete system from the design of the algorithm model to the practical application, and then brings its value into full play in an efficient and intelligent production and living model.

**Acknowledgement.** This research is partly supported by the National Defense Equipment Advance Research Shared Technology Program of China (41402050301-170441402065), and Technological Equipment Mobilization Program of Dongguan (KZ2017-06).

# References

1. Shi, J., Wan, J., Yan, H., Suo, H.: A survey of cyber-physical systems. In: Proceedings of International Conference on Wireless Communications and Signal Processing, pp. 1–6 (2011)
2. Chen, Y., Chen, C., Liu, Z., et al.: Methodological function of knowledge map based on CiteSpace. Stud. Sci. Sci. **33**(02), 242–253 (2015)
3. Wang, Q., Zhou, X., Yang, G., et al.: Behavior modeling of cyber-physical system based on discrete hybrid automata. In: IEEE International Conference on Computational Science and Engineering, pp. 680–684. IEEE (2013)
4. Wan, J., Zhang, D., Sun, Y., et al.: VCMIA: a novel architecture for integrating vehicular cyber-physical systems and mobile cloud computing. Mobile Netw. Appl. **19**(2), 153–160 (2014)
5. Chen, C., Yan, J., Lu, N., et al.: Ubiquitous monitoring for industrial cyber-physical systems over relay-assisted wireless sensor networks. IEEE Trans. Emerg. Top. Comput. **3**(3), 352–362 (2015)
6. Xie, F., Lu, T., Guo, X., et al.: Security analysis on cyber-physical system using attack tree. In: International Conference on Intelligent Information Hiding and Multimedia Signal Processing, pp. 429–432. IEEE (2013)
7. Wu, F.-J., Kao, Y.-F., Tseng, Y.-C.: Review: from wireless sensor networks towards cyber physical systems. Pervasive Mobile Comput. **7**(4), 397–413 (2011)
8. Wang, J., Abid, H., Lee, S., et al.: A secured health care application architecture for cyber-physical systems. Control Eng. Appl. Inform. **13**(3), 101–108 (2011)
9. Wan, J., Chen, M., Xia, F., et al.: From machine-to-machine communications towards cyber-physical systems. Comput. Sci. Inf. Syst. **10**(3), 1105–1128 (2013)
10. Lv, L., Lu, J., Zhang, Z., et al.: Looking into complex networks. Complex Syst. Complex. Sci. (Z1), 173–186 (2010)
11. Sridhar, S., Hahn, A., Govindarasu, M.: Cyber-physical system security for the electric power grid. Proc. IEEE **100**(1), 210–224 (2011)
12. Li, J., Chen, C.: CiteSpace: Text Mining and Visualization in Scientific Literature. Capital University of Economics and Business Press (2016)
13. Wei, R.: An empirical study of keywords network analysis using social network analysis. J. Intell. **28**(9), 46–49 (2009)

# Modeling Method of Space Information Network Architecture Based on TaaC

Xiangli Meng[✉], Lingda Wu, Shaobo Yu, and Xitao Zhang

Space Engineering University, Beijing 101416, China
10211193@bjtu.edu.cn

**Abstract.** Along with the development of space information technology, "space-ground integration information network" has risen to national strategy, the space information network has become a new research hotspot. The current research status quo of spatial information network architecture are summarized and analyzed, A modeling method based on TaaC (Task as a Center, Task centered) was proposed exploratory, the modeling ideas and modeling process are studied, different space missions are divided into different subtasks, the same child tasks were restructured, the task planning and resource invocation process is designed, in order to improve the execution efficiency of space mission. This paper is to provide the support structure for the basic theory and key technology of space information network development.

**Keywords:** Space information network · Task as a Center · Architecture · The subtasks

## 1 Introduction

At present, with the gradual deepening of space science exploration and the continuous development of space information technology, the construction of space information system presents a state of explosive development. However, the construction of various kinds of space information systems is still separate, forming a situation of repeated construction and "chimney development". Various kinds of navigation, communication, remote sensing and other satellites occupy a large number of orbital resources. After a single satellite system completes a given task, there will be more idle state, resulting in the waste of space resources [1]. The proposal of space information network provides a solution to the above problems. The construction of "space-earth integrated information network" has formally become the ninth item of the "13th Five-Year Plan" National Strategic Hundred Project, and has become a research hotspot in the global field.

Space information network is a network system that acquires, transmits and processes space information in real time on various space platforms (such as synchronous satellites or medium-orbit satellites, flat-layer balloons and manned or unmanned aerial vehicles, etc.) [2]. Because of its unique spatial location advantages, compared with the ground network, the space information network plays an irreplaceable role in earth observation, emergency communications, air transport, space TT&C and the expansion

© Springer Nature Singapore Pte Ltd. 2019
Q. Yu (Ed.): SINC 2018, CCIS 972, pp. 42–51, 2019.
https://doi.org/10.1007/978-981-13-5937-8_6

of national strategic interests, and has gradually become a high frontier of national strategic interests [3].

In 1964, G. Amdahl first proposed the concept of architecture, which made people have a unified and clear understanding of computer systems, and laid a good foundation for the design and development of computer systems. In the past sixty years, the discipline of architecture has made considerable progress. In the construction of C4ISR system, the U.S. Army firstly designs the system architecture to determine the corresponding investment and development plans and guide the development and construction of the system [4].

Similar to the construction of spatial information network, the architecture design of spatial information network is an important link in the construction and development of spatial information network. However, the spatial information network is still in the primary stage of development, the design of the architecture has not yet formed a unified idea. For this reason, this paper aims at the characteristics of complicated spatial information network structure and many kinds of tasks, a Taac (Task-as-a-Center) architecture modeling method is proposed to support the development of basic theory and key technologies of spatial information network.

## 2  Research Status

According to the current architecture of the spatial information network, through the analysis of the research status at home and abroad, it can be summarized to the following three categories:

(1) Star-Earth network: Star-Earth network refers to the ability to serve the world by connecting ground stations instead of networking the satellites in the sky. It is the main way adopted by the satellite communication network with global coverage abroad. Typical systems include Intelsat, Inmarsat, WGS [5, 6] and so on, which are the most mature architecture at present.

(2) Space Network and Earth Station: Space Network and Earth Station refers to a relatively independent space-based network formed by means of inter-satellite networking. The whole system can operate independently without relying on the ground network. Information processing and exchange functions are completed on the satellite. Typical systems include Iridium, AEHF and so on. This architecture has strong survivability, but the cost of construction and maintenance is high.

(3) Skynet and Ground Network: Skynet and Ground Network refers to the integration of space and ground networks, a typical representative of the United States Transfer Satellite (TSAT) communication system. Space-based networks and ground stations cooperate with each other, can cover the world, but also has a strong information processing and transmission capacity.

Of the above three types, the Skynet and Ground Network can make full use of the global coverage of the space-based network and the powerful transmission and processing capabilities of the ground network, which is a more appropriate reference for the construction of space information network.

Based on the design idea of Skynet and Ground Network, domestic and foreign relevant institutions and research teams have made some preliminary explorations. Zhang Wei and others of the Army Engineering University proposed a hierarchical autonomous domain network structure model. According to the different nodes in the network, the highly dynamic spatial information network was divided into sub-networks with weak dynamic changes, which improved the efficiency of management and control. Yan Jian and others of Tsinghua University proposed a software-defined network-based protocol architecture for spatial information networks to overcome the challenges of discontinuous, long-delay, heterogeneous and multi-service spatial information networks by separating business, control and management [7]. Sun Chenhua of the 54th Research Institute of China Electric Power Group put forward a grid network structure, which calls the dual planes of foundation and space-based core "core grid" and the multi-plane mobile access network between them, including space-based, space-based and ground-based networks, is called "mobile grid". Others, such as Wuhan University, Beihang University, Xidian University and other research institutes have also done some research on the architecture of space information network, and achieved a series of research results [8, 9].

Spatial information network is a network system that serves a wide range and a wide range of services. The requirements of various space services are changing with the tasks. Especially with the increasing of new application scenarios, such as ocean escort, emergency rescue, joint operations, etc, higher requirements for the architecture of spatial information network are put forward. Current architecture description methods are not designed for different tasks, and lack of perception and adaptation to different tasks. Therefore, this paper proposes an architecture modeling method based on TaaC, the modeling idea and process, task decomposition and reorganization, task planning and resource invocation are discussed in detail.

## 3 Modeling of Spatial Information Network Architecture Based on TaaC

The architecture of spatial information network refers to the structure, relationship, design criteria and guidelines of the components of spatial information network. The description and modeling of the architecture of spatial information network are the premise and basis for the development of spatial information network.

### 3.1 Modeling Thought

Space information networks include geostationary satellites, low-and medium-earth-orbit satellites, stratospheric balloons, manned or unmanned aerial vehicles and various ground equipment to complete communications, remote sensing, navigation and other tasks. In the future, apart from the development of communication, remote sensing, navigation and other professional terminals, the development of multi-network inte-gration of space-terrestrial user terminals will become an important research direction, the latter will be a multi-functional (communication/navigation/remote sensing), multi-service (data/time-frequency/Internet), multi-mode (satellite communications/satellite navigation/ground terminal positioning) integrated terminal [10]. Therefore, there is bound to be a convergence of space tasks. The spatial information network architecture is shown in Fig. 1:

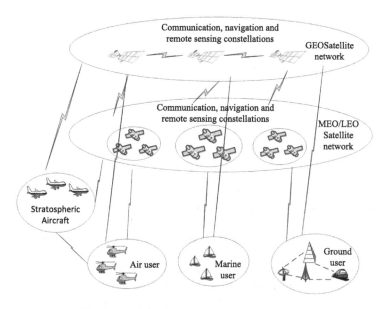

**Fig. 1.** Spatial information network architecture

Different space missions have different requirements for speed and reliability. Taking typical tasks such as remote sensing and communication as an example, the following conclusions can be drawn:

**Table 1.** Characteristics of different space tasks

|  | Speed | Reliability | Other characteristics |
|---|---|---|---|
| Remote sensing task | Higher | Lower | Short period |
| Measurement and control task | Lower | Higher | Long arc section |
| Operation and control task | Lower | Higher | Real time, no interruption |
| Communication task | Secondary | Secondary | Comprehensive and strong |

As shown in Table 1, different spatial tasks have different characteristics. There are many kinds of spatial information network resources. As a whole, the resources of spatial information network can be divided into node resources and link resources. Node resources include sensor resources, antenna resources, frequency resources, power resources, computing resources, energy resources, storage resources and so on. Link resources include inter-satellite link resources, inter-satellite link resources of the same layer, satellite ground link resources, ground link resources and so on. Different space tasks require different resources, constraints and task standards. Therefore, it is necessary to establish an effective task centered modeling method [11].

Task-centric modeling concept shifts information technology from traditional "system-centric" to "task-centric", and achieves the goal of system integration through the combination and reuse of tasks. The task oriented architecture is shown in Fig. 2:

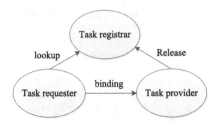

**Fig. 2.** TaaC architecture

The architecture contains three roles: (1) Task Provider - Provides data and services in the form of task publication and responds to requests for tasks. (2) Task Registry - Registers the tasks that have been released, and provides classification, search and other services. (3) Task requestor - Using task center to find the tasks needed and get the required services.

In the task-centric architecture, technology is viewed from the perspective of business process, the implementation process of information service is decomposed into business process under task-centric architecture, the operations and operations involved in the implementation process are encapsulated into corresponding task interfaces, and the data and business are separated, the process and the implementation are separated. This flexible operation mechanism can solve the problem of information interoperability and information sharing. The task oriented architecture has the following characteristics and advantages:

(1) Encapsulating spatial resources in the form of tasks and describing the dynamic interaction of services are helpful to analyze the dynamic connection relationship between different systems.
(2) The task model is accurately expressed to better support business process analysis.
(3) Task-oriented architecture provides a new way to share resources and carriers, reflecting the idea of integration of sky and ground [12].

## 3.2 Modeling Process

In this paper, different spatial tasks are modeled from five aspects: task resources, task objectives, task description, constraints and task standards. Different spatial tasks can be described by the following formula:

$$Task = \{R, G, E, L, St\} \tag{1}$$

R: Represents the resources required for the mission, including remote sensing satellites, relay satellites and different ground stations. These resources can be further divided into the next level of resources, such as remote sensing satellite resources can be further divided into sensors, antennas, data storage media and so on.

G: Represents mission objectives, objectives can be divided into point objective, regional objective and moving objective.

E: Indicating task description, indicating the desired target state.

L: Represents the constraints, refers to the satellites, stratospheric aircraft, ground stations in the implementation of the mission by the various constraints.

St: Represents the mission standard, refers to the mission implementation needs to achieve certain indicators, such as navigation and positioning satellite positioning accuracy of the target.

Spatial tasks can be subdivided into several subtasks. For example, remote sensing tasks can be further divided into information acquisition, information transmission, information processing and other subtasks. From the above five aspects of the space mission modeling process as shown in Fig. 3, different air, ground and sea users submit tasks, pretreat the tasks, after the completion of the pretreatment to get a reasonable set of tasks, and then select sub-tasks from the task set to model, forming a Task-aware model.

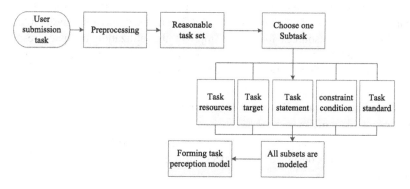

**Fig. 3.** Modeling process based on Taac

According to the above task modeling process, the sub-task is modeled to form a Task-aware model, which lays the foundation for the task decomposition and reorganization in the following [13].

### 3.3 Task Decomposition and Reorganization

Due to the problems of uneven resources and capabilities, resource constraints and resource shortages in satellites, different tasks may contain the same sub-tasks or require the same resources after the establishment of a space information network. Therefore, according to the task characteristics, the task can be decomposed and reorganized, and the same resources can be invoked to improve the execution efficiency. The schematic diagram of task decomposition and reorganization is shown in Fig. 4:

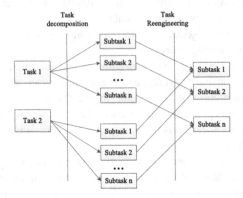

**Fig. 4.** Schematic diagram of task decomposition and reorganization

When subtasks are still complex, they can be further decomposed into two sub tasks according to the actual situation. When space resources are limited, services can be provided according to the priority of tasks. The purpose of task decomposition and reorganization is to reduce the complexity of different space missions and combine the tasks of the same resources to further improve the utilization of space resources. However, the interaction between decomposed sub-tasks should be reduced as much as possible to avoid conflicts between cooperative satellites.

### 3.4   Task Planning and Resource Invocation

### 3.4.1   Structural Process

On the basis of task decomposition and reorganization, the process of task planning and resource invocation is designed. The process of task planning and resource invocation is shown in Fig. 5:

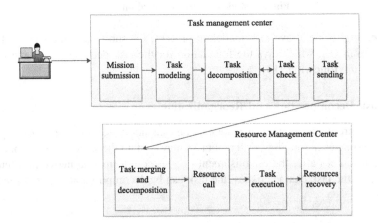

**Fig. 5.** Task planning and resource invocation flow chart

As shown in Fig. 5, the task management center and resource management center are set up. In the task management center, after the user submits the task, the task is modeled according to the Sect. 3.2 modeling process to form a Task-aware model. Then, according to the task characteristics, the task is decomposed into different subtasks, and then the task is checked to eliminate the impossible tasks or tasks whose attributes do not meet the global constraints. Finally, the task is sent.

In the resource management center, different tasks are sorted according to the resource requirement category and priority, and different tasks are merged according to the resource type to improve the efficiency of task execution. For example, when both subtasks A and B require the same computing resource, the two subtasks are merged into task C. Similarly, when subtask A needs to invoke different resources, it is further divided into secondary subtasks according to resource requirements. After the task is merged and decomposed, the resources can be called and the corresponding tasks can be completed.

In the process of task execution, for the case of using the same resource, when a new sub-task arrives, and the current sub-task is not completed, allowing waiting time, the new sub-task can only be carried out after the completion of the previous sub-task. After the task is executed, the resources are recovered and waiting for the next task [14]. Next, we focus on mathematical modeling of resource call process.

### 3.4.2    Mathematical Model

After the task is decomposed into subtasks, set the collection as $T = \{task_1, task_2, \cdots task_n\}$; $R_i = \{r_{ij} | j \in [1, m_i]\}, i = 1, 2, \cdots n$ represents the resource set that can complete the subtask $task_i, m_i$, represents the amount of resources that can be loaded with the task $task_i$. Set $Pr_{ij} = \{t_{ij}, c_{ij}, q_{ij}, b_{ij}, \cdots\}$, $i \in [1, n]$, $j \in [1, mi]$, indicates the performance parameters of resource $r_{ij}$ when executing sub task $task_i, t_{ij}$, represents time, $c_{ij}$ represents the cost of resources, $q_{ij}$ represents quality, $b_{ij}$ represents reliability, other indicators can be increased according to the actual situation.

Let $T_m$ represents the total time to complete all tasks, C represents the total cost of using resources, Q represents the total quality index, and B represents the total reliability. The goal of resource optimization is to get $E = \{e_1, e_2, e_3 \cdots e_n\}$, and $E \cap R = \{e_i\}$, make:

$$\begin{cases} \min(T_m) \\ \min(C) \\ \max(Q) \\ \max(B) \end{cases} \tag{2}$$

It can be seen that the selection of optimal resources is a multi-objective optimization problem. In most cases, it is impossible to exist such that all the objectives of Eq. (2) are satisfied. Therefore, the multi-objective optimization function can be used as follows:

$$\begin{cases} \min(J) \\ J = \alpha T_m + \beta C + \eta Q^{'} + \varepsilon B^{'} \end{cases} \tag{3}$$

In the formula, $\alpha, \beta, \eta, \varepsilon$ represents the weighting coefficient, $\alpha + \beta + \eta + \varepsilon$ is usually equal to 1. Among, $C = \sum c(Task_i, e_i)$, $i = 1, 2 \cdots n$; $Q' = \sum (1 - q(Task_i, e_i))$, $i = 1, 2 \cdots n$; $B' = \sum (1 - b(Task_i, e_i))$, $i = 1, 2 \cdots n$; Among, $c(Task_i, e_i)$ indicates the resources used by $e_i$ to complete the task $Task_i$, $q(Task_i, e_i)$ indicates the quality of $e_i$ completing the task $Task_i$, $b(Task_i, e_i)$ indicates the reliability of $e_i$ completing the task $Task_i$, and $q, b \in [0, 1]$. Because there are concurrent and parallel tasks in the process of task execution, $T_m$ can not be expressed analytically. In fact, $T_m$ mainly depends on the use and invocation of resources. Therefore, as the use of resources is determined, $T_m$ is also determined.

At this point, to get the optimal solution of $J$, it can be divided into three situations: (1) Sub task types are different, for example, now there are three sub tasks of remote sensing, communication and computation. Then the optimal solution can be obtained by finding the largest resource $e_i$ of $c(Task_i, e_i)$, $1 - q(Task_i, e_i)$, $1 - b(Task_i, e_i)$ in remote sensing resources, communication resources and computing resources. (2) If the subtasks are of the same type, optimization strategies such as artificial search algorithm, local search algorithm and genetic algorithm can be used to solve the problem, so that Eq. (3) achieves the maximum value. (3) If there are both the same type and different subtasks, then proceed according to steps (1) and (2) [15, 16].

## 4   Concluding Remarks

Aiming at the architecture design of spatial information network, this paper proposes a task-centered modeling method, which aims to provide a basis for the construction of spatial information network. The idea and principle of modeling are expounded. Modeling is carried out from five aspects: task resources, task objectives, task description, constraint conditions and task standards. Spatial tasks are decomposed and reorganized. The flow of task planning and resource invocation is designed, and the process of resource invocation is mathematically modeled, which improves the efficiency of resource utilization and the efficiency of space tasks in spatial information networks. China has initially built a multi-track and multi-functional space-based information system, which lays a foundation for the construction of space information network, but the construction of the whole system will be a huge and long process. This paper is only a preliminary exploration of the architecture of spatial information network. For the Taac modeling method, further modeling, topology control and network protocol research is the next key research direction.

## References

1. Zhang, W.: Topological control theory and method of space information network. Nanjing, PLA University of Science and Technology (2016)
2. National Natural Science Foundation. The program guidance of the basic theory and key technology research of space information network in 2006 [EB/OL]. http://www.nsfc.gov.cn/publish/portal0/tab38/info51946.htm. Accessed 25 Mar 2016

3. Wang, J.C., Yu, Q.: System architecture and key technology of space information network based on distributed satellite clusters. ZTE Technol. J. **22**(4), 9–13 (2016)
4. Jian, P., Xiong, W.: Research on activity based methodology of modeling C4ISR system architecture. J. Equip. Acad. **20**(5), 50–55 (2009)
5. Axford, R., Short, S., Shchupak, P., Muhammad, N.: Wideband global SATCOM (WGS) earth terminal interoperability demonstrations. In: Milcom IEEE Military Communications Conference, pp. 1–6 (2008)
6. Nishiyama, H., Tada, Y., Kato, N., Yoshimura, N., Toyoshima, M., Kadowaki, N.: Toward optimized traffic distribution for efficient network capacity utilization in two-layered satellite networks. IEEE Trans. Veh. Technol. **62**(3), 1303–1313 (2013)
7. Lin, P., Kuang, L., Chen, X., et al.: Adaptive subsequence adjustment with evolutionary asymmetric path-relinking for TDRSS scheduling. J. Syst. Eng. Electron. **25**(5), 800–810 (2014)
8. Dong, F.H.: Optimal design and research of space information network structure. PLA University of Science and Technology, Nanjing (2016)
9. Zhang, D.Y., Liu, S.S.: Research on mesh – based architecture for space information network. Comput. Technol. Dev. **19**(8), 69–73 (2009)
10. Min, S.Q.: An idea of China's space-based integrated information network. Spacecr. Eng. **22**(5), 1–14 (2013)
11. Li, D.R., Shen, Y., Gong, J.Y., et al.: On Construction of China's space information network. Geomat. Inf. Sci. Wuhan Univ. **40**(6), 711–715, 766 (2015)
12. Xiong, W., Liu, D.S., Jian, P., et al.: Spatial information system modeling and simulation technology assessment, pp. 62–66. National Defense Industry Press, Beijing (2016)
13. Xu, K., Zhang, W.B., Liu, Z.G., et al.: Study of resources optimization algorithm for tasks in satellite network. J. ShenYang LiGong Univ. **29**(3), 55–59 (2010)
14. Wang, Y., Sheng, M., Zhuang, W., et al.: Multi-resource coordinate scheduling for earth observation in space information networks. IEEE J. Sel. Areas Commun. **36**(2), 268–279 (2018)
15. Jiang, Y.Q., Pan, C.S., Li, H., et al.: Resource management and task management based on space networks. Acta Arm Amentarh **25**(5), 595–599 (2004)
16. Fonseca, C.M., Fleming, P.J.: An overview of evolutionary algorithms in multiobjective optimization. Evol. Comput. **3**(1), 1–16 (2014)

# Overview of the International Satellite-Based COSPAS-SARSAT System

Wei Wang[1] and Shuming Wang[2(✉)]

[1] Intelligent Transportation Department,
China Transport Telecommunication & Information Center,
No. 1 Rear Road, Anwaiwaiguan, Chaoyang District, Beijing, China
[2] Research and Development Center (Beijing),
Shandong Institute of Aerospace Electronics Technology, Yiheng Building,
North 3rd Ring East Road, Chaoyang District, Beijing, China
wangshm@513bj.cn

**Abstract.** In order to provide emergency distress altering capacity from an aircraft, vessel or individual in distress, the COSPAS-SARSAT (COSPAS is an acronym for the Russian words "Cosmicheskaya Sistema Poiska Avariynyh Sudov," which translates to "space system for the search of vessels in distress"; SARSAT is an acronym for search and rescue satellite-Aided tracking) international satellite system has been operational for many years. In this paper, we give a detailed description of the system, looking at beacons, the space segment, and the ground segment; we also compare the system performance by using first generation and second generation of 406 MHz beacons, respectively.

## 1 Introduction

Too many persons lose their lives due to accidents and their fatal situation cannot be informed efficiently. The detection and location of an aircraft crash or maritime distress is of paramount importance to the search and rescue (SAR) teams and to the potential survivors. Studies show that if rescue is delayed beyond two days, the survival rate of an aircraft crash will be less than 10%. If the rescue can be accomplished within eight hours, the survival rate will be over 60%. Similar urgency can apply in maritime distress situations, particularly where injuries have occurred. Therefore, locate the distress rapidly can significantly improve rescue efficiency [1, 2].

In the 1970s, light aircraft were carrying emergency locator transmitters (ELTs), and these ELTs could be activated without human intervention in an emergency distress situation. Marine vessels also started carrying similar distress beacons, called Emergency Position Indicating Radio beacons (EPIRBs), which could float off a sinking ship and automatically emit a distress signal. However, if a plane or ship went down in a remote area or in inclement weather, the distress signal could not be detected for days or even weeks, which could be long after the distress beacon's batteries were depleted [1, 3, 4].

In the view of this, an intergovernmental organization, the international COSPAS-SARSAT programme, is established to coordinate satellite-aided search and rescue activities. This system use spacecraft and ground facilities to detect and locate the

Q. Yu (Ed.): SINC 2018, CCIS 972, pp. 52–61, 2019.
https://doi.org/10.1007/978-981-13-5937-8_7

signals of 406 MHz or 121.5 MHz distress beacons. In an emergency situation, the distress beacon emit a signal to the satellite constellation of the system, and then this signal is retransmitted to the nearest local user terminal (LUT), the LUT process the received signal and determine the beacon's position. When the position is already estimated, it is passed to the Mission Control Center (MCC) which automatically sends the information to the nearest Rescue Coordination Center (RCC). The informed RCC will coordinate the SAR forces to find out what had happened and rescue possible survivors [5–8].

In this paper, we introduce the origin and structure of the COSPAS-SARSAT system; and give a detailed description of the main three components of the system, including the distress beacons, the space segment and the ground stations, and then compare the system performance between using the first generation 406 MHz beacons and using the second generation 406 MHz beacons. We finally conclude this paper.

## 2   Origin and Structure

In order to locate the distress accurately and rapidly, particularly from remote areas, a satellite-based receiving system was proposed. In the mid-1970s, experiments were conducted in Canada. In these experiments, the Communication Research Centre and the Department of National Défence used an amateur radio satellite, called OSCAR, to demonstrate the feasibility of using satellites for detecting and locating the source of distress signals. Similar experiments at NASA in the United States and the French Space Agency (CNES) further showed the technical viability of such a satellite system. These agencies agreed to set up a joint experiment for SARSAT. In 1979, the former USSR (and later Russia) joined the experiment and developed a compatible system called COSPAS, and the COSPAS-SARSAT system was born [6, 9]. In order to ensure the continuity of the system, these four states ratified the International COSPAS-SARSAT Programme Agreement in July 1988 and make it available to all nations on a non-discriminatory basis. The programme now includes 43 participating countries and organizations worldwide. At the end of 2010, more than 30,000 people had been rescued through the use of the System [1].

As shown in Fig. 1, there are three main components to the COSPAS-SARSAT system [6],

- the beacons transmit the distress signals,
- the satellites detect and retransmit the distress beacon signals; and
- the ground component includes the LUTs that automatically receive and distribute the satellite-captured alerts to mission control centres (MCCs) worldwide, and the MCC execute the signals from the LUT and transfer them to the rescue coordination centers (RCC) and the SAR point of contact (SPOC).

The detailed information of these three components will be given in the following sections.

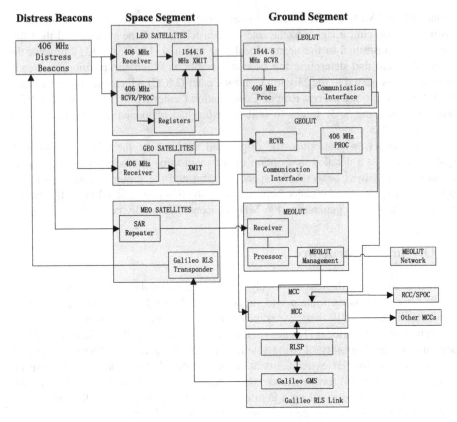

**Fig. 1.**  The system structure of the COSPAS-SARSAT

## 3  Distress Beacons

### 3.1  121.5/243 MHz Beacon

A beacon with a characteristic audio signal transmitted at 121.5 or 243 MHz can be
located to within 20 km. However, these emergency transmitters must be within a
3220-km radius of a ground terminal in order to be received. A major problem with the
121.5/243 MHz transmitters has been the large number of "false alarm" caused by
unintentional activation and by equipment failure [9]. Therefore, based on recom-
mendations from the International Maritime Organization (IMO) and the International
Civil Aviation Organization (ICAO), COSPAS-SARSAT decided to terminate the
satellite processing of 121/243 MHz signals [4]. From Feb. 2009, all these rescue
beacons transmit on 406 MHz [11].

### 3.2  406 MHz Beacon

In order to track down false alarm, a second system, using 406 MHz transmission, has
been designed specifically for use with satellites. This system provides the following

improvements over the 121.5/243 MHz system: global monitoring, location determination to within 5 km, and a beacon-specific message [10]. Because each beacon-specific message contains a user certification code, false alarm can be quickly tracked by contacting the beacon user. The 406 MHz beacon usually includes an auxiliary transmitter to enable suitably equipped SAR forces to home on the distress beacon [12]. For different purpose, two generations of 406 MHz beacons have been developed [9, 12].

**The first generation 406 MHz Beacon:** The carrier frequency is phase-modulated positive and negative $1.1 + 0.1$ radians peak with a digital message. The digital message transmitted by the first generation 406 MHz beacon consists of [4] (Fig. 2):

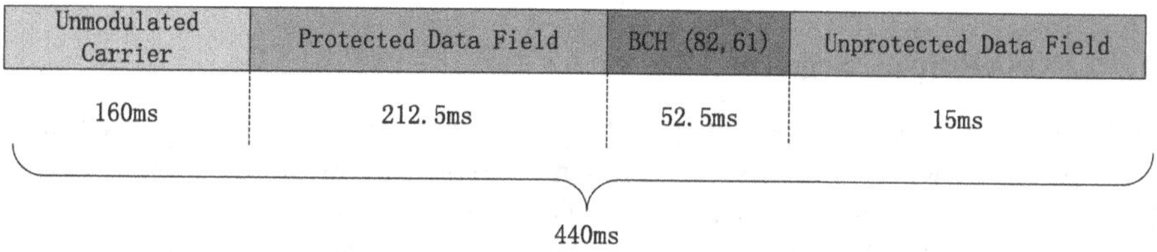

| Unmodulated Carrier | Protected Data Field | BCH (82, 61) | Unprotected Data Field |
|---|---|---|---|
| 160ms | 212.5ms | 52.5ms | 15ms |

440ms

**Fig. 2.** The short message structure

(a)  112 bits for the short message; and
(b)  144 bits for the long message (Fig. 3).

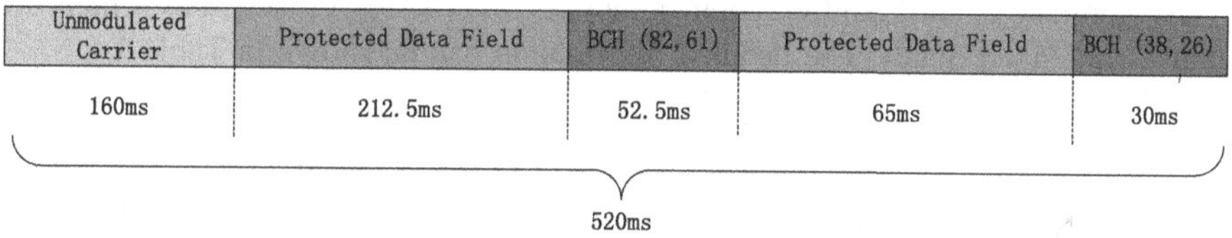

| Unmodulated Carrier | Protected Data Field | BCH (82, 61) | Protected Data Field | BCH (38, 26) |
|---|---|---|---|---|
| 160ms | 212.5ms | 52.5ms | 65ms | 30ms |

520ms

**Fig. 3.** The long message structure

**The second generation 406 MHz Beacon:** As the development of the third constellation of medium-earth orbit (MEO) COSPAS-SARSAT satellites, the second generation 406 MHz beacon has been proposed, and is expected to use in 2020. For the second generation 406 MHz beacon, the carrier frequency is modulated by offset quadrature phase shift keying (OQPSK) with a direct sequence spread spectrum spread digital message [13].

As shown in Fig. 4, the digital message consists of 202 information bits and 48 bits for Bose–Chaudhuri–Hocquenghem (BCH) (250, 202) error correction. The 202 information bits are further divided into [13]:

(a)  154 bits within the main data field (transmitted in every burst),
(b)  48 bits within a rotating data field (may be 1 of 16 different content types).

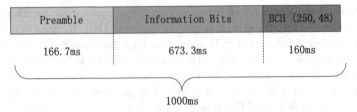

**Fig. 4.** The second generation 406 MHz Beacons' message structure

# 4 Space Segment

## 4.1 LEOSAR Space Segment

The COSPAS-SARSAT system of satellites in low earth orbit (LEO) is referred to as the COSPAS-SARSAT LEOSAR system. In order to stay in orbit, satellites at low altitude must move quickly over the earth. This movement causes a shift in the radio frequency called the "Doppler effect". The relative motion between the satellites and the beacon can be used to locate the distress beacons. When the satellite is at its time of closet approach to the beacon, the "Doppler curve" of frequency versus time has an inflection point. The LEOSAR system with polar orbiting satellites can provide a global, but the satellite may not be in a position to pick up a distress signal the moment a user activates the beacon. Delay of two hours or longer are possible, especially near the equator [1, 3].

The nominal system configuration comprises five SARSAT satellites which are operated by United States. The detailed information can be shown in Table 1.

**Table 1.** The space segment of LEOSAR (2018)

| No. | Name | Transmitted date | Status | Information |
|-----|------|------------------|--------|-------------|
| Sarsat-7 | NOAA-15 | May, 1998 | Operational | Exceed the design-working-life |
| Sarsat-10 | NOAA-18 | May, 2005 | Operational | Exceed the design-working-life |
| Sarsat-11 | Metop-A | Oct. 2006 | Operational | Exceed the design-working-life |
| Sarsat-12 | NOAA-19 | Feb. 2009 | Operational | Exceed the design-working-life, frequently failures in 2016 |
| Sarsat-13 | Metop-B | Sept. 2012 | Operational | |

## 4.2 GEOSAR Space Segment

In 1998, following several years of testing, geostationary satellites are employed by the COSPAS-SARSAT Council for detecting 406 MHz beacons (referred to as the GEOSAR system) [1]. The detailed information of geostationary satellites can be shown in Table 2.

**Table 2.** The space segment of GEOSAR (2018)

| Satellites | Longitude position | Status | Supplement |
|---|---|---|---|
| GOES-13 | 60° W | OFF | For backup |
| GOES-14 | 105° W | OFF | For backup |
| GOES-15 | 135° W | Operational | |
| GOES-16 | 75.2° W | Operational | |
| INSAT-3D | 82° E | Operational | Will be replaced by INSAT-3DR, and for backup |
| INSAT-3DR | 74° E | Operational | Will be used to replace INSAT-3D |
| GSAT-17 | 93.5° | Under test | |
| MSG-1 | 41.5° E | Operational | |
| MSG-2 | 3.5° E | Operational | Will be replaced by MSG-3 |
| MSG-3 | 9.5° E | Operational | |
| MSG-4 | 0° | Operational | Replace MSG-3 |
| Electo-L NO. 2, Louch-5A & 5 V | 76° E, 167° E & 95° E | Under test | |

With respect to the Earth's surface, the footprints of geostationary satellite are fixed; therefore, each satellite provides continuous coverage over the geographic region defined by its footprint. This reduces the detection delays associated with the LEOSAR system. However, GEOSAR systems can only obtained the location information from an external source which is transmitted in the 406 MHz beacon message. Because of their altitude each GEOSAR satellite provides coverage of a very large area (about one third the surface of the Earth excluding the Polar Regions) [1, 3].

### 4.3   MEOSAR Space Segment

The COSPAS-SARSAT system of satellites in medium-altitude earth orbit is referred to as the COSPAS-SARSAT MEOSAR system. This system can process the current COSPAS-SARSAT data and can function compatibly with the Galileo and Glonass satellites, and is planned to be run soon. The enhanced Galileo SAR service offers return link service with an integrated feedback channel [14]. Thus, besides executing only the information from the GEOLUT and the LEOLUT, by monitoring the information from the MEOSAR, the location of emergency will be determined with 99% success and it will serve to save more lives [15]. Currently, there are 40 MEO cospas-sarsat satellites, but only 35 can be used for COSPAS-SARSAT system. And, besides that, China has 6 Beidou MEO satellites are allowed to join the COSPAS-SARSAT system. The detailed information can be shown in Table 3.

There will be many possible SAR alerting benefits for using a MEOSAR system, including [14, 15]:

- near instantaneous global coverage with accurate independent location capability,
- robust beacon to satellite communication links, high levels of satellite redundancy and availability,

**Table 3.** The space segment of MEOSAR (2018)

| Satellites Constellation | Status | Bandwidth | Supplement |
|---|---|---|---|
| Galileo 401/402/403/404/405/407/408/409/414/418/419/420/424/426/430 | Fully operational | Wideband filter and automatic amplitude control | |
| Galileo 411/412 | Not applicable | Not applicable | No SAR repeater but can provide RLS |
| Glonass 501 | | Wideband filter and automatic amplitude control | Only can be used for test |
| Glonass 502 | Applicable | Wideband filter and automatic amplitude control | Can be used for test and location |
| GPS DASS S-band 301/302/303/306/308/309/310/312/315/316/317/319/323/324/326/327/329/330/332 | Fully operational | Not applicable | DASS tested repeater |
| GPS DASS S-band 318 | OFF | Not applicable | |

- resilience against beacon to satellite obstructions, and
- the possible provision for additional (enhanced) SAR services, such as a ground to beacon return link.

## 5  Ground Segment

The ground segment includes LUT and MCC.

### 5.1  LUT

Cospas-Sarsat LUTs receive the signal which is retransmitted by the satellites, process the received signal and determine the beacon's position. When the position is already estimated, it is passed to MCC [1]. Currently, in the worldwide, there are 42 LEOLUTs and 20 GEOLUTs (Mainly distribute over Americas and Europe) in service. For MEOSAR systems, there are 30 MEOLUTs, including built and under planned.

Note that, China has two LUTs (CNLUT-1 and CNLUT-2). Both can only receive distress signals from LEO satellites. However, the need to build a new MEOLUT has been approved by Ministry of Transport in July, 2017.

## 5.2   MCC

The main functions of an MCC are to [1, 4]:

- collect, store and sort the data from LUTs and other MCCs;
- provide data exchange within the Cospas-Sarsat System; and
- distribute alert and location data to associated RCCs or SPOCs.

Currently, China has one MCC, and this MCC can only receive signals from LEOLUTs. However, it will be updated to serve the MEOSAR system in the future.

# 6   Performance Analysis

In this section, we investigate the BER performance of the system between using the first generation 406 MHz distress beacons and the second generation 406 MHz distress beacons. For expository purpose, we assume the distress signals are transmitted through AWGN channel and are resent 1000 times. Under this assumption, we obtained the BER curves versus signal-to-noise ratios (SNRs) as shown in Fig. 5. We note that the system using the second generation 406 MHz distress beacons can attain a BER of 0.2 at SNR $= -35.4$ dB, while the system using the first generation 406 MHz distress beacons requires an SNR of 11.9 dB to achieve the same BER performance.

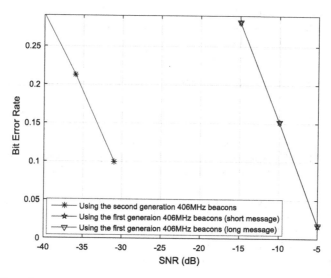

**Fig. 5.** BER performance comparison of the system using different type of beacon message

# 7   Future

Unfortunately, the Cospas-Sarsat system cannot necessarily save the distress situation as a malfunction of the beacon. For example, Air France 447 carrying 228 persons crashed into Atlantic in 2009. The beacons carried in this jet failed to transmit emergency signals. Also, the SOS signal from the missing Malaysia Airlines Flight 370 never came [16]. Thus, as many experts suggest, beacons need to be designed to allow detach from the sinking wreckage and remain floating on the water's surface. Also, the beacons should be able to begin transmission as fast as they can.

# 8   Conclusions

Cospas-sarsat system has been credited with saving thousands of lives. The development and evolution of the cospas-sarsat system are outlined in this paper, including the principle of operation and the current status. A performance comparison of using the first generation and second generation of 406 MHz distress beacons is also presented in this paper.

# References

1. Introduction to the COSPAS-SARSAT system, Issue 6, C/S G.003, October 2009
2. Katz, D.A.: Locating recording system. United States Patent Application Publication, No. US 7,855,654 B2, December 2010
3. King, J.V.: Cospas-Sarsat: an international satellite system for search and rescue. Space Commun. **18**, 139–150 (2002)
4. Specification for COSPAS-SARSAT 406 MHz distress beacons, Issue 4-Revision 1, C/S T.001, May 2017
5. Fernandez Prades, C., Closas Gomez, P., Fernandez-Rubio, J.A.: Time-frequency estimation in the Cospas/Sarsat system using antenna arrays: variance bounds and algorithms. In: 13th European Signal Processing Conference, Antalya, Turkey, April 2015, pp. 1–4 (2015)
6. COSPAS-SARSAT: saving lives with higher frequency-information for the Canadian aviation community about the switch to 406 MHz, No. D94-2 (2011). www.nss-snrs.gc. canada
7. Lee, J., Lee, S.: Emergency position indicating radio beacon terminal and apparatus and method for monitoring operating state thereof. United States Patent Application Publication, No. US 9,102,388 B2, August 2015
8. Cox, W., Pack, T.J.: Method of providing additional information to emergency services about emergency locator beacons. United States Patent Application Publication, No. US 9,049,585 B1, June 2015
9. Ivancic, W.D.: Cospas-Sarsat 406 MHz emergency beacon digital controller, NASA Technical Memorandum, No. 100859, August 1988
10. Street, W.A.: 406 MHz emergency beacon with in-band homing transmitter. United States Patent Application Publication, No. US2004/0087284 A1, May 2004
11. Cakaj, S.: Communication duration and missed passes among terminals and satellites for search and rescue services. Br. J. Math. Comput. Sci. **4**, 1771–1785 (2014)

12. Holmes, K., Street, W.A.: COSPAS-SARSAT beacon tester in a removable expansion card for a handheld computing device. United States Patent Application Publication, No. US 7,162,395 B1, January 2007
13. Specification for second generation COSPAS-SARSAT 406 MHz Distress Beacons, C/S T.018, Issue 1-Revision 1, May 2017
14. Lewandowski, A., Niehoefer, B., Wietfield, C.: Performance evaluation of satellite-based search and rescue services: Galileo vs. Cospas-Sarsat. In: 68th IEEE Vehicular Technology Conference, Calgary, September 2008
15. Kilic, O., Solik, A.: Recent performance in satellite networks for search and rescue: MEOSAR. In: Advanced Satellite Mobile Systems, Bologna Italy, pp. 317–319, 26–28 August 2009
16. COSPAS-SARSAT: Life saving beacons fail to save. Space Saf. Mag. (2014)

# Research on SINs Topology Evolution Mechanism: Considering Local-World

Shaobo Yu, Lingda Wu$^{(\boxtimes)}$, Xiangli Meng, and Xitao Zhang

Space Engineering University, Beijing 101416, China
Qilinbo2020@yeah.net, wld@nudt.edu.cn

**Abstract.** As an infrastructure of national strategy, the space information networks (SINs) is an important platform for information support. We analyze the demand for studying dynamic topology evolution of SINs, and we analyze the local-world phenomenon of SINs. Meanwhile, we propose the dynamic topology model, and based on its evolution characteristics, we propose dynamic evolution algorithm of SINs. Simulation results show that it has similar topology performance with real networks, and it verify the validity and feasibility of the proposed evolution mechanism. Finally, we summarize the content of this article, and prospect the future development.

**Keywords:** Space information networks · Topology · Mechanism · Local-world

## 1 Introduction

As a new research object, SINs mostly focus on the top-level design of the architecture and the construction of networks, and few literatures have reported the topology structure and evolution modeling [1]. However, the topology evolution of SINs refer to the description of the nascent, extinction and evolution of nodes and edges of SINs topology over time. It also refers to the process and mechanism of the formation, update, and change of topology structure of SINs. The SIN is an integrated information network system, and it is composed of satellite system, other information systems or terminals. It provides integrated investigation, navigation, communications and other services, and realizes battlefield situational awareness and so on [2].

The main purpose of researching the evolution of SINs is to establish a dynamic model and understand the key factors affecting the topology structure to understand the dynamic process of SINs, and gain a deeper understanding of the topology of SINs. The structure provides an effective basis for the construction and management of SINs. Structural decision function is the basic viewpoint of system science. How to combine the composition and characteristics of SINs, establish an effective model to analyze the topology structure and dynamic evolution characteristics, while providing theoretical guidance for the construction and management of the SINs, has evolved into the important part of SINs major theory and key technology research [3].

With a deeper research on complex networks, people gradually find a phenomenon. That is, a node is closely to some nodes, while is loosely to other nodes. Therefore, a local-world is formed between the closely nodes with each other. Within the local-world, there

© Springer Nature Singapore Pte Ltd. 2019
Q. Yu (Ed.): SINC 2018, CCIS 972, pp. 62–67, 2019.
https://doi.org/10.1007/978-981-13-5937-8_8

is a preferential connection mechanism, and this phenomenon is called local-world. This phenomenon is ubiquitous, such as economic networks, trade networks and mobile communication networks, etc. Study of local-world phenomena can be traced back to the year of 2003 [4]. Combining the compositional structure of SINs and the overall structural topology [5], the heterogeneity of network structure and business scope, and multi-layer and cross-domain of space distribution make the SINs show a more obvious local-world phenomenon. By comparison, because of the large number of nodes in the adjacent space layer and the complexity and uncertainty of the formation of the aircraft, the hot air balloon network, and the trajectory, the local-world phenomenon is more obvious, and the overall performance of the network is affected [6].

## 2  SINs Evolution Mechanism

The aim of this section is to describe SINs dynamic topology model, analysis SINs dynamic evolution characteristics and propose an evolution framework of SINs.

### 2.1  SINs Dynamic Topology Model

Network is usually represented by a graph. SINs are different from simple network, and the complexity of its compositional structure and the diversity of its functions make it a more complex network topology. SINs contain multi-nodes and multiple information exchange relationships. Therefore, according to the set of nodes and edges, a static topology model $G$ of SINs is established as follow.

$$G := <V, E> \tag{1}$$

where, symbol $V$ represents a limited set of network nodes, and $E(E \subseteq V \times V)$ represents a limited set of edges. A time factor introduced can define the dynamic topology model of SINs, and one 5-tuple is used to describe the model in this article, and its mathematical representation is

$$G_i := <V_i, Av_i, E_i, Ae_i, t_i> \tag{2}$$

where, symbol $t_i$ represents ordered time point, and $0 \leq i \leq T$. Symbol $T$ represents the set of time point, and symbol $V_i$ and $E_i$ represents a finite set of nodes and edges at time $t_i$, and symbol $Av_i$ and $Ae_i$ represents the node attribute set and edge attribute set at time $t_i$. Meanwhile, defining these time points does not need to be equally spaced, that is, they may change at consecutive times between two time points $(t_{i+1} - t_i)$.

### 2.2  SINs Dynamic Evolution Framework

Based on the dynamic features and the local-world phenomenon, we design its evolutionary framework as follow (Fig. 1).

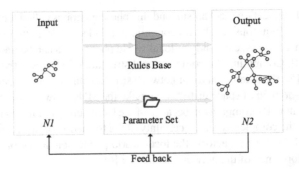

**Fig. 1.** SIN topology evolution framework.

In the evolution framework, *N1* represents the initial state of evolution, and *N2* represents the end of evolution. By controlling different parameters, the corresponding evolution rules are selected so as to achieve dynamic evolution. In the evolution process, feedback is also required at all times in order to achieve a better evolutionary effect.

### 2.3    SINs Dynamic Evolution Characteristics

The aim of this section is to analysis SIN dynamic evolution characteristics. From the perspective of time and space, dynamic is one of prominent features of SINs, and its dynamic feature can be further refined into time-varying of time domain and space-varying of space domain. For SINs, its time-varying features and space-variant features exist simultaneously, and this leads to its topology in real-time dynamic changes, and greatly increases the irregularity of its network topology. At the same time, changes also affect the properties of the nodes and edges of the network. Therefore, to establish a local-world evolution model for SIN dynamic topology, the following four evolution characteristics need to considered, and it can be more accurately and effectively study the dynamic evolution.

- Feature 1: Time-varying of topology
- Feature 2: Space-varying of topology
- Feature 3: Change of edge-weight
- Feature 4: Priority choice of local-world

### 2.4    SINs Dynamic Evolution Algorithm

Combining with the inseparability of topology structure and evolution, we believe that the topology model of SINs are the initial moment of its dynamic evolution model, that is, the model with $t = t_0 = 0$. Therefore, based on the previous research contents, the steps to implement the algorithm as follows.

**Step 1:** At the initial time $t_0 = 0$, the initial topology model of SIN is generated, and the initial time is a fully-coupled network with $n$ nodes and $e_0$ edges, and each edge is given an initial value $w_0$.

**Step 2:** At the time $t = t_0 + \Delta t$, randomly select $M(M < n)$ nodes as a local-world from the generated SIN, and proceed with the following operation with a certain probability. Assume that the time $t$ obeys the exponential distribution of the parameter of $\beta$, and when the evolution time $t = t_n$, the evolution is complete.

Adding a new node $v_i$ to the local-world with probability of $p_1$, and this node establishes a connection with the existing $m$ nodes in the local-world. The connected nodes are preferably taken in accordance with the probabilistic

$$p_1 = \prod_{i,j \in local}(i \to j) = \frac{s_j}{\sum_{k \in local} s_k - s_i} \tag{3}$$

The dynamic evolution of edge-weight is the same as that of bidirectional selection rule. Adding $m_1$ as a new edge to the local-world with the probability of $p_2$, and in the local-world, one node is randomly selected as one end of the edge, and the other end is selected in the local-world by the content of evolutionary rule.

$$\omega_{ij} \to \omega_{ij} + \Delta\omega_{ij} \tag{4}$$

where, $\Delta\omega_{ij} = \alpha_i \frac{\omega_{ij}}{s_i}$, and each time a new edge $e_i$ is introduced, additional traffic $\alpha_i$ will be brought to node $v_i$. The connected edges share a certain amount of traffic according to their own weight $\omega_{ij}$. So the strength of node $v_i$ is readjusted to

$$s_i \to s_i + \alpha_i + \omega_0 \tag{5}$$

where, the meaning of symbols are the same as above. Increasing the number of new edges $m_2$ inside the local-world and outside the local-world with probability of $p_3$, and increasing the number of connections inside and outside the local-world. In the local-world, the node of the network is selected as the end of the edge probability

$$p_2 = \prod_{i \in local} = \frac{s_i}{\sum_{k \in local} s_k} \tag{6}$$

and the other end is selected outside the local domain probability

$$p_3 = \prod_{j \in local\text{-}world} = \frac{s_j}{\sum_{k \in local\text{-}world} s_k} \tag{7}$$

Deleting $m_3$ links with probability of $p_4$, randomly selecting one point as the edge of the edge in the local-world, and selecting the other probability in the local-world.

$$p_4 = 1 - \prod_{j \in local} = 1 - \frac{s_j}{\sum_{k \in local} s_k} \tag{8}$$

Among them, $p_1 + p_2 + p_3 + p_4 = 1$, and $p_1, p_2, p_3, p_4 > 0$.

**Step 3:** Repeating Step 2, and until $t = t_n$, ending the evolution.

## 3  Simulation Analysis

To verify the validity and feasibility of the proposed evolutionary model, this section carries on the simulation verification analysis to this model based on MATLAB R2015b platform. Based on initial generation of SINs, the changes in the properties of the network topology are analyzed by analyzing the different values of the parameters $p_1, p_2, p_3, p_4, \beta, M, \alpha, m$. The focus will discuss separately from the following situations from local-world.

Assumptions: $t$ obeys the exponential distribution with $\beta$, and $\beta = 1$. The probability of values in the model is $p_1 = 0.5$, $p_2 = 0.2.5$, $p_3 = 0.15$, $p_4 = 0.05$.

**Situation (About Local-World):** Other conditions are determined, changing the value of the local-world $M$, and analyzing its impact on the features of the network topology. Determining the initial value is that $n = 30, w_0 = 1, m = 3, m_1 = m_2 = m_3 = 3, \alpha = 1, N = 1000$. Comparative analysis of the similarities and differences of the distribution of node degree, node strength, edge weight and correlation of strength and degree by changing the value of $M$ as shown in Fig. 2 below.

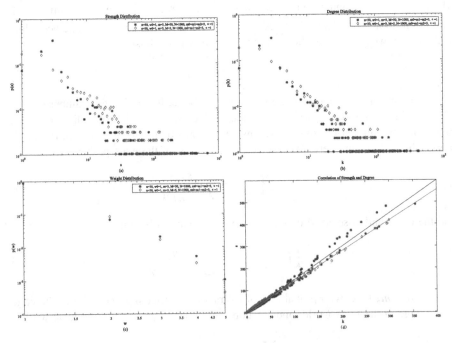

**Fig. 2.**  Analysis of the influence of local-world $M$

As shown in Fig. 2, keeping the other parameters unchanged, give the assignments $M = 30$ and $M = 5$ to observe the changes in the power law exponential distribution. From Fig. 2(a) and (b), it can be seen that in the case where the assignment of other parameters is determined, the larger the value of the local-world $M$ is, the more nodes with the stronger intensity are. From Fig. 2(c) and (d), we can see that the size of the local-world $M$ does not affect the effectiveness of the merit selection, nor does it affect the trend and the law of the distribution of edge-weight.

To sum up, this article focuses on the phenomenon of local-world. Therefore, the proposed model was evaluated experimentally using the parameters local-world. What needs to be said is that due to the limited length of the article, we also carried not out the simulation analysis of weight $w_0$. However, the simulation results show a similar pattern with extra traffic load $\alpha$, so we do not show and analyze the related simulation results again.

## 4  Conclusion

The dynamic topology evolution of SIN is a new direction formed by the intersection of SIN and complex network theory. This paper addresses the needs of topology evolution modeling for SIN and conducts research on the dynamic evolution framework. It is hoped to lay a theoretical foundation for the study of the dynamic evolution model of SIN through the analysis of dynamic topology evolution features and evolution rules.

In the future research, we should further improve the evolution rules and combine the local-world phenomenon and edge-weight characteristic of SIN to improve the weighted dynamic evolution model for SIN. Finally, it provide some methods and technical support for the construction and management of SIN.

## References

1. Zhou, J.G.: Research on key technology of spatial information network based on DTN, pp. 1–5. Wuhan University, Wuhan (2013)
2. Yu, S.B., Wu, L.D., Zhang, X.T.: Data as a center: an architecture modeling of space information network. J. Commun. **38**(Z1), 165–170 (2017)
3. Li, D.R., Shen, X., Gong, J.Y., et al.: On construction of China's space information network. Geomat. Inf. Sci. Wuhan Univ. **40**(6), 711–715 (2015)
4. Li, X., Chen, G.R.: A local-world evolving network model. Phys. A **328**, 274–286 (2003)
5. Yu, S.B., Wu, L.D., Zhang, X.T., et al.: Survey of multi-feature visualization for space information network. J. CAEIT **13**(2), 201–208 (2018)
6. Mu, X.Q., He, H., Wang, J.H.: Research on the model of the financial network evolution based on the weighted local-world. J. Syst. Sci. Math. Sci. **37**(5), 1272–1286 (2017)

# Theories and Methods of High-Speed Transmission

# Research on Multi-layer Satellite Network QoS Routing Strategy Based on Logical Clustering

Lifang Liu, Xiaoyan Chen[✉], Yan Wang, Zeyu Liu,
and Xiaogang Qi

Xidian University, Xi'an 710071, Shaanxi, China
15529017950@163.com

**Abstract.** In order to meet the QoS requirements of broadband communication services of the space information network, efficient routing strategies need to be designed. Due to different businesses have different requirements on QoS, the existing on-board routing strategies cannot solve the problem simply and efficiently. Therefore, we design a multi-layer satellite network architecture based on logical cluster management model. Then a dynamic bandwidth adaptive QoS routing algorithm based on multi-queue scheduling and link state is designed on the multi-layer satellite network architecture. The simulation results show that the QoS routing algorithm proposed in this paper can better meet the QoS requirements of various services.

**Keywords:** Satellite network · QoS · Logical clustering · Link state

## 1 Introduction

The satellite network undertakes the acquisition, transmission and distribution of a large amount of information. Meanwhile, the increase in the types and the traffics requires satellite network to provide more reliable and efficient services. Many of these services need the guarantee of Quality of Service (QoS), such as real-time services have high requirements for delay and delay jitter at the same time, while other services have limitations on packet loss rate and bandwidth [1]. Therefore, it is necessary to study the satellite network routing strategy that can provide QoS guarantee.

The single-layer centralized QoS routing strategy pre-calculates the routing table by predicting the network topology. For example, the LEO satellite network intelligent routing protocol proposed by Firouzj et al. is that when the network is congested, the satellite node will send its own status information to the ground control center for route recalculation [2]. In the single-layer distributed QoS routing strategy, a cross-layer design and ant-colony optimization routing algorithm based load-balancing for LEO satellite networks (CAL-LSN) proposed by Houtian et al. establishes a multi-objective optimization model to solve the multi-objective QoS routing problem [3]. The satellite network group routing protocol SGRP proposed by Chen et al. inherits the grouping idea of MLSR [4]. And this protocol is mainly to optimize the delay index and does not consider other QoS requirements. The multi-service routing algorithm based on GEO/LEO satellite network proposed by Yang, Sun et al. defines the link initial weight, delay, residual bandwidth, and it introduces the concept of the key link [5]. Because the

© Springer Nature Singapore Pte Ltd. 2019
Q. Yu (Ed.): SINC 2018, CCIS 972, pp. 71–76, 2019.
https://doi.org/10.1007/978-981-13-5937-8_9

algorithm is computationally complex and has a slow converges speed, it is not suitable for real-time business with large volume.

## 2  QoS Requirement and Satellite Network Structure

### 2.1  QoS Requirement Analysis

We define the QoS requirement for the i-th service as the following three constraints:

$$\text{End-to-end delay constraint:} D(p(s,d)) <= D_{QoSi} \qquad (1)$$

$$\text{Packet loss rate constraint:} L(p(s,d)) <= L_{QoSi} \qquad (2)$$

$$\text{Residual bandwidth constraint:} B(p(s,d)) >= B_{QoSi} \qquad (3)$$

Different types of businesses have different QoS requirements. According to the actual business conditions, the corresponding QoS constraints are shown in the following table [6] (Table 1):

**Table 1.** QoS classification and constraint indicators

| QoS level i | Business type | $D_{QoSi}$ (ms) | $L_{QoSi}$ (%) | $B_{QoSi}$ (Mbps) |
|---|---|---|---|---|
| 0 | Real-time voice data | <200 | <0.1 | None |
| 1 | Real-time multimedia data | <500 | <0.1 | None |
| 2 | General file | >1000 | 0 | >5 |

### 2.2  Multi-layer Satellite Network Model Based on Logical Clustering

In order to provide a more concise and efficient multi-layer satellite network structure, we design a multi-layer satellite network model based on logical clustering. The schematic diagram is shown as Fig. 1. In order to better describe the multi-layer satellite network model, the following concepts are defined:

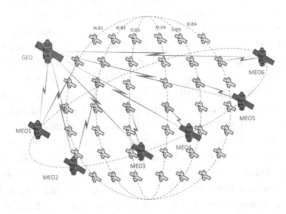

**Fig. 1.** Multi-layer satellite network architecture based on logical clustering

- $L_{clusteri}$: All LEO satellites in the same orbit become a cluster. $L_{clusteri}(x) = \{x|x \in LEO \text{ orbit } i\}$. In the LEO satellite layer, an orbit is represented as a cluster.
- $M_i$: Each $L_{clusteri}$ corresponds to a MEO satellite as its manager.
- $L_{clusteri\_head}$: It is defined as a specific intra-cluster LEO with the longest connection time of the MEO manager corresponding to the current cluster.

# 3 QoS Routing Algorithm Description

The essence of network QoS lies in the management of resources, which is to control the allocation and the use of network resources such as buffer queue and link bandwidth. Since this paper only considers the network of fixed-length data packet, combining the three kinds of QoS level obtained from the analysis of the satellite network business requirements of the second part, an appropriate multi-queue scheduling strategy is defined on the basis of [2].

In order to solve the problem of increasing the end-to-end delay of QoS level 0 and QoS level 1 businesses and reducing the throughput of QoS level 2 business when the real-time business data volume becomes larger, we propose a dynamic bandwidth adaptive routing algorithm based on link status (LSDBA). In order to describe the implementation of LSDBA, the following concepts are defined:

- $Route_{DBA}$: The routing table is used for the QoS level 2 business. It is the same as $Route_{DSP}$ at the beginning. As the remaining bandwidth of the network link changes, the computing node removes the link that does not satisfy the remaining bandwidth requirement in the network topology.
- $LSR_{LEO}$: The link state report $LSR_{LEO}(x)$ of LEO satellite x is represented by a quadruple $(rb_0, rb_1, rb_2, rb_3)$, where $rb_i$ represents the remaining bandwidth of the sending link of the LEO satellite node port i. The report is sent by the LEO satellite to the cluster head in the same orbit.
- $LSR_{clusterj\_head}$: $L_{clusterj\_head}$ collects all $LSR_{LEO}(x)$ of the same $L_{clusterj}$, and generates $LSR_{clusterj\_head} = \{LSR_{LEO}(x)|\forall x \in L_{clusterj}\}$. The report will be sent to the $M_j$ corresponding to this cluster.
- $LSS_{GEO}$: As a global computing node, GEO is responsible for collecting the link state information of each cluster sent by 6 MEO satellites. $LSS_{GEO} = \{LSR_{clusterj}|\forall j \in \{1, 2, 3, 4, 5, 6\}\}$.
- LSM: Searching $LSS_{GEO}$, if the remaining bandwidth between two nodes $b_{ij} < B_{QoS}$, then update the Link State Matrix, so that $\omega_{ij} = \infty$.

The pseudo-code of the algorithm is shown as below (Fig. 2):

---

**Algorithm 1. Dynamic Bandwidth Adaptive Routing Algorithm on Link State**

---

Input: one packet need to forward $Packet_{fwd}$

Output: find the next hop of the packet to the destination

1: while (TRUE)

2: 　　if (TypeofQoS($Packet_{fwd}$) == 0 ‖ 1)

3: 　　　　Search($Route_{DSP}$);

4: 　　else if (TypeofQoS($Packet_{fwd}$) ==2)

5: 　　　　　Search($Route_{DBA}$);

6: 　　end if

7: 　end if

8: 　if ($rb_i < B_{QoS}$)

9: 　　　LEO(x) send $\text{LSR}_{LEO}(x)$ to $L_{clusterj\_head}$;

10: 　　$L_{clusterj\_head}$ send $\text{LSR}_{clusterj\_head}$ to $M_j$;

11: 　　$M_j$ send $\text{LSR}_{clusterj\_head}$ to GEO;

12: 　　GEO use $\text{LSS}_{GEO}$ update LSM;

13: 　　GEO update $Route_{DBA}$ = Dijkstra(LSM);

14: 　end if

15: end while

---

**Fig. 2.** Dynamic bandwidth adaptive routing algorithm based on link state

## 4　Performance Analysis and Comparison

We analyze and compare the packet loss rate, average end-to-end delay and average throughput of the three types of business.

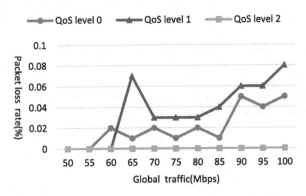

**Fig. 3.** Packet loss rate of three types of business with global traffic changes

As shown in Fig. 3, with the growth of global business volume, the packet loss rate of the two types of real-time businesses is on the rise within a certain range of business volume, and both of them are less than 0.1% of the QoS requirements. For general files, the packet loss rate continues to be 0.

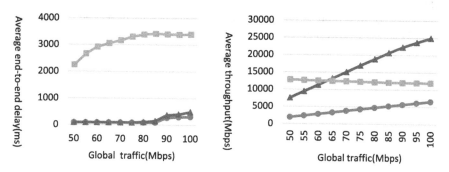

**Fig. 4.** Average end-to-end delay (left) and throughput (right) of three types of business with global traffic changes

From Fig. 4 (left) we can see that the average end-to-end delay of real-time voice data is basically kept below 300 ms. For general file data, it increases with the increase of global business volume, and the overall delay is in seconds. As shown in Fig. 4 (right), since the volume of the real-time type data is gradually increased, the average throughput is also gradually increased. Due to the volume of general file remains constant, it can be seen that although the average throughput is slightly lower, the decline is not large.

## 5   Conclusions

We design a multi-layer satellite network architecture based on logic clustering, which makes the collection of state information in the network more simple and efficient. we combined the queue scheduling algorithm and the dynamic bandwidth adaptive routing algorithm based on link state. In the future research, GEO and MEO can also be used to forward user data.

## References

1. Matasaru, P.D., Scripcariu, L., Diaconu, F.: An up-to-date overview on QoS for Satellite IP networks. In: International Symposium on Signals, Circuits and Systems, pp. 1–4 (2017)
2. Firouzja, S.A.N., Yousefnezhad, M., Othman, M.F., et al.: A wised routing protocols for LEO satellite networks (2015)
3. Houtian, W., Qi, Z., et al.: Cross-layer design and ant-colony optimization based routing algorithm for low earth orbit satellite networks. China Commun. **10**(10), 37–46 (2013)

4. Chen, C., Ekici, E., Akyildiz, I.F.: Satellite grouping and routing protocol for LEO/MEO satellite IP networks. In: International Workshop on Wireless Mobile Multimedia, pp. 109–116 (2002)
5. Yang, L., Sun, J.: Multi-service routing algorithm based on GEO/LEO satellite networks. In: International Conference on Network and Information Systems for Computers, pp. 80–84. IEEE (2017)
6. Baohong, H.: IP network performance parameters and target requirements. Telecommun. Eng. Technol. 5, 26–29 (2001)

# The Investigation of Resource Allocation on Heterogeneous Space-Based Networks Based on SDN Framework

Boyu Deng[1,2,3], Chunxiao Jiang[2(✉)], Linling Kuang[2], and Shanghong Zhao[3]

[1] Department of Electronic Engineering,
Tsinghua University, Beijing 100084, China
[2] Tsinghua Space Center, Tsinghua University, Beijing 100084, China
jchx@tsinghua.edu.cn
[3] Air Force Engineering University, Xi'an 710077, China

**Abstract.** To overcome the problem about lacking space resource for our country, the integrated resource allocation management on heterogeneous space-based networks can break through the barrier of single service on a satellite system, which has become a hotspot in the space information network. This paper improves the SDN framework with three layers into a four-layer-framework based on heterogeneous space-based networks. Moreover, an integrated resource scheduling framework also with four layers is proposed to realize the management on services and resource, including the operations of defining unified service features, describing unified heterogeneous resource and constructing service-resource matching model. Meanwhile, a service-on-demand decoupling heterogeneous resource allocation algorithm is proposed to solve the coupling matching model. Simulation results show that the proposed algorithm has better performance in terms of resource utilization and convergence. Compared with the improved greedy algorithm, the resource utilization ratio of proposed algorithm is improved by 3.81%, 6.66%, 9.00%, 10.85%, 12.88%, 18.40%, 21.74%, 21.58%, 21.45% and 21.29%, meanwhile, the resource utilization ratio is increased by 28.86% on average. Therefore, the proposed algorithm has strong applicability on resource allocation in heterogeneous space-based networks.

**Keywords:** Heterogeneous space-based networks ·
Integrated resource scheduling · Multi-domain coupling · Service on demand

## 1 Introduction

With the increasing communication demands around the world, Space Information Network (SIN) is widely applied in multiple research areas, such as pelagic communications, emergency rescue and aerospace, especially can provide high dynamic service for terrestrial users and intensive service for hot spot region, which has become an important research direction in recent years [1]. Since the early studies of SIN, The United States currently has plenty of satellite resource, including more than one-fifth of

© Springer Nature Singapore Pte Ltd. 2019
Q. Yu (Ed.): SINC 2018, CCIS 972, pp. 77–88, 2019.
https://doi.org/10.1007/978-981-13-5937-8_10

Geostationary Earth orbit (GEO) satellites and much more low-orbit and medium-orbit constellations, such as Iridium, Globalstar, Orbcomm and O3b. Depending on the sufficient satellites as well as ground stations spread all over the world, The United States constructs a satellite communication architecture called global information center with satellite-terrestrial networks [2–6]. In comparison, there are two reasons constrained the development of SIN in China: (1) limited number of satellites; (2) ground stations are only distributed within the territory, for which the resource of orbits, frequency and ground stations far behind that of the United States and European countries [7]. Furthermore, since different satellite systems have developed independently, it is difficult to realize the real-time access and fast respond between different satellite systems for users. Therefore, integrating the communication satellite system and relay satellite system to construct a Heterogeneous Satellite Communication network (HSCN), which can provide services of efficient satellite coordination and unified resource management, has become a way that can improve the resource utilization of the whole network. However, the future satellite network combined the advantages of coverage and communication links is able to break through the limitation of specific service served by the specific satellite system and to maximize the benefit of resource utilization, which can support various network functions, including access anytime and anywhere, resource allocation on demand and fast response for users.

For different satellite systems in HSCN, their resources have obvious difference in terms of feature, usage and restriction, which is difficult to depict by unified model or formulation. In addition, statistical properties of service are seen as important reasons to allocate resource of SIN, which results in the low allocation efficiency and serious resource waste. Software Defined Network (SDN) suggests to disassociate the data plane from the control plane and abstracts the physical network into multiple virtual networks, which is widely applied in terrestrial networks and is also appropriate for HSCN due to the flexibility of network configuration [8, 9]. In order to further realize the efficient resource management for the whole network, virtualization technology is used to extract and integrate the network resources.

The rest of this paper is organized as follows. In Sect. 2, we extend the typical three-layer architecture of SDN into a novel SDN framework with four-layer design. Based on the improved SDN framework, a resource management architecture of HSCN is investigated in Sect. 3. In order to further improve the resource utilization, we study the resource allocation algorithm in Sect. 4, and the performance of the proposed algorithms is evaluated by simulations in Sect. 5. Finally, the paper concludes with a summary in Sect. 6.

## 2    SDN Framework in HSCN

As considering the features of different satellite systems, we combine SDN and virtualization technology to propose an SDN Framework in HSCN, which is shown in Fig. 1. The Framework consists of four layers, including Application Layer (AL), Control Layer (CL), Virtualized Function Layer (VFL) and Infrastructure Layer (IL), where AL and CL are connected by Northbound Interface as well as CL and VFL are connected by Southbound Interface. Northbound Interface is able to extract service demands from AL and Southbound Interface is used to obtain the information of resource usage from VFL, and finally we realize the matching between service and resource in CL. Furthermore, the unit of Integrated Service-Resource Management is used to the four layers, which is described in Sect. 3.

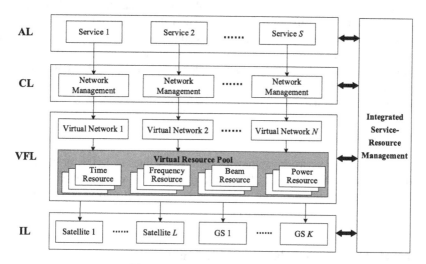

**Fig. 1.** Improved SDN framework

## 2.1 AL

In this framework of SDN, AL undertakes the mission of service collection and classification for HSCN. Satellite services in HSCN can be categorized into user services and management service, where user services consist of communication services, data transmission services and TT&C services, etc., management services include network configuration services, network monitoring services and network maintenance service, etc. By extracting features and demands of services, AL applies for network management in CL and realizes the efficient resource utilization. Since the process of feature extraction is appropriate for various types of space services, AL has strong expansibility to accommodate the increasing services in HSCN.

## 2.2 CL

CL is used to collect the requirements of services as well as maintain the management, allocation and monitoring for network resources, and especially realize the matching between services and resource, which can satisfy the different service demands of AL as well as guarantee the utilization of various resources in VFL. However, the centralized network management can be realized by setting and cooperating multiple controllers as well as defining protocol for their communications, in which each controller is served for a virtual network that defined in VFL.

## 2.3   VFL

VFL can provide virtualization function for the network, which is used to construct virtualized resource pool and divide virtual network. In order to construct virtualized resource pool, we first apply virtualization technology to extract logical resources (time, frequency, beam, power, etc.) to physical resources (satellite and GS, etc.), then, all the logical resources are collected and put into the virtualized resource pool, by which the resources from different satellite systems are managed intensively and efficiently. Based on the virtualized resource pool, network virtualization technology is also applied to abstract the HSCN into multiple virtual networks. Moreover, by considering the demand of services, the flexibly dynamic resource allocation can be realized by network management in CL.

## 2.4   IL

IL consists of various network equipment, such as satellites and GSs, or even smaller devices, such as satellite platforms, terminal payload and antennas, but we focus more on the coarse-grained physical unit which can be abstracted into virtualized resource and construct mapping relationship with VFL.

## 3   Integrated Service-Resource Management

In order to guarantee the communication between different satellite systems in HSCN, the efficient resource management method is require to be investigated. An architecture of integrated service-resource management is proposed and shown at Fig. 2, which consists of four layer and corresponds with the layers of SDN framework, respectively, including service feature management, network control management, virtualized resource management and physical resource management. In the layers of virtualized resource management and physical resource management, we study the unified description of heterogeneous resources, as well as, we study the unified description of service feature in the layer service feature management. Finally, we model the mapping relationship between service feature description and heterogeneous resource description.

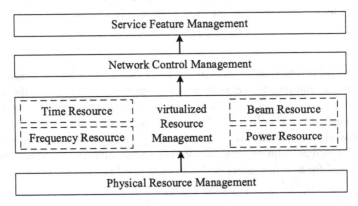

**Fig. 2.** The architecture of integrated service-resource management

## 3.1    Heterogeneous Resource Description

In HSCN, unified description is require to be applied for the satellites and GSs in different satellite systems, which is necessary to construct a universal model to realize the unified description of resource features and constraint conditions. Depending on this uniform model, heterogeneous resource can be managed or used in a centralized manner, which removes the influence of heterogeneity on physical resources.

(1)  Satellite resource description

The parameters of satellite have been determined when it enters into an orbit. Therefore, we can describe the satellite feature by its parameters, such as system type, orbit coordinate and coverage range. Generally, a satellite consists of platform and payload. In order to facilitate the management of logical resources, we focus more on the payload. Taking relay satellites and high-orbit communication satellites as examples, the payload mainly includes transparent transponders and processing transponders, which serve in different frequency bands, including Ku, Ka, S and UHF. Transparent transponders are usually used for amplification and forwarding of signals, which can support information interaction between different technical systems and network systems as well as satisfies various transmission requirements. The processing transponders can only support special network transmission because it is mainly used for signal processing under specific system.

In order to further improve the flexibility resource usage, we virtualize the physical heterogeneous resources into logical resources for description, including time domain, frequency domain, space domain and power domain. In the time domain, we can assign the start time and end time, or multiple different transfer period of a service. In the frequency domain, a carrier band can be divided into several available sub-channels and serve different services at the same time, respectively. Furthermore, technologies of frequency division multiplexing and OFDM can also be adopted to further improve the spectrum utilization. Beams are used to describe the resource in space domain. Since different satellites usually carry different types of antennas, their beams also have different transmission capabilities. In addition, if two beams with the same frequency are overlapped, the co-channel interference will be generated and will affect their spectral efficiency. The power domain can also be understood as the signal domain, where we can realize the maximization of spectral efficiency by reasonably allocating power while transferring the service. Obviously, there is a coupling relationship between the four resource domains. Therefore, it is necessary to design a reasonable resource allocation method in virtualized resource management, which can realize the optimization of four domains and achieve the global optimization.

(2)  GS resource description

The studies of resources allocation on satellite concentrate more on the optimization of satellite resources and have less consideration on GS resource optimization. However, the space service is always forwarded on satellites, and collected, processed and distributed at ground stations. Therefore, the communication capability of ground station directly affects the resource allocation efficiency of whole system. The features of ground station include type, position, frequency band, power and antenna gain, etc.

When the influence of ground station is incorporated into the resource optimization problem, it can be considered as a series of constraint conditions, which is defined as follows: (1) the technical standard of GS is appropriate for the matching satellite; (2) the GS is visible to the matching satellite while transmitting data; (3) the frequency band of GS is appropriate for the matching satellite; (4) the transmission rate between the GS and the matching satellite is larger than data transmission rate on satellites.

## 3.2 Service Feature Description

Service feature description is to extract the common features from various services and define the unified model to represent the services, which is beneficial to unify the description of resource allocation on demand. In addition, the constraint of services is also required to be constructed for the specific service feature which is difficult to describe. We select five features to realize the unified description, including coordinate, timeliness, QoS, priority and decomposability.

Coordinate represents the position of generated service, which is used to determine the visible time window between the service and satellites, where the time window of service $n$ can be defined as $[Ws_n, We_n]$, obviously, the assigned time of service must be in the time window. Moreover, the service is required to be satisfied timeliness, which represents that a service may lost its value if the service exceed its valid time, thus, $[Vs_n, Ve_n]$ is defined as the valid time of service $n$. The studies of QoS are pay more attention to the requirements of delay and transmission rate, for which different types of services, such as text, voice, video, etc., also have different transmitted demand. Priority is used to determine that the processing order of services, which is also related with timeliness. When a conflict is generated between multiple services, the high-priority service is prior to be assigned. Decomposability is used to represent whether a service could be served at multiple periods or can not be interrupted while transmitting data. In other words, the complexity of service assignment is increasing with the growing decomposed sub-service, which is also a tradeoff problem for the resource optimization.

## 3.3 The Matching Model of Service and Resource

Under the conditions of coupled multiple-dimension resources, the service demand is determined as the important factor to construct the matching model of service and resource. The definition of model and parameters are shown as follow (Table 1).

**Table 1.** Parameter definition

| Parameter | Physical meaning |
|---|---|
| $N, T, M, B$ | Number of services, time slots, beams and frequency bands |
| $x_{n,t,m,b}$ | Resource allocation indicator, if service $n$ is served by beam $m$ on frequency $b$ at time slot $t$, $x_{n,t,m,b} = 1$; otherwise, $x_{n,t,m,b} = 0$ |
| $y^m_{n_i,n_j}$ | Service switch indicator, if beam $m$ is switched from service $n_i$ to $n_j$, $y^m_{n_i,n_j}=1$; otherwise, $y^m_{n_i,n_j}=1$ |
| $[Vs_n, Ve_n]$ | The valid time of service $n$ |
| $[Ws_{n,m}, We_{n,m}]$ | The visible time window of service $n$ to beam $m$ |

*(continued)*

**Table 1.** (*continued*)

| Parameter | Physical meaning |
|---|---|
| $st_n, et_n$ | The start time and end time of service $n$, $st_n = \{\min t \mid x_{t,m,b}, \forall t, m, b\}$, $et_n = \{\max t \mid x_{t,m,b}, \forall t, m, b\}$ |
| $T_n^c$ | The maximized delay value for service $n$ |
| $R_n^c$ | The minimized transmission rate for service $n$ |
| $Q_n$ | The quantity of service $n$ |
| $BS_{t,m}(n_i, n_j)$ | The switch time of beam $m$ from service $n_i$ to $n_j$ at time slot $t$ |
| $M_E$ | The beam number of infrastructure $E$ |
| $BW_{m,b}$ | The bandwidth of $b$th frequency band on beam $m$ |
| $B_E$ | The maximized bandwidth of infrastructure $E$ |
| $P_{n,t,m,b}$ | The allocated power of service $n$ served by beam $m$ on frequency $b$ at time slot $t$ |
| $P_E$ | The maximized power of infrastructure $E$ |
| $R_{n,t,m,b}$ | The rate of service $n$ served by beam $m$ on frequency $b$ at time slot $t$ |
| $R_{t,m,b}$ | The maximized rate of a service served by beam $m$ on frequency $b$ at time slot $t$ |

$$\max \frac{\sum_{n=1}^{N}\sum_{t=1}^{T}\sum_{m=1}^{M}\sum_{b=1}^{B} R_{n,t,m,b} x_{n,t,m,b}}{\sum_{t=1}^{T}\sum_{m=1}^{M}\sum_{b=1}^{B} R_{t,m,b}}$$

$s.t.$

$$C_1 : Vs_n \leq st_n, et_n \leq Ve_n, \qquad \forall n,$$

$$C_2 : Ws_{n,m} \leq st_n, st_n \leq We_{n,m}, \qquad \forall n, m,$$

$$C_3 : et_n - st_n \leq T_n^c, \qquad \forall n$$

$$C_4 : R_{n,t,m,b} x_{n,t,m,b} \geq R_n^c, \qquad \forall n, t, m, b,$$

$$C_5 : \sum_{t=1}^{T}\sum_{m=1}^{M}\sum_{b=1}^{B} R_{n,t,m,b} x_{n,t,m,b} = Q_n, \quad \forall n,$$

$$C_6 : st_{n_j} \geq et_{n_i} + BS_{t,m}(n_i, n_j), \quad if \ y_{n_i,n_j}^m = 1,$$

$$C_7 : y_{n_i,n_j}^m \in \{0,1\}, \qquad \forall n_i, n_j, m,$$

$$C_8 : \sum_{m \in S} x_{n,t,m,b} \leq M_E, \qquad \forall n, t, b,$$

$$C_9 : \sum_{m \in S}\sum_{b=1}^{B} BW_{m,b} x_{n,t,m,b} \leq B_E, \quad \forall n, t,$$

$$C_{10} : \sum_{m \in S}\sum_{b=1}^{B} P_{n,t,m,b} x_{n,t,m,b} \leq P_E, \qquad \forall n, t,$$

$$C_{11} : P_{n,t,m,b} \geq 0, \qquad \forall n, t, m, b,$$

$$C_{12} : x_{n,t,m,b} \in \{0,1\}, \qquad \forall n, t, m, b,$$

Service Demands

Resource Constraint

(1)

Where $C_1$ is valid time constraint, which represents that a service must be completely transmitted at its valid time. $C_2$ is time window constraint, which represents that service can be served at its visible time window between the service and selected beam. $C_3$ and $C_4$ are QoS constraints, where $C_3$ is delay constraint, i.e., a service should not transfer with long time delay, $C_4$ is service quality constraint, i.e., transmission rate of service is require to satisfy the demand of users. $C_5$ is service execution constraint, i.e., the quantity of service equal to the sum of quantities of sub-services served by all the resource. A beam successively serves two services that may generates payload, thus, $C_6$ and $C_7$ are defined as beam switch constraint and beam switch indicator, respectively, which is to describe the process of beam switch. $C_8$ is beam number constraint, the number of beam used at the same time on an infrastructure can not larger than the number beam on the infrastructure. $C_9$ is frequency band constraint, i.e., the sum of used bands at the same time can not exceed the practical frequency band of each infrastructure. $C_{10}$ and $C_{11}$ represent the power constraint, the sum of allocated power for services at the same time can not larger than total of each infrastructure, meanwhile, the allocate power for service must exceed 0. $C_{12}$ represents the resource allocation indicator, which consists of $x_{n,t,m,b}$ and becomes a sparse solution space.

## 4   Decoupled Resource Allocation Algorithm

Obtaining service requirements is the premise of allocating resources. Reasonable resource allocation can achieve the matching between services and resources by considering the service requirements and resource status. However, in HSCN, resources in different domains resources are coupling, which may affect each other in the process of resource allocation, thus, it is difficult to obtain global optimization. For example, in the process of resource allocation, the typical greedy algorithm takes the single factor of priority, completion, capacity and channel state information as the judgment of optimizing the time, space, and frequency domain resources, which has poor applicability for the multi-domain resource optimization [3, 10–13]. On the other hand, if we optimize the resource allocation accurately, the overall resource optimization can be realized, but it undoubtedly increases the complexity of the algorithm.

According to the above analysis, beam is the basis of resource allocation in multi-domain. Due to the sparsity, beam with same frequency has few opportunities to overlap by apply beam allocation algorithm at the same time. Moreover, power allocation always based on the spectrum allocation scheme, which is processed after optimizing time, space and frequency resource. Therefore, we prior couple the beam resource in the large time-space scale, which realizes the beam allocation and corresponding time scheduling, then, we allocate frequency band for each beam to reduce the conflict between beams. After that, power allocation for each services is determined to further eliminate the interference among beams and to improve the resource efficiency (Fig. 3).

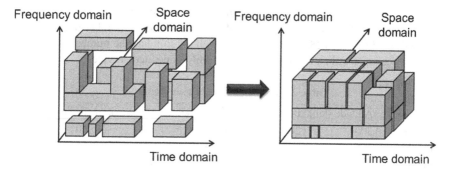

**Fig. 3.** Decoupled resource allocation

According to the above analysis, a decoupled resource allocation algorithm is proposed to solve the resource allocation problem in HSCN, which is described as follows:

Step 1: Initializing services and resource. Obtain service set $S$, which includes $N$ services, then, obtain resource states from virtualized resource pool, where space resource is divided into $M$ beams, time resource is divided into $T$ time slots, frequency resource is divided into $B$ bands. Meanwhile, set the power allocation as the manner of equal power allocation.

Step 2: Beam scheduling. Apply beam scheduling algorithm to possibly avoid the overlapping between different beams at time domain.

Step 3: Frequency allocation. Allocate frequency resources to each beam, where the technologies of OFDM and multiplexing are used to reduce the interference in beam density areas.

Step 4: Beam allocation. Compute the surplus degree of freedom of resource blocks for each beam, where the beams need to satisfy the constraints $C_1$–$C_5$ in (1). Find the service with minimum surplus degree of freedom to prior assign, until all the service traversed.

Step 5: Power allocation. Applying the algorithm in [13] to allocate power for each service, which guarantees that the number of services exceed the three-dimension blocks as little as possible.

Step 6: Adjustment of time resource for beams. Adjust the beam allocation for the fail assigned service, and repeat execute step 4 and step 5 until the resource allocation scheme converged.

## 5  Simulation and Analysis

The simulation scenario is composed by a relay satellite, a high-orbit communication satellite and 16 user satellites whose orbits information is from the American Geosciences Institute (AGI) database. The altitude and inclination of user satellites are shown at Table 2. The positions of the relay satellite and high-orbit communication satellite are defined as $0°$ and $162.324°E$, respectively. Meanwhile, we assume that the relay satellite generates 3 beams, where 2 spot beam work at Ka band and 1 spot beam works at S band, the communication satellite carries 10 spot beams worked at Ka band. In this section, we simulate the resource utilization curve at the number of services 16, 32, 48, 64, 80, 96, 112, 128, 144 and 160, as well as, simulate the number of iterations versus the resource utilization under 100 randomly generated services.

**Table 2.** The parameters of user satellites

| User satellite | Altitude (km) | Inclination (°) | User satellite | Altitude (km) | Inclination (°) |
|---|---|---|---|---|---|
| LEO 01 | 300 | 20 | LEO 09 | 700 | 60 |
| LEO 02 | 350 | 25 | LEO 10 | 750 | 65 |
| LEO 03 | 400 | 30 | LEO 11 | 800 | 70 |
| LEO 04 | 450 | 35 | LEO 12 | 850 | 75 |
| LEO 05 | 500 | 40 | LEO 13 | 900 | 80 |
| LEO 06 | 550 | 45 | LEO 14 | 950 | 85 |
| LEO 07 | 600 | 50 | LEO 15 | 1000 | 90 |
| LEO 08 | 650 | 55 | LEO 16 | 1050 | 95 |

As shown in the Fig. 4, the proposed algorithm has better performance than the greedy algorithm in the term of resource utilization. Comparison with greedy algorithm, the proposed algorithm improves 3.81%, 6.66%, 9.00%, 10.85%, 12.88%, 18.40%, 21.74%, 21.58%, 21.45% and 21.29% under the 10 situations of service number. Under the small number of service, the performance of proposed algorithm has obvious improvement, meanwhile, when the number of services is larger than 100, the resource utilization of two algorithms become stable. Comparing with the improved greedy algorithm, the proposed algorithm optimizes 28.86% in the term of resource utilization on average.

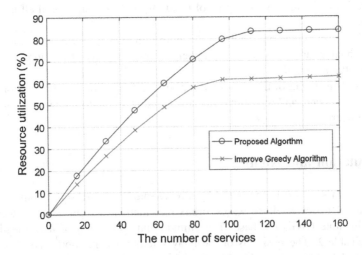

**Fig. 4.** The number of service versus the resource utilization under the different number of service.

As shown in the Fig. 5, under the condition of 100 randomly generated services, the resource utilization of the algorithm is optimized with continuous iterations and converged at the 35th iteration. Obviously, the proposed algorithm has strong convergence and the resource utilization reaches 80.64%. Meanwhile, there is a situation that the value of resource utilization is not improved in some iterations, which represents that the algorithm is trapped in the local optimization during these iterations, but then it jumps out of the local optimization through the reliable optimization strategy and finally reaches convergence.

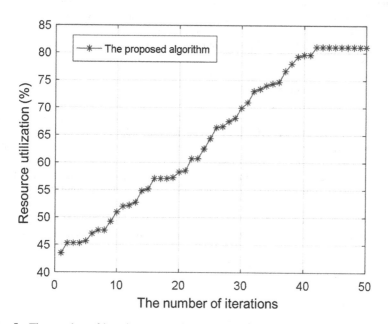

**Fig. 5.** The number of iteration versus the resource utilization under the 100 services.

## 6   Conclusion

By improving the typical SDN framework, this paper proposes an integrated service-resource management architecture, which realizes the unified description of heterogeneous resources, the unified description of service features and the matching model between services and resources, meanwhile, a decoupled resources allocation algorithm is proposed to solve the heterogeneous resource allocation problem. The results show that the algorithm proposed in this paper can realize the efficient resource allocation of the heterogeneous satellite network when the small scale resources are require to be allocated. Considering the continuous increasing of resources and service in HSCN, we plan to make use of the machine learning in the next work and focus on the research of resource allocation based on deep reinforcement learning.

# References

1. Deren, L.I., Xin, S., Gong, J., et al.: On construction of China's space information network. Geomat. Inf. Sci. Wuhan Univ. **40**, 711–715 (2015)
2. Axford, R., Short, S., Shchupak, P., et al.: Wideband global SATCOM (WGS) earth terminal interoperability demonstrations. In: 2008 IEEE Military Communications Conference, MILCOM 2008, pp. 1–6. IEEE (2008)
3. Bisio, I., Marchese, M.: Power saving bandwidth allocation over GEO satellite networks. IEEE Commun. Lett. **16**(5), 596–599 (2012)
4. Defense Industry Daily. Special Report: The USA's Transformational Communications Satellite System (TSAT) [EB/OL]. http://www.defenseindustrydaily.com/special-report-the-usas-transformational-communications-satellite-system-tsat-0866/. Accessed 19 Mar 2015
5. Cheah, J.: Contributions to MUOS communication link assessments at the Arctic Circle locations. In: Military Communications Conference, Milcom 2015, pp. 187–192. IEEE (2015)
6. ITU Telecommunication Standardization Sector. http://www.itu.int/en/ITU-T/Pages/default.aspx
7. Bertaux, L., Medjiah, S., Berthou, P., et al.: Software defined networking and virtualization for broadband satellite networks. IEEE Commun. Mag. **53**(3), 54–60 (2015)
8. Open Networking Foundation. Software-defined networking: the new norm for networks (2012)
9. Sheng, M., Wang, Y., Li, J., et al.: Toward a flexible and reconfigurable broadband satellite network: resource management architecture and strategies. IEEE Wirel. Commun. **24**(4), 127–133 (2017)
10. Lin, P., Kuang, L., Chen, X., et al.: Adaptive subsequence adjustment with evolutionary asymmetric path relinking for TDRSS scheduling. J. Syst. Eng. Electron. **25**(5), 800–810 (2014)
11. Rojanasoonthon, S., Bard, J.F., Reddy, S.D.: Algorithms for parallel machine scheduling: a case study of the tracking and data relay satellite system. J. Oper. Res. Soc. **54**(8), 806–821 (2003)
12. Chandhar, P., Das, S.S.: Multi-objective framework for dynamic optimization of OFDMA cellular systems. IEEE Access **4**, 1889–1914 (2016)
13. Zhu, X., Jiang, C., Kuang, L., et al.: Non-orthogonal multiple access based integrated terrestrial-satellite networks. IEEE J. Sel. Areas Commun. **PP**(99), 1 (2017)

# Performance of Systematic Convolutional Low Density Generator Matrix Codes over Rayleigh Fading Channels with Impulsive Noise

Meiying Ji[1,3], Shengxiao Chen[2,3], and Xiao Ma[1,3(✉)]

[1] School of Data and Computer Science, Sun Yat-sen University,
Guangzhou 510006, China
maxiao@mail.sysu.edu.cn
[2] School of Electronics and Information Technology, Sun Yat-sen University,
Guangzhou 510006, China
[3] Guangdong Key Laboratory of Information Security Technology,
Sun Yat-sen University, Guangzhou 510006, China

**Abstract.** We investigate the systematic convolutional low density generator matrix (SC-LDGM) codes over Rayleigh fading channels with symmetric alpha-stable (S$\alpha$S) impulsive noise. The performance is analyzed by deriving a lower bound based on an equivalent genie-aided (GA) system. Numerical simulations show that the SC-LDGM codes can achieve a significant gain compared to the convolutional codes over Rayleigh fading channels with impulsive noise. Numerical results also show that the performance of the SC-LDGM codes can be around one dB away from Shannon limits at the bit-error rate (BER) of $10^{-5}$ and matches well with the GA lower bound in the low BER region.

**Keywords:** Genie-aided (GA) lower bound · Impulsive noise ·
Rayleigh fading channels · Symmetric alpha-stable (S$\alpha$S) model ·
Systematic convolutional low density generator matrix (SC-LDGM)
codes

## 1 Introduction

The additive white Gaussian noise (AWGN) channel model is widely used in communication systems. However, the noise is not always Gaussian in practical communication systems, such as powerline communication networks [1], shallow water communications [2] and satellite communications [3]. The noise caused by the superposition of electromagnetic radiation in these systems is typically non-Gaussian and impulsive [4]. Recently, it has been proved that the symmetric

X. Ma—This work was supported by the National Natural Science Foundation of China (No. 91438101).

© Springer Nature Singapore Pte Ltd. 2019
Q. Yu (Ed.): SINC 2018, CCIS 972, pp. 89–98, 2019.
https://doi.org/10.1007/978-981-13-5937-8_11

alpha stable (S$\alpha$S), based on generalized central limit theorem [5], is a proper model for the impulsive noise. Moreover, we also need to consider the fading effect in such wireless channels, such as Rayleigh fading [6,7]. Therefore, we consider Rayleigh fading channel with the impulsive noise in this paper.

Channel coding is an important technology to transmit data reliably in communication systems. In non-Gaussian impulsive channels, a modified extrinsic information transfer chart (EXIT) method was proposed in [8] for performance analysis of turbo codes, while an iterative analysis method based on an EXIT chart was developed in [9] for low-density parity check (LDPC) codes. In [10], the authors proposed joint channel estimation and LDPC decoding over impulsive noise channels. In [11], the authors analyzed the performance of LDPC-coded diversity combining over Rayleigh fading channels with impulsive noise. In [12], we investigated the performance of block Markov superposition transmission (BMST) scheme over channels with S$\alpha$S impulsive noise. This paper is the extension of [12]. On the one hand, we consider the channel model with the fading coefficients, which is more practical. On the other hand, we use systematic convolutional low density generator matrix (SC-LDGM) codes instead of BMST codes, because the systematic structure is more robust in the fading environment [13]. Moreover, SC-LDGM codes have a predictable lower bound and can be constructed flexibly with any given (rational) code rate.

In this paper, we investigate the SC-LDGM codes over Rayleigh fading channels with S$\alpha$S impulsive noise. We also present a BER lower bound of the proposed scheme based on a GA equivalent system. Numerical results show that the performance of the SC-LDGM codes can approach the corresponding Shannon limits over Rayleigh fading channels with impulsive noise and matches well with the GA lower bound in the low BER region.

## 2   System Model

### 2.1   System Model

Consider a system model consisting of transmitter, Rayleigh fading channel with impulsive noise and receiver. A source sequence is encoded by an SC-LDGM encoder resulting in a coded sequence, and then the coded sequence is modulated in binary phase shift keying (BPSK) manner. At the receiver, the received sequence $y$ is expressed as

$$y = hx + z, \tag{1}$$

where $h$ is a sequence of Rayleigh fading coefficients, $x$ is a bipolar sequence, and $z$ is a noise sequence which obeys S$\alpha$S distribution.

### 2.2   Noise Model

The S$\alpha$S distribution model is a steady-state distribution model with mean zero [5]. The probability density function (pdf) of S$\alpha$S distribution is

$$f_\alpha(z) = \frac{1}{2\pi} \int_{-\infty}^{\infty} \exp(i\delta t - \gamma^\alpha |t|^\alpha) e^{-itz} dt, \tag{2}$$

where $\alpha$ is the characteristic exponent with a range $(0, 2]$ which measures the tail heaviness of the pdf. From the pdfs of S$\alpha$S distributions for different $\alpha$, as shown in Fig. 1, we find that the smaller the parameter $\alpha$ is, the heavier the tail is. The parameter $\gamma$ is the dispersion which represents the spread of the S$\alpha$S pdf. The parameter $\delta$ is the mean, which depends on the value of $\alpha$. There are two special cases of S$\alpha$S distribution model. (1) When $\alpha = 2$, the distribution is Gaussian. (2) When $\alpha = 1$, the distribution is Cauchy. For practical communication systems, $\alpha$ is typically in the range $(1, 2]$.

Note that the complexity of the integral in formula (2) is very high, so a look-up table method is adopted in the simulations to reduce the computational complexity.

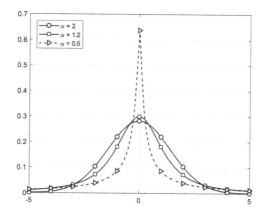

**Fig. 1.** Standard S$\alpha$S distribution$(\gamma = 1, \delta = 0)$

## 2.3   Geometric Signal-to-Noise Ratio

The power, as a second order moment, measures the signal strength generally, but the second order power is infinite in the S$\alpha$S distribution$(\alpha < 2)$. Hence the zero-order statistics (ZOS),

$$\mathbb{E}\{\log|Z|\} < \infty, \tag{3}$$

were proposed to characterize the S$\alpha$S process in [14], where $\mathbb{E}\{\cdot\}$ is the expectation operator. The geometric signal-to-noise ratio (SNR$_G$) is given as

$$\text{SNR}_G = \frac{1}{2C_g}\left(\frac{A}{S_0}\right)^2, \tag{4}$$

where $A$ is the signal amplitude, and the normalization constant $2C_g$ is used to ensure that the definition of the SNR$_G$ corresponds to that of the standard SNR if the channel noise is Gaussian. Since BPSK is used, $E_b/N_0$ can be given as

$$\frac{E_b}{N_0} = \frac{\text{SNR}_G}{2R} = \frac{1}{4RC_g}\left(\frac{A}{S_0}\right)^2, \tag{5}$$

where $R$ denotes a code rate.

## 2.4    Mutual Information Analysis

Mutual information analysis is a vital method in the study of coding and modulation. In general, when system model and channel are given, we can obtain the theoretical maximum transmission rate of communication systems by calculating mutual information, and then get the minimum signal to noise ratio (SNR), namely Shannon limit, required to achieve a given rate. We can analyze the performance of the proposed coding scheme compared to the Shannon limits. Assume that $X$ and $Y$ are the random variables corresponding to the transmitted symbol $x$ and the received symbol $y$, respectively. The mutual information between $X$ and $Y$ can be defined as

$$I(X;Y) = H(X) - H(X|Y), \tag{6}$$

where $H(\cdot)$ is entropy.

The mapping of bits to transmitted symbols can be expressed by a one-to-one mapping $\varphi : \mathbb{F}_2^N \to \mathcal{X}$, where $N$ is the number of bits per symbol. Suppose that the bits are independent and uniformly distributed. Therefore, the probability mass function (pmf) of $X$ is given as

$$\Pr\{X = x\} = \frac{1}{2^N}, x \in \mathcal{X}. \tag{7}$$

So

$$H(X) = \sum_{x \in \mathcal{X}} \Pr\{X = x\} \log_2 \frac{1}{\Pr\{X = x\}} = N, \tag{8}$$

and

$$H(X|Y) = \int_y p(y) \sum_{x \in \mathcal{X}} p(x|y) \log_2 \frac{1}{p(x|y)}, \tag{9}$$

which can be estimated by Monte Carlo simulations.

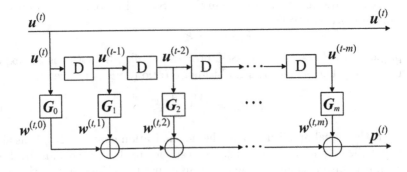

**Fig. 2.** The encoding diagram of the SC-LDGM codes with memory $m$

# 3    SC-LDGM Codes

## 3.1    Encoding

Let $\mathbb{F}_2 = \{0,1\}$ be the binary field. A binary linear code $\mathcal{C}[n,k]$ with length $n$ and dimension $k$ can be defined as a $k$-dimensional subspace on $\mathbb{F}_2^n$, which can be characterized a generator matrix of size $k \times n$. A low density generator matrix (LDGM) code is a binary linear code which has a sparse generator matrix.

Let $\boldsymbol{u}^{(t)} (0 \leq t \leq L-1)$ be $L$ blocks of information sequence to be transmitted, and the length of $\boldsymbol{u}^{(t)}$ is denoted as $k$. For $i = 0, 1, \ldots, m$, let $\boldsymbol{G}_i$ be the random matrix of size $k \times (n-k)$ with each column drawn independently and uniformly from the collection of all binary column vectors of weight 0 or 1. The encoding algorithm of the SC-LDGM codes of rate $R = k/n$ with encoding memory $m$ is described in Algorithm 1. See Fig. 2 for reference.

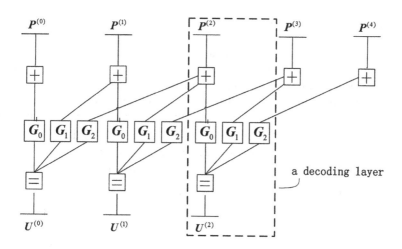

**Fig. 3.** Normal graph for an SC-LDGM decoder($L = 3, m = 2$)

## 3.2    Decoding

Assume that $\boldsymbol{y}^{(t)}$ are received, an iterative sliding-window decoding algorithm, which is a message passing algorithm over the normal graph, can be implemented to obtain the decoding result $\hat{\boldsymbol{u}}^{(t)}$. Figure 3 shows the normal graph [15] of the SC-LDGM codes with $L = 3$ and $m = 2$. The normal graph of the SC-LDGM codes can be divided into *layers*, where each layer typically consists of three types of constraint nodes, which are node $\boxed{=}$, node $\boxed{G_i}$ and node $\boxed{+}$. The node $\boxed{=}$ represents the constraint that all connecting variables must take the same value. The node $\boxed{G_i}$ represents the $i$-th generator matrix. The node $\boxed{+}$ represents the constraint that all connecting variables must be added up to zero. The decoding process of the SC-LDGM codes with decoding delay $d$ is described in Algorithm 2.

## 4   Performance Analysis

### 4.1   Genie-Aided Upper Bound

Similar to [13,16], we can obtain a genie-aided lower bound for the proposed scheme over Rayleigh fading channels with impulsive noise based on the GA equivalent system. Let $U = (u^{(0)}, u^{(1)}, \cdots, u^{(L-1)})$ be the transmitted sequences. For any given $t$, we assume that a genie tells the decoder all the transmitted sequences $u^{(\ell)} (0 \leq \ell \leq L - 1, \ell \neq t)$, except $u^{(t)}$. Let $f_{eq}(\lambda)$ and $f_{SC-LDGM}(\lambda)$ be the BER performance functions of the GA equivalent system and the proposed system, respectively, where $\lambda$ is $E_b/N_0$. Then $f_{SC-LDGM}(\lambda)$ can be lower-bounded by

$$f_{SC-LDGM}(\lambda) \geq f_{eq}(\lambda). \tag{10}$$

### 4.2   Complexity Analysis

Consider an SC-LDGM system with memory $m$. At the receiver, an iterative sliding-window decoding algorithm with decoding delay $d$ is used. The size of the generator matrix is $k \times (n-k)$. The complexity of the SC-LDGM codes can be analyzed from the normal graph. Let $Opt(A)$ denote the number of operations at a generic node $A$. Each decoding layer actually has $k$ parallel nodes $\boxed{=}$ of degree $m+2$, $n-k$ parallel nodes $\boxed{+}$ of degree $m+2$, and $m+1$ parallel nodes $\boxed{G_i}$ of degree $n-k$. In each iteration, the total number of operations for each decoding layer is $k \cdot Opt\left(\boxed{=}\right) + (n-k) \cdot Opt\left(\boxed{+}\right) + (m+1) \cdot Opt\left(\boxed{G_i}\right)$, where both the node $\boxed{=}$ and the node $\boxed{+}$ have computational complexity $O(m+2)$ and the node $\boxed{G_i}$ has computational complexity $O(n-k)$. To recover a target layer with a decoding delay $d$, the adjacent $d+1$ layers are involved. Hence, in each iteration, the total decoding complexity is given by $O((n(m+2) + (n-k)(m+1))(d+1))$. Note that the decoding complexity also relies on the iteration numbers. In our simulations, we found that, in the high-SNR region, $3 \sim 5$ iterations are sufficient on average to decode one layer with a properly designed stopping criterion.

## 5   Numerical Results

The results presented in this section are based on Monte Carlo simulations over Rayleigh fading channels with S$\alpha$S impulsive noise. We use SC-LDGM codes with rate 1/2 and BPSK modulation. The encoder terminates for every $L = 1000$ data blocks, and the length of each data block is set to 2048. The decoding algorithm performs with a maximum iteration number $J_{max} = 18$, a decoding delay $d = 3m$, and an entropy stopping threshold $\sigma = 10^{-5}$.

---

**Algorithm 1.** The encoding algorithm of the SC-LDGM codes

- **Initialization:** For $t < 0$, set $\boldsymbol{u}^{(t)} = \boldsymbol{0} \in \mathbb{F}_2^k$.
- **Loop:** For $t = 0, 1, \cdots, L - 1$,
  1) For $0 \leq i \leq m$, encode $\boldsymbol{u}^{(t-i)}$ into $\boldsymbol{w}^{(t-i)} \in \mathbb{F}_2^{n-k}$ by $\boldsymbol{w}^{(t-i)} = \boldsymbol{u}^{(t-i)} \boldsymbol{G}_i$.
  2) Compute $\boldsymbol{p}^{(t)} = \sum_{i=0}^{m} \boldsymbol{w}^{(t-i)}$ and take $\boldsymbol{c}^{(t)} = (\boldsymbol{u}^{(t)}, \boldsymbol{p}^{(t)}) \in \mathbb{F}_2^n$ as the $t$-th block to be transmitted.
  3) Map $\boldsymbol{c}^{(t)}$ into a transmission signal sequence $\boldsymbol{x}^{(t)}$ by BPSK.
- **Termination:** For $t = L, L + 1, \cdots, L + m - 1$, set $\boldsymbol{u}^{(t)} = \boldsymbol{0} \in \mathbb{F}_2^k$ and compute $\boldsymbol{x}^{(t)}$ following Step. **Loop**.

---

**Algorithm 2.** The iterative sliding-window decoding algorithm for SC-LDGM codes

- **Global initialization:** Assume that $\boldsymbol{y}^{(t)}$ have been received for $0 \leq t \leq d - 1$. First, compute the *a posteriori* probabilities of the information sequence $P_{U^{(t)}}^{(|\rightarrow=)}\left(\boldsymbol{u}^{(t)}\right)$ and the parity sequence $P_{P^{(t)}}^{(|\rightarrow+)}\left(\boldsymbol{p}^{(t)}\right)$ for $0 \leq t \leq d - 1$. Then initialize all messages over the other edges within and connecting to the $t$-th layer $(0 \leq t \leq d - 1)$ as uniformly distributed variables. Finally, set a maximum iteration number $J_{\max} > 0$. Set a threshold $\sigma > 0$ and initialize the entropy rate $H_0\left(\boldsymbol{Y}^{(t)}\right) = 0$, where $\boldsymbol{Y}^{(t)}$ is the random vector corresponding to $\boldsymbol{y}^{(t)}$.
- **Loop:** For $t = 0, 1, \cdots, L - 1$,
  1. **Local initialization:** If $t + d \leq L + m - 1$, compute $P_{U^{(t)}}^{(|\rightarrow=)}\left(\boldsymbol{u}^{(t)}\right)$ and $P_{P^{(t)}}^{(|\rightarrow+)}\left(\boldsymbol{p}^{(t)}\right)$. Initalize all messages over other edges within and connecting to the $(t + d)$-th layer as uniformly distributed variables.
  2. **Iteration:** For $J = 1, 2, \cdots, J_{\max}$,
     (a) *Forward recursion:*
         For $i = 0, 1, \cdots, \min(d, L + m - 1 - t)$, the $(t + i)$-th layer performs a message passing algorithm scheduled as
         $$\boxed{+} \rightarrow \boxed{G} \rightarrow \boxed{=} \rightarrow \boxed{G} \rightarrow \boxed{+}. \tag{11}$$
     (b) *Backward recursion:*
         For $i = \min(d, L + m - 1 - t), \cdots, 1, 0$, the $(t + i)$-th layer performs a message passing algorithm scheduled as
         $$\boxed{+} \rightarrow \boxed{G} \rightarrow \boxed{=} \rightarrow \boxed{G} \rightarrow \boxed{+}. \tag{12}$$
     (c) *Hard decision:*
         Make hard decisions to obtain the estimation $\hat{\boldsymbol{u}}^{(t)}$ corresponding to $\boldsymbol{u}^{(t)}$. Estimate the entropy rate $H_J\left(\boldsymbol{Y}^{(t)}\right)$ of $\boldsymbol{Y}^{(t)}$ [16]. If $\left|H_J\left(\boldsymbol{Y}^{(t)}\right) - H_{J-1}\left(\boldsymbol{Y}^{(t)}\right)\right| \leq \sigma$, output $\hat{\boldsymbol{u}}^{(t)}$ and exit the iteration.

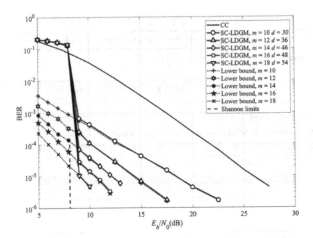

**Fig. 4.** The performance of the SC-LDGM codes with different memory $m$ over Rayleigh fading channels with impulsive noise

**Example 1:** Figure 4 is the performance of the SC-LDGM codes with different memory $m$ over Rayleigh fading channels with impulsive noise ($\alpha = 1.5$). We find that the SC-LDGM codes can provide a significant gain compared to the convolutional codes (CC) and that the larger the memory is, the higher the gain is. We also observe that the performance of the SC-LDGM codes matches well with the GA lower bound in the low BER region. Moreover, we provide the Shannon limits with rate 1/2 over Rayleigh fading channels with impulsive noise in Fig. 4. The performance of the proposed scheme can be 0.9 dB away from Shannon limits at the BER of $10^{-5}$ when memory is 18.

**Example 2:** First, we study the mutual information performance over Rayleigh fading channels with impulsive noise of different characteristic exponents. As shown in Fig. 5, the higher the characteristic exponent is, the higher the spectral efficiency is in the wide range of $SNR_G$. However, all three channels can achieve the same spectral efficiency in the high $SNR_G$ region. Moreover, from Fig. 5, we can obtain the Shannon limits with rate 1/2 over the three channels.

Second, we investigate the performance of the SC-LDGM codes over Rayleigh fading channels with impulsive noise of different characteristic exponents ($\alpha = 1.2, 1.5, 1.8$). The simulation results are given in Fig. 6. We see that the BER performance of SC-LDGM systems improves with the increase of $\alpha$ and that the SC-LDGM codes can provide higher gains over the three channels compared to the convolutional codes. We also observe that the performance of the proposed scheme with $\alpha = 1.2, 1.5, 1.8$ can be 2.6 dB, 2.4 dB, 2.0 dB, respectively, away from Shannon limits at the BER of $10^{-5}$ and matches well with the GA lower bound in the low BER region.

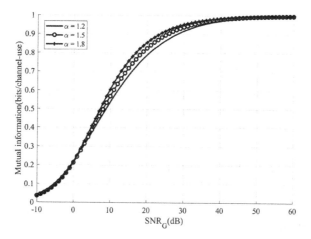

**Fig. 5.** The mutual information performance over Rayleigh fading channels with impulsive noise of different characteristic exponents ($\alpha = 1.2, 1.5, 1.8$)

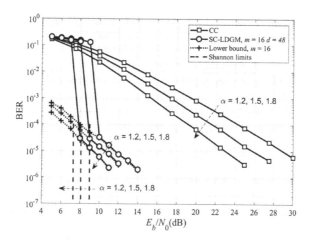

**Fig. 6.** The performance of the SC-LDGM codes over Rayleigh fading channels with impulsive noise of different characteristic exponents ($\alpha = 1.2, 1.5, 1.8$)

## 6   Conclusions

In this paper, we investigate the performance of SC-LDGM codes over Rayleigh fading channels with symmetric alpha-stable impulsive noise. The performance is analyzed by deriving a lower bound based on an equivalent GA system. Simulation results demonstrate that the SC-LDGM codes can perform well over Rayleigh fading channels with impulsive noise. Moreover, the results show that the performance of the SC-LDGM codes matches well with the GA lower bound in the low BER region.

# References

1. Nassar, M., Gulati, K., Mortazavi, Y., Evans, B.L.: Statistical modeling of asynchronous impulsive noise in powerline communication networks. In: 2011 IEEE Global Telecommunications Conference, pp. 1–6. IEEE (2011)
2. Chitre, M.: A high-frequency warm shallow water acoustic communications channel model and measurements. J. Acoust. Soc. Am. **122**(5), 2580–2586 (2007)
3. Weinberg, A.: The impact of pulsed RFI on the coded BER performance of the nonlinear satellite communication channel. IEEE Trans. Commun. **29**(5), 605–620 (1981)
4. Mei, Z., Johnston, M., Le, S., Chen, L.: Density evolution analysis of LDPC codes with different receivers on impulsive noise channels. In: 2015 IEEE/CIC International Conference on Communications in China, pp. 1–6. IEEE (2015)
5. Nikias, C.L., Shao, M.: Signal processing with alpha-stable distributions and applications. Wiley-Interscience, New York (1995)
6. Rajan, A., Tepedelenlioglu, C.: Diversity combining over Rayleigh fading channels with symmetric alpha-stable noise. IEEE Trans. Wireless Commun. **9**(9), 2968–2976 (2010)
7. Mei, Z., Johnston, M., Le Goff, S., Chen, L.: Error probability analysis of M-QAM on Rayleigh fading channels with impulsive noise. In: 2016 IEEE 17th International Workshop on Signal Processing Advances in Wireless Communications, pp. 1–5. IEEE (2016)
8. Luo, K., Zhao, M.: Modified EXIT chart method for performance analysis of turbo equalization in non-gaussian impulsive noise environments. J. Electron. Inf. Technol. **31**(6), 1386–1389 (2009)
9. Dai, B., Liu, R., Hou, Y., Zhao, L., Mei, Z.: EXIT chart aided LDPC code design for symmetric alpha-stable impulsive noise. IEEE Commun. Lett. **21**(3), 464–467 (2017)
10. Hou, Y., Liu, R., Dai, B., Zhao, L.: Joint channel estimation and LDPC decoding over time-varying impulsive noise channels. IEEE Trans. Commun. **66**(6), 2376–2383 (2018)
11. Mei, Z., Johnston, M., Le Goff, S., Chen, L.: Performance analysis of LDPC-coded diversity combining on Rayleigh fading channels with impulsive noise. IEEE Trans. Commun. **65**(6), 2345–2356 (2017)
12. Ji, M., Chen, S., Ma, X.: Performance of block Markov superposition transmission over non-Gaussian impulsive channels. J. Commun. (in Chinese, 2018)
13. Ma, X., Huang, K., Bai, B.: Systematic block Markov superposition transmission of repetition codes. IEEE Trans. Inf. Theory **64**(3), 1604–1620 (2018)
14. Gonzalez, J.G., Paredes, J.L., Arce, G.R.: Zero-order statistics: a mathematical framework for the processing and characterization of very impulsive signals. IEEE Trans. Signal Process. **54**(10), 3839–3851 (2006)
15. Forney, G.D.: Codes on graphs: normal realizations. IEEE Trans. Inf. Theory **47**(2), 520–548 (2001)
16. Ma, X., Liang, C., Huang, K., Zhuang, Q.: Block Markov superposition transmission: construction of big convolutional codes from short codes. IEEE Trans. Inf. Theory **61**(6), 3150–3163 (2015)

# Coordinated Earth Observation Task Scheduling Algorithm for Multiple Controlling Platforms

Jiaxin Wu[1], Runzi Liu[1($\boxtimes$)], Min Sheng[1], Jiandong Li[1], Kai Chi[2], and Wanyong Tian[2]

[1] The State Key Lab of ISN, Xidian University, Xi'an 710071, Shaanxi, China
rzliu@xidian.edu.cn
[2] Electric Information Network Laboratory, CETC the 20th Research Institute, Xi'an 710068, Shaanxi, China

**Abstract.** In view of the current situation that different Earth Observation Satellite systems are independent in our country, which results in the failure to share resources and to cope with numerous emergency tasks effectively, the paper proposes a Multi-platform Distributed Coordinate Task Scheduling Algorithm (MDCTS Algorithm) via consensus ADMM (Alternating Direction Method of Multipliers). Firstly, the problem of maximizing the overall value of multi-platform is modelled as a mixed-integer linear programming problem. Then, the global optimization problem is decomposed into the scheduling of each platform based on local information and public task price issued by collaborative center. On the basis, MDCTS Algorithm is proposed. The simulation results show that compared to existing algorithm, the value of local and public tasks achieved by MDCTS Algorithm is higher under the premise that the local tasks and resource information of each controlling platform do not have to be disclosed.

**Keywords:** Task Scheduling · Distributed coordinate · Consensus ADMM

## 1 Introduction

Earth Observation Satellites (EOSs) are an important part of Space Information Networks (SIN). Due to their wide ranges of observation and free limitations of complex geographical environments, the role of EOSs play in environmental monitoring and national security has become more and more significant [1], which has received increasing attention from various countries [2, 3]. China's current on-orbit EOSs include Haiyang Constellation, Ziyuan Constellation, Gaofen Constellation, etc. [4], which belong to different administrative units and are controlled by their respective controlling platforms. These satellite constellations are designed for different types of observation tasks and the management systems are different. Meanwhile, there is no effective collaborative interaction mechanism among them. With the explosive growth of tasks and the emergence of new kinds of tasks, the problem of this chimney-type of EOSs management architecture is becoming more and more obvious: on the one hand, due to the large cost of EOSs manufacture, operation and maintenance, the resources of

© Springer Nature Singapore Pte Ltd. 2019
Q. Yu (Ed.): SINC 2018, CCIS 972, pp. 99–112, 2019.
https://doi.org/10.1007/978-981-13-5937-8_12

each satellite system are limited and it is difficult to cope with large-scale emergency tasks relying only on a single system; on the other hand, since the emergence of tasks in the network is unpredictable and uneven, it occurs that a large number of tasks arrive at a single controlling platform in specific areas at a certain time while the rest is relatively idle. Therefore, this isolated resource management model leads to low resource utilization efficiency in the network and the failure to effectively deal with emergencies such as natural disasters and armed conflicts.

In response to this drawback, an intuitive solution is to merge all the platforms into one central controlling platform, which manages all satellite resources and centrally schedules observation tasks. However, due to the high computational complexity of all tasks in the unified scheduling and the limitation of the governmental management system, it is difficult to achieve the unified management of EOS systems belonging to different administrative departments. Therefore, the aforementioned method is not realistically feasible at this stage [5].

Because both the isolated and centralized planning framework are insufficient, it is necessary to study the method of distributed collaboration to realize resource sharing yet without changing the existing management system. Wu et al. proposed a collaborative planning framework for multiple controlling platforms, wherein the collaborative center assigns tasks based on observation opportunities, and designs a simulated annealing algorithm combined with taboo tables to achieve task assignment [6]. Although this method realizes resource sharing without changing the existing system, each EOS system cannot provide specific information of local tasks and observation resources to the collaborative center due to their closedness. Therefore, in the case that the effective information learned by the collaborative center is very limited, especially when the conflict relationship among the tasks is very complicated, blindly assigning public tasks to controlling platforms can easily lead to conflicts with the local tasks, of which the execution is affected, leading to inefficiencies of the overall planning algorithm.

Aiming at the multi-platform collaborative task planning problem to be solved, this paper proposes a distributed multi-platform collaborative planning method that is efficient and suitable for the current situation of satellite management in China: First, the global task planning problem is modeled as a mixed-integer linear programming problem. Then, use the idea of ADMM algorithm to decompose the global problem into sub-problems of each platform: under the coordination of the price issued by the collaborative center, each platform independently decides whether or not to execute the public task according to local information. Finally, the optimal solution of the original problem is obtained by integrating the results of sub-problems and thereby achieving a desirable resource scheduling scheme. Under the premise that the resource privacy of each platform do not have to be disclosed, the method can not only coordinate all the satellite resources to ensure the efficient completion of public tasks, but also minimize the impact on local tasks to achieve the goal of maximizing the overall value of finished tasks.

The remainder of this paper is organized as follows. Section 2 gives the network model and mathematical model of the problem. Section 3 transforms the model into a distributed optimization problem which is solved by using the ADMM Algorithm. Through the simulation in Sect. 4 and compared to HWFA Algorithm designed by Wu et al. in literature [6], the conclusion is drawn, followed by a summary of the full text in Sect. 5.

# 2 System Model

## 2.1 Network Model

We consider the scenario shown in Fig. 1 which contains:

- A few controlling platforms (CPs) denoted by $A = \{1, 2, \ldots, a, \ldots\}$, which the total number is $M$.
- A set of tasks that are divided into public tasks and local tasks. The local task of a controlling platform is defined as tasks that can only be performed by satellites controlled by the platform. Assume that CP $a$ has $N_a$ local tasks. The public tasks are defined as tasks that can be performed by any platform in the network, of which the number is denoted by $N_{M+1}$. Thus, the total number of tasks is $I = \sum_{a=1}^{M+1} N_a$. For convenience, the subscript set of the local task of CP $a$ is denoted by $I_a$, and the one of public tasks is $I_{M+1}$. Task $om_i$ can be represented by a four-dimensional vector $om_i = (ob_i, w_i, et_i, lt_i)$, where $ob_i$ is the point target included in the observation task (We assume that all targets have been preprocessed), $w_i$, $et_i$, $lt_i$ is the value, earliest start time and latest end time of it, respectively. Namely, $[et_i, lt_i]$ is the scheduling window of task $om_i$.
- A set of EOSs denoted by $OS = \{os_1, os_2, \ldots, os_j, \ldots\}$, with $H$ indicating the total number of them. Note that $OS_a$ is the collection of EOSs controlled by CP $a$. Therefore, $OS = OS_1 \cup OS_2 \cup \ldots \cup OS_M$.

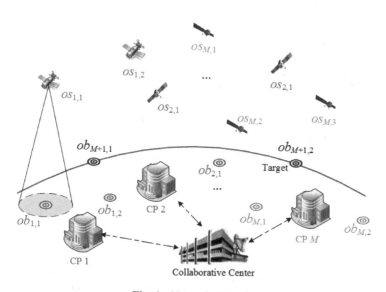

**Fig. 1.** Network scenario

We divide the simulation duration $T$ into a plurality of time slots of the same length $\tau$, then there are a total of $K = T/\tau$ time slots. Assuming that the network topology is fixed in each time slot while it can change at the instant of time slot switching. We define a new variable $x_{ij}^k$, where $x_{ij}^k = 1$ means that task $i$ is performed by EOS $j$ in the $k$-th slot, and $x_{ij}^k = 0$ otherwise. We use $K(i,j) = \{k | \text{task } i \text{ is visible to EOS } j \text{ in the } k\text{-th slot}, \forall i \in I, \forall j \in J\}$ to indicate the set of time slots that task $i$ can be performed by EOS $j$.

In addition, for the public tasks, we introduce a new variable $y_{ia}$, where $y_{ia} = 1$ indicates that public task $i$ is performed by an EOS controlled by CP $a$; otherwise $y_{ia} = 0$. According to the definition, $y_{ia}$ can be calculated by the following formula:

$$y_{ia} = \sum_{j \in OS_a} \sum_{k \in K(i,j)} x_{ij}^k, \forall i \in I_{M+1}, a \in A \qquad (1)$$

After obtaining the visible relationship between each task and each EOS, we can find the collision set $O\left(x_{ij}^k\right) = \{(m,l)\}$ of each possible observation action $x_{ij}^k$, where $m, l$ is the task number and slot number of the observation action that conflicts with $x_{ij}^k = 1$. Here, according to the factors, the conflicts we consider in this article are divided into two types:

- Resource contention conflicts. Since a single EOS is equipped with only one set of imaging equipment, the imager can only be aimed at one observation target at a certain time slot. If two (or more) tasks request to call the EOS simultaneously in the same time slot, then there is a resource contention conflict between the two (or more) tasks. It is described mathematically as follows: assuming that task $i$ and task $m$ are both visible to EOS $j$ at the $k$-th slot, then $(m,k) \in O\left(x_{ij}^k\right)$, $(i,k) \in O\left(x_{mj}^l\right)$.

- Action switching conflicts. Because the EOS rotates at a slow speed, it takes some time to switch from one task to another. If the difference between the start time of the second task of the two successive tasks and the end time of the first task is smaller than the time needed for the EOS to switch between them, then there is an action switching conflict. The mathematical form is described as follows: assume that task $om_{i_1}$ and $om_{i_2}$ are performed by the same EOS $j$ successively, an action switching conflict exists if $\gamma_{i_1,i_2} + ast \geq tst_{i_2} - ten_{i_1}$ or $\gamma_{i_1,i_2} + ast \geq tst_{i_1} - ten_{i_2}$, where $\gamma_{i_1,i_2}$ is the time required for EOS $j$ to switch from task $om_{i_1}$ to task $om_{i_2}$, $ast$ is the attitude stability time of EOS $j$, $tst_{i_1}, ten_{i_1}, tst_{i_2}, ten_{i_2}$ are the start and end time of the observation action for task $om_{i_1}$ and $om_{i_2}$ respectively. Therefore, $(i_2, k_2) \in O\left(x_{i_1 j}^{k_1}\right)$, $(i_1, k_1) \in O\left(x_{i_2 j}^{k_2}\right)$.

## 2.2 Optimization Problem Model

Based on the network model proposed in Sect. 2.1, we formulate the task planning problem as a mixed-integer linear optimization problem with the objective function of maximizing the overall value of finished tasks. Since the public tasks are often important and urgent, we need to prioritize their observation and then consider trying to complete the local tasks of each platform. In other words, if $w_1$ represents the value of all local tasks and $w_2$ for all public tasks, then $w_1 \ll w_2$. Thus, the optimization objective function of the planning algorithm is:

$$\max w_1 \sum_{a \in A} \sum_{i \in I_a} \sum_{j \in OS_a} \sum_{k \in K(i,j)} x_{ij}^k + w_2 \sum_{a \in A} \sum_{i \in I_{M+1}} y_{ia} \tag{2}$$

which should satisfy

$$y_{ia} = \sum_{j \in OS_a} \sum_{k \in K(i,j)} x_{ij}^k, \forall i \in I_{M+1}, a \in A \tag{3}$$

$$\sum_{a \in A} y_{ia} \leq 1, \forall i \in I_{M+1} \tag{4}$$

$$\sum_{j \in OS_a} \sum_{k \in K(i,j)} x_{ij}^k \leq 1, \forall i \in I_a, a \in A \tag{5}$$

$$x_{ij}^k + \sum_{(m,l) \in O(x_{ij}^k)} x_{mj}^l \leq 1, \forall x_{ij}^k \in X \tag{6}$$

In constraint (6), $X = \left\{ x_{ij}^k | i \in I_{M+1}, j \in S, k \in K(i,j) \right\} \cup \left( \bigcup_{a=1}^{M} X_a \right)$ is the set of available opportunities for all tasks while $X_a = \left\{ x_{ij}^k | i \in I_a, j \in OS_a, a \in A, k \in K(i,j) \right\}$ is the available opportunities for local tasks of CP $a$.

Among the constraints listed above, constraint (3) is the mathematical relationship between $y_{ia}$ and $x_{ij}^k$ given by Eq. (1). Constraint (4) guarantees that for any public task, it should be considered successfully observed if it is performed by one of the $M$ platforms. That is, a public task cannot be executed multiple times. Constraint (5) guarantees that for a local task of CP $a$, it can be considered executed as long as it is performed by one satellite affiliated to CP $a$. Namely, a local task cannot be executed multiple times, either. Constraint (6) ensures that for any EOS, only one observation task can be performed in a time slot, and the tasks that conflict with the executed task cannot be performed by it in the same slot.

In the objective function, $x_{ij}^k$ and $y_{ia}$ are both 0–1 variables. Observing Eqs. (3)–(6), we can find that the constraints are all linear. To ensure the convexity of the problem, we relax the variables $x_{ij}^k$ and $y_{ia}$ to continuous variables with a value range of $[0, 1]$. Since Eq. (2) is a function of $x_{ij}^k$ and $y_{ia}$, we can write the optimization model as following:

$$g(x,y) = \begin{cases} -w_1 \sum_{a \in A} \sum_{i \in I_a} \sum_{j \in OS_a} \sum_{k \in K(i,j)} x_{ij}^k - w_2 \sum_{a \in A} \sum_{i \in I_{M+1}} y_{ia}, & (x,y) \in X \\ +\infty, & otherwise \end{cases} \tag{7}$$

where $X$ is the set of $(x,y)$ that satisfies constraints (3)–(6). In this way, the original problem can be abbreviated to its equivalent form:

$$(P1) \; \min \; g(x,y) \tag{8}$$

## 3 Distributed Coordinate Task Scheduling Algorithm via Consensus ADMM

We use the ADMM algorithm to solve problem (P1) in a distributed fashion. Since (P1) is a global problem, it is decomposed into sub-problems of each controlling platform according to the idea of the ADMM. However, the variable $y_{ia}$ cannot be further split, thereby a new variable $\hat{y}_{ia}^b, \forall i \in I_{M+1}, \forall a, b \in A$ is introduced, which is the decision made by CP $b$ of whether public task $i$ is performed by CP $a$. By duplicating $y_{ia}$ $M$ times, (P1) can be decomposed into sub-problems of each platform:

$$g_a(x_a, \hat{y}_a) = \begin{cases} -w_1 \sum\limits_{i \in I_a} \sum\limits_{j \in OS_a} \sum\limits_{k \in K(i,j)} x_{ij}^k - w_2 \sum\limits_{i \in I_{M+1}} \sum\limits_{b \in A} \hat{y}_{ib}^a, & (x_a, \hat{y}_a) \in X_a \\ +\infty, & otherwise \end{cases} \tag{9}$$

where $X_a$ is the set of $(x_a, \hat{y}_a)$ that satisfies the optimization constraints on CP $a$, which can be written as

$$X_a = \left\{ (x_a, \hat{y}_a) \left| \begin{array}{l} C1: \hat{y}_{ia}^a = \sum\limits_{j \in OS_a} \sum\limits_{k \in K(i,j)} x_{ij}^k, \forall i \in I_{M+1} \\ C2: \sum\limits_{b \in A} \hat{y}_{ib}^a \le 1, \qquad \forall i \in I_{M+1} \\ C3: \sum\limits_{j \in OS_a} \sum\limits_{k \in K(i,j)} x_{ij}^k, \forall i \in I_a \\ C4: x_{ij}^k + \sum\limits_{(m,l) \in O(x_{ij}^k)} x_{mj}^l \le 1, \forall x_{ij}^k \in X_a \end{array} \right. \right\} \tag{10}$$

The constraints in Eq. (10) are essentially the results of constraints (3)–(6) decomposed into $M$ controlling platforms. Specifically, in Eq. (10), C1 gives the relationship between $\hat{y}_{ia}^a$ and $x_{ij}^k$; C2 indicates that for any public task, it cannot be executed multiple times in the view of CP $a$; C3 indicates that for a local task of CP $a$, it can be regarded as finished as long as it is successfully executed by an EOS controlled by the platform; C4 guarantees that for any EOS of CP $a$, it can only perform one observation task in a time slot.

Therefore, (P1) is equivalent to obtain the minimum of the sum of multiple sub-problems $g_a(x_a, \hat{y}_a)$, i.e.

$$(P2) \; \min \; \sum_{a \in A} g_a(x_a, \hat{y}_a) \tag{11}$$
$$s.t. \; \hat{y}_{ib}^a = y_{ib}, \forall i \in I, \forall a, b \in A$$

where the constraint $\hat{y}_{ib}^a = y_{ib}$ is the core idea of the ADMM algorithm, consensus constraint, which guarantees that each local variable $\hat{y}_{ib}^a$ is consistent with its corresponding global variable $y_{ib}$.

After that, we use the constraint to extend problem (P2) into its augmented Lagrangian form [7]:

$$
L_\rho\left((x_a, \hat{y}_a)\big|_{a\in A}, y, \lambda_{ib}^a\big|_{i\in I_{M+1}}^{a,b\in A}\right)
$$

$$
= \sum_{a\in A}\left(g_a(x_a, \hat{y}_a) + \sum_{i\in I_{M+1}}\sum_{b\in A}\lambda_{ib}^a\left(\hat{y}_{ib}^a - y_{ib}\right) + \frac{\rho}{2}\sum_{i\in I_{M+1}}\sum_{b\in A}\left(\hat{y}_{ib}^a - y_{ib}\right)^2\right) \tag{12}
$$

where $\lambda_{ib}^a, i\in I_{M+1}, a, b \in A$ is the Lagrange multipliers of the consistency constraint of the equivalence problem (P2), called the dual variable; and $\rho \in \mathbb{R}_{++}$ can be seen as the penalty factor for augmented Lagrangian expression, which can adjust the convergence speed of ADMM algorithm.

We can find that the augmented Lagrangian not only includes a series of consistency constraints weighted by dual multiplier, but also a regularized quadratic term (thus augmented) to ensure strict convexity.

After obtaining the augmented Lagrangian form of each sub-problem, we can get the following variable iteration steps:

1. Minimize the augmented Lagrangian over the local variables for each controlling platform:

$$
\left\{x_a^{t+1}, \hat{y}_a^{t+1}\right\}_{a\in A}
$$

$$
= \underset{x_a, y_a}{\arg\min}\left\{g_a(x_a, \hat{y}_a) + \sum_{i\in I_{M+1}}\sum_{b\in A}\lambda_{ib}^{a,t}\left(\hat{y}_{ib}^{a,t} - y_{ib}^t\right) + \frac{\rho}{2}\sum_{i\in I_{M+1}}\sum_{b\in A}\left(\hat{y}_{ib}^{a,t} - y_{ib}^t\right)^2\right\} \tag{13}
$$

It can be seen from Eq. (13) that (P2) has been completely decomposed into subproblems for each platform. After neglecting the constant term which does not affect the final solution, Eq. (13) can be written as

$$
\text{(P3)} \quad \min \ -w_1\sum_{i\in I_a}\sum_{j\in OS_a}\sum_{k\in K(i,j)}x_{ij}^k - w_2\sum_{i\in I_{M+1}}\sum_{b\in A}\hat{y}_{ib}^a + \sum_{i\in I_{M+1}}\sum_{b\in A}\left[\lambda_{ib}^{a,t}\hat{y}_{ib}^{a,t} + \frac{\rho}{2}\left(\hat{y}_{ib}^{a,t} - y_{ib}^t\right)^2\right] \tag{14}
$$

$$
s.t. \ (x_a, \hat{y}_a) \in X_a
$$

2. Minimize the augmented Lagrangian over the global variables:

$$
y^{t+1} = \underset{y}{\arg\min}\left\{\sum_{i\in I_{M+1}}\sum_{b\in A}\left(\sum_{a\in A}\lambda_{ib}^{a,t}\left(\hat{y}_{ib}^{a,t+1} - y_{ib}\right) + \frac{\rho}{2}\sum_{a\in A}\left(\hat{y}_{ib}^{a,t+1} - y_{ib}\right)^2\right)\right\} \tag{15}
$$

Similarly, we decompose (15) into sub-problems of $M$ controlling platforms and ignore the constant term $y_{ib}^t$, it can be written as

$$y_{ib}^{t+1} = \arg\min_{y_{ib}} \left[ -\sum_{a \in A} \lambda_{ib}^{a,t} y_{ib} + \frac{\rho}{2} \sum_{a \in A} \left( y_{ib}^2 - 2 y_{ib} \hat{y}_{ib}^{a,t+1} \right) \right] \qquad (16)$$

Since a regularized quadratic term is added to the augmented Lagrangian formula, the function in (16) is strictly convex. Therefore, the minimum value with respect to $y_{ia}$ can be obtained by letting the derivative function of (16) be equal to zero:

$$-\sum_{a \in A} \lambda_{ib}^{a,t} + \rho M y_{ib} - \rho \sum_{a \in A} \hat{y}_{ib}^{a,t+1} = 0 \qquad (17)$$

which leads to

$$y_{ib}^{t+1} = \frac{1}{M} \sum_{a \in A} \left( \frac{1}{\rho} \lambda_{ib}^{a,t} + \hat{y}_{ib}^{a,t+1} \right) \qquad (18)$$

3. Update of dual variables:

$$\left\{ \lambda_{ib}^{a,t+1} \right\}_{a,b \in A}^{i \in I_{M+1}} = \lambda_{ib}^{a,t} + \rho \left( \hat{y}_{ib}^{a,t+1} - y_{ib}^{t+1} \right) \qquad (19)$$

In the superscript of Eqs. (13)–(19), $t$ is the number of iterations.

Therefore, the steps of the entire ADMM algorithm are roughly described as follows:

(1) Each controlling platform obtains the values of the local variables $x_{ij}^k$ and $\hat{y}_{ib}^a$ by solving the convex optimization problem (P3).
(2) Each platform delivers the obtained local variable $\hat{y}_{ib}^a$ to the collaborative center.
(3) Then, according to Eq. (18), the collaborative center can get the value of the global variables $y_{ib}^{t+1}$ through the dual variables $\lambda_{ib}^a$ and the local variables $\hat{y}_{ib}^a$ obtained in step 1, according to which we can determine public task $om_i$ is executed by which controlling platform.
(4) Finally, each platform iteratively updates the value of the dual variable $\lambda_{ib}^a$ by Eq. (19).

Algorithm 1 describes in detail a distributed coordinate scheduling method based on consensus ADMM, where $j1$, $j2$, $i1$, $i2$ are the EOS and task indices corresponding to the observation actions $num1$ and $num2$, respectively.

**Algorithm 1.** Distributed Coordinate Scheduling Algorithm via Consensus ADMM

1: Initiate simulation parameters, such as task number, satellite number, task value, etc.

2: Obtain the latitudes and longitudes of tasks.

3: **for** $j \in S_a$, $i \in I_a$ or $i \in I_{M+1}$, $j \in OS$ **do**

4:    Calculate observation time windows of all tasks, record them in *twindex*.

5: **end for**

6: *ntwin*=size( *twindex*, 1 );

7: **for** *num1*=1:*ntwin*, *num2*=*num1*+1:*ntwin* **do**

8:    **if** $j1 = j2$, $i1 \neq i2$ **do**

9:       Calculate the switching time *slewtime* required between the two observation actions.

10:   **end if**

11: **end for**

12: **for** *num*=1:*ntwin* **do**

13:    Calculate the set of collision *collision(num)*.

14: **end for**

15: Initialize: $t \leftarrow 1$, dual variables $\lambda_{ib}^a$ and global variables $y_{ib}$.

16: **repeat**

17:    Solve (P4), obtain global variables, update dual variables.

18:    $t \leftarrow t + 1$。

19: **until** stopping criteria is met.

20: Output: $x_{ij}^{k*}$ and $y_{ia}^*$.

As mentioned earlier, in order to ensure the convexity of the problem, we have relaxed the variables $x_{ij}^k$ and $y_{ia}$, which need to be reduced to 0 or 1 after Algorithm 1 gets the optimal solution. The detailed steps are given in Algorithm 2, where $M_f$ denotes the fixed tasks and $M_u$ the opposite.

**Algorithm 2.** Relaxation-Reduction Algorithm

1: Initialize $M_f \leftarrow \emptyset$, $M_u \leftarrow OM$.

2: **if** variable $y$ need to be fixed exists **then**

3:    $a_0 \leftarrow \mathrm{argmax}_a y_{ia}$, $\{j_0, num_0\} \leftarrow \mathrm{argmax}_{j \in S_{a_0}} x_{ij}^k$.

4:    Update: $M_f \leftarrow M_f \cup om_i$, $M_u \leftarrow M_u \backslash om_i$.

5:    Fix: $y_{ia_0} \leftarrow 1$, $x_{ij_0}^k \leftarrow 1$.

6:    **for** $a \neq a_0$, $j \in S_{a_0}$ and $j \neq j_0$ **do**

7:        Fix: $y_{ia} \leftarrow 0$, $x_{ij}^{k_0} \leftarrow 0$.

8:    **end for**

9:    **for** $num \in collision\{num_0\}$ **do**

10:        Fix: $x(collision\{num_0\}) \leftarrow 0$.

11:    **end for**

12: **else if** variable $x$ need to be fixed exists **then**

13:    $\{j_0, num_0\} \leftarrow \mathrm{argmax}_j x_{ij}^k$.

14:    Update: $M_f \leftarrow M_f \cup om_i$, $M_u \leftarrow M_u \backslash om_i$.

15:    Fix: $x_{ij_0}^k \leftarrow 1$.

16:    **for** $j \neq j_0$ and $num \in collision\{num_0\}$ **do**

17:        Fix: $x_{ij}^k \leftarrow 0$, $x(collision\{num_0\}) \leftarrow 0$.

18:    **end for**

19: **end if**

20: Output: $x_{ij}^k$ and $y_{ia}$.

# 4   Simulation

## 4.1   Simulation Parameters

We consider the following scenario: 3 controlling platforms, where CP 1 controls 2 EOSs, CP 2 controls 1 and CP 3 controls 2. The planning period is set to 86400 s, which is divided into 288 equal-length slots, each of which equals 300 s. Other simulation parameters are shown in Table 1.

**Table 1.** Simulation parameters

| Parameter | Value |
|---|---|
| Task number | [200, 400, 600, 800, 1000] |
| Satellite rotation rate | 0.5 (deg/s) |
| Attitude stability time | 5 (s) |
| Local task value | 1 |
| Public task value | 10 |

## 4.2   Simulation Results

In order to verify the effectiveness of the proposed method in this paper, we compare the MDCTS Algorithm with the HWFA Algorithm in [6], the idea of which is that the collaborative center determines the allocation of public tasks based on observation opportunities. We use STK and MATLAB to build the simulation scenario, and analyze the advantages of the MDCTS Algorithm by comparing the number of tasks completed by the two algorithms and the overall value of finished tasks.

**(1) Comparison of the number of tasks completed by each algorithm.**
The number of local tasks, public tasks and total tasks completed by the HWFA Algorithm and the MDCTS Algorithm are shown in Figs. 2, 3 and 4. It can be clearly seen from the figures that as the total number of arrived tasks increases, the numbers of completed tasks of the two algorithms go upward. This is because as the number of tasks increases, so does the number of tasks that can be completed. Meanwhile, it is apparent that the upward trends of the tasks completed by the two algorithms become slower as the tasks increases. This is because when the number of tasks is relatively small, the observation resources are sufficient enough to guarantee the demand of most tasks. But when the number increases, the utilization of observation resources gradually becomes saturated. In addition, as can be seen from each figure that the number of tasks completed by the MDCTS Algorithm is always greater than the one of the HWFA Algorithm. The reason is that the capacity information of each controlling platform known by the collaborative center is very limited. Therefore, in the HWFA Algorithm, it is probable that a large number of tasks fail to be executed caused by conflicts with the local tasks when the collaborative center allocates public tasks. The MDCTS Algorithm designed in this paper, however, transfers the decision-making right of the public task assignment to the controlling platforms, which can reduce the impact of the assignment on the local task to a certain extent, thus ensuring the successful execution of the tasks.

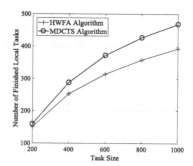

**Fig. 2.** Comparison of finished local tasks

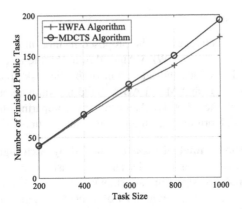

**Fig. 3.** Comparison of finished public tasks

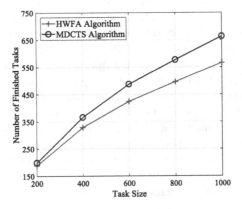

**Fig. 4.** Comparison of finished tasks

**(2) Comparison of overall value achieved by each algorithm.**
The total values of the tasks completed by the two algorithms under different task numbers are shown in Fig. 5. As depicted in the figure, the values obtained by the two algorithms gradually increase as the task scale becomes larger. This is because the number of completed local tasks and the one of completed public tasks increase as the size of the task goes up, so does the total value. In addition, the value of the MDCTS Algorithm is also greater than that of the HWFA Algorithm and the advantages become more obvious as the task size increases. This is because the collaborative center utilizes the coordination among the decisions made by each controlling platform in the MDCTS Algorithm, which reduces the degree of conflict between the public tasks and the local tasks so that the performance of total value is better than the HWFA algorithm. When the task size continues to increase, the conflict relationship among tasks becomes more complicated which turns out that the advantage embodied by the MDCTS algorithm that reduces the conflict becomes more and more obvious.

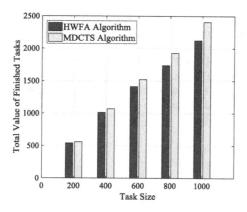

**Fig. 5.** Comparison of total value of two algorithms

## 5   Conclusion

Aiming at the problem of earth observation mission planning for multiple controlling platforms, this paper designs a distributed coordinate scheduling algorithm via consensus ADMM. Firstly, the scheduling problem is modeled as a mixed-integer linear programming problem that maximizes the total value of finished tasks. Secondly, using the idea of ADMM, the modeled global problem is decomposed into sub-problems of multiple controlling platforms. By solving the sub-problems, local optimal solutions are obtained to calculate the global optimal solution by the collaborative center, and thus generates the final scheduling scheme. Finally, the simulation verifies the gain in the number of tasks completed and the total task value.

**Acknowledgments.** This work is supported by the National Natural Science Foundation of China (No. 61701365, 61801365, 91638202), China Postdoctoral Science Foundation (No. 2017M623121, No. 2018M643581), Postdoctoral Foundation in Shaanxi Province of China, Fundamental Research Funds for the Central Universities.

## References

1. Wang, Y., Sheng, M., Zhuang, W.H., et al.: Multi-resource coordinate scheduling for earth observation in space information networks. IEEE J. Sel. Areas Commun. **36**(2), 268–279 (2018)
2. Jiang, C., Wang, X., Wang, J., et al.: Security in space information networks. IEEE Commun. Mag. **53**(8), 82–88 (2015)
3. Yu, J.: Research on Key Technologies of Cooperative Task Scheduling for Airborne and Spaceborne Earth Observing Assets. National University of Defense Technology, Changsha (2011)
4. Hou, S., Liu, H.: Chinese satellite programs: an internal view. In: Schrogl, K.-U., Hays, P.L., Robinson, J., Moura, D., Giannopapa, C. (eds.) Handbook of Space Security, pp. 885–898. Springer, New York (2015). https://doi.org/10.1007/978-1-4614-2029-3_33

5. Wang, H.L., Wu, G.H., Ma, M.H.: Coordinated task planning method of multiple heterogeneous Earth-observation platforms. Acta Aeronautica et Astronautica Sinica **37**(3), 997–1014 (2016)
6. Wu, G.H., Pedrycz, W., Li, H.F., et al.: Coordinated planning of heterogeneous earth observation resources. IEEE Trans. Syst. Man Cybern. Syst. **46**(1), 109–125 (2016)
7. Boyd, S., Parikh, N., Chu, E., et al.: Distributed optimization and statistical learning via the alternating direction method of multipliers. Found. Trends Mach. Learn. **3**(1), 1–125 (2010)

# Beam-Hopping Based Resource Allocation Algorithm in LEO Satellite Network

Wanying Liu[1,2,3], Feng Tian[3], Zaiyang Jiang[1,2,3], Guotong Li[3,4(✉)], and Quanjiang Jiang[3]

[1] Shanghai Institute of Micro-system and Information Technology Chinese Academy of Science, Shanghai 200050, China
[2] University of Chinese Academy of Sciences, Beijing 100049, China
[3] Shanghai Engineering Center for Micro-satellite, Shanghai 201203, China
[4] ShanghaiTech University, Shanghai 201210, China
ligt@mail.sim.ac.cn

**Abstract.** Beam hopping Low Earth Orbit (LEO) Satellite Network can augment terrestrial wireless networks to provide global broadband services to users regardless of the users' locations. Compared with Geostationary Earth Orbit (GEO) Satellite, the LEO satellite has limited on board resource, e.g., power, battery, and weight. In this paper, we propose a beam hopping scheme for resource limited LEO satellite to improve the performance of throughput. Compared with the traditional fixed point beam scheme, the beam hopping scheme provides better performance of capacity throughput when the distribution of users is uneven. First, we review the related work about beam hopping, and shows that most of the existing beam hopping schemes are for GEO satellite and cannot be used for the LEO satellite. Then, we propose the system model and formulate the resource allocation problem in beam hopping scheme. Various simulations are constructed to verify that the Beam Hopping Scheme has better performance of throughput than the fixed beam scheme, and the performance improvement is more significant when the distribution of users is uneven.

**Keywords:** Beam hopping · LEO satellite · QoS

## 1 Introduction

Terrestrial wireless network (cellular and WiFi networks) provides mobile communication services with limited geographic coverage. The LEO satellite networks can augment these networks to provide global communication services such as flight WiFi, cruise WiFi, and remote communication. It has attracted a lot of interest from both the academia and industry to build LEO satellite network to provide the global communication services [1,2].

© Springer Nature Singapore Pte Ltd. 2019
Q. Yu (Ed.): SINC 2018, CCIS 972, pp. 113–123, 2019.
https://doi.org/10.1007/978-981-13-5937-8_13

Generally, the on-board resource of LEO satellite is limited. Beam hopping is a promising approach to improve the throughput of broadband satellite communication under limited on-board resource. The authors of [3] has shown that the beam hopping can improve the efficiency of satellite resource usage in terms of bandwidth and power. Further more, beam hopping can improve the performance of throughput and make flexible use of satellite power by focusing the beam only on where it is needed. Additionally, beam hopping uses the entire allocated frequency band and is able to hop from one block to another, which is an efficient way of resource allocation [4,5]. In this paper, we study how to use beam hopping technology to improve the service capabilities of LEO satellite.

At present, most of research about beam hopping is mainly used in GEO satellite communication system. Due to the difference between the GEO satellite communication system and the LEO satellite communication system, these existing beam hopping scheme cannot be used in the LEO satellite communication system directly. For example, beam hopping technology has been successfully applied in Spaceway-3 broadband satellite communication [6], it serves each cell in a fair polling mode and lacks the optimization of throughput. Since the electromagnetic environment in the LEO satellite network is much more complex and changeable than what in the GEO satellite network, the beam hopping scheme in [6] cannot be applied for the LEO satellite network directly. In this paper, we propose a beam hopping scheme for broadband LEO satellite communication by analyzing the characteristics of LEO satellite network and study the beam-hopping based resource allocation algorithm.

The main contributions of the paper are as follows.

- To the best of our knowledge, we are the first to propose the beam hopping scheme for broadband LEO satellite communication. and analyze the corresponding resource allocation algorithm.
- We construct various simulations to evaluate the efficiency of beam hopping technology in the LEO satellite. Simulation results show that our proposed beam hopping scheme outperforms the fixed beam scheme.
- Moreover, we not only consider about the throughput-first to select the unit to be illustrated by the hopping beam, but also put the quality of service (QoS) into consideration.

The remainder of our paper is organized as follows. In Sect. 2, we briefly review the related work. Then we propose the model and theoretical analysis in Sect. 3. We present the evaluation results about the beam hopping based resource allocation in Sect. 4. Section 5 concludes our work and propose our future work.

## 2   Related Work

As one of the next generation satellite communication technologies, beam hopping (BH) can illuminate separated cells by small beams in time domain flexibly, and each beam can only illuminate one cell at one time [7]. Research institutes, government and business researchers are studying and developing the algorithm to realize the beam hopping with great enthusiasm. European Space Agency (ESA) carried out the study of beam hopping techniques for multi-beam satellite system in 2004. Hughes Network Systems (HNS) company in the United Sates used the technology to design and build the Sapceway-3 broadband satellite communication system in 2007. At the same time, many American patents [8,9] also have discussed the application of the technology. T. Pecorella designed a realizable beam hopping framework [10], while J. Anzalchi completed the detailed system simulation and performance comparison [11], which verified the advantages of beam hopping. [12] proposed a more practical Focal-array-fed beam hopping antenna based on cell reuse mechanism. Recently, the combination of beam hopping technology with cognitive radio technology has been regarded as the most promising research to improve the spectral efficiency of future satellite system [13].

According to the DVB protocol, there is possibility that the beam hopping technology can be applied in the low rail and is able to enrich the traditional multi-beam technology. In this paper, based on LEO satellite fast moving scene, we compare the hopping beam technology and fixed point beam technology and propose a resource scheduling management method based on hopping beam.

# 3   LEO Satellite System Model

The satellite communication system has wide coverage, large transmission capacity, high reliability, flexible network, and many other advantages, which has become one of the most important means of modern wireless communication. In particular, with the rapid development of mobile communication business, the ground mobile communication system cannot satisfy the communication in remote areas, mountains, island, disaster area, ships sailing in oceans and any other emergency occasions. Therefore, it is necessary to establish a perfect global multi-media satellite mobile communication system, which can realize the seamless coverage of global system for mobile communications (GSM).

In fast moving low-earth orbit (LEO) satellite modes, this section carried out the basic system model in LEO satellite situation and try to simplify the system model in order to understand the beam hopping theory more clearly.

## 3.1   Satellite Cell Model

As shown in Fig. 1, we divide the LEO satellites coverage areas into many rectangle blocks lined up neatly, namely we call it cells, and for the convenience of modeling, we set the cell shape as rectangle. The LEO satellite coverage area can be divided into neat rectangle blocks, as shown in Fig. 1. We let Cell $i$ represents the division and each Cell $i$ is a communication district where the satellite covers for a period of T at a time.

Each user in $cell_i$ is random distribution and we set that the number of users in $cell_i$ is $number_i$.

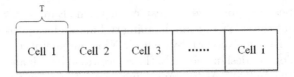

**Fig. 1.** Satellite coverage area division

We label every user in the current $cell_i$ by $user_{ij}$ where $j = 1, 2, \ldots, number_i$. Assume that the bandwidth required by each user is $b_{ij}$, and the user's time of live (TOL) is presented by $\tau_{ij}$. Additionally, the user's service status is valid if and only if

$$\tau_{ij} < T \tag{1}$$

Otherwise, the user's survival time exceeds the maximum length time of the current satellite coverage and the user cannot be effectively served by the current satellite.

### 3.2   Satellite Unit Model

For each rectangle area cell, we further divide it into a number of smaller rectangular blocks which are $M$ rows and $N$ columns, and let $unit_{ij}$ represent each smaller block illuminated by a beam from the satellite. In order to simplify, the shape of each beam is assumed to be the rectangular shape, and in each spot-beam covering range, the user is still the random distribution. The units in each cell are as shown in Fig. 2.

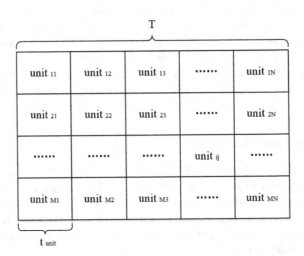

**Fig. 2.** A cell divided into units

Although the units in each cell shown in Fig. 2 are simple and easy to understand, this division is not perfect when combine the rectangle units with circle beams in the practice. Here, we give an example of the further division of each cell. Based on the original division, we use rectangle diagonal method to get the diameter of the each circle, namely, the diagonal of each rectangle is just the diameter of each beam circle. The further division of each cell is as shown in Fig. 3. This method of division will cause the conflicts at the border coverage, which will be our future work.

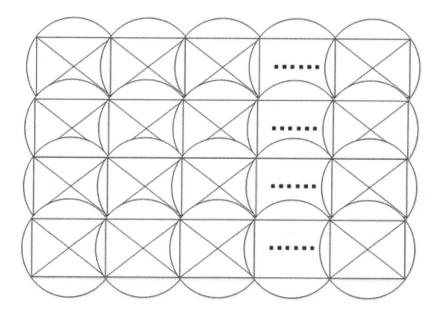

**Fig. 3.** Further division of each cell

Assume that $S$ is the number of hopping beams provided by the satellite in a coverage area. Considering the resources allocation among the beams, the channel differences between different users in the beam are calculated on average and the channel capacity parameters of the beams are as follows, namely the $C_s$. For the convenience of modeling, the ideal Shannon capacity approximates to the capacity for each unit provided by the satellite

$$C_s = B \log(1 + \frac{\alpha_s P}{BN_0}) \tag{2}$$

where $B$ is the bandwidth used in the beam hopping system, $\alpha_s$ is the quasi-static signal power attenuation due to the weather effects, $N_0$ is the noise power density, and $P$ is the fixed equivalent downward transmission power.

Define $A = min\{R, C\}$, where $R$ is the needed capacity matrix for all users in a unit, $C$ is the capacity each beam can provide and $A$ is the actual capacity matrix for each channel. Assume that the average packet arrival rate of each beam is $\lambda_i$, and the arrival process obeys the Poisson arrival process.

### 3.3   Problem Formulation

The three-dimensional (3-D) matrix can correspond to an x-y-z three-dimensional coordinate, as shown in Fig. 3.

For given $R$ and $C$, our problem is formulated as

$$TC(s)_{max} = \sum_m \sum_n \sum_k B(m,n,k;s) * A(m,n,k) \tag{3}$$

where $TC(s)_{max}$ is the maximum of the capacity, $B(m,n,k;s)$ is a three-dimensional matrix with elements 0 or 1, s is the number of elements 1. As shown in Fig. 4, $B(m,n,k;s)$ is the optimization matrix that must be first confirm to achieve the objective function. The dimension $k$ is a time domain and $k \in [1,K]$, where $K = \frac{T}{t_{unit}}$, $t_{unit}$ is the duration each hopping-beam serves the unit at one time (Fig. 5).

For example, when the value of element in $B(m,n,k;s)$ is 1, it means that the corresponding position is illuminated by the hopping beam. On the contrary, it is not illuminated when the value is 0. The number of 1 in every page equals to the number of hopping beams that the system can synchronously provide.

A is also a three-dimensional matrix whose form is the same with $B(m,n,k;s)$, namely $A(m,n,k)$. Meanwhile, every page of matrix $A(m,n,k)$ corresponds to the actual capacity matrix $A(m,n,k)$ among the $cell_i$. Figure 6 shows the example of the way to describe the process $B(m,n,k;s) * A(m,n,k)$, which means to multiply A's each unit with B's unit correspondingly in these two three-dimensional matrixes.

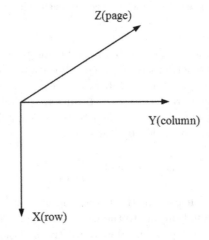

**Fig. 4.** Matrix coordinates

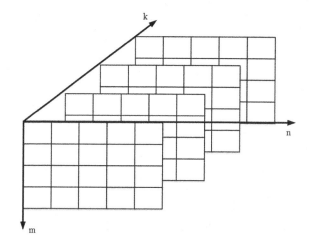

**Fig. 5.** Matrix coordinates

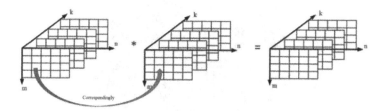

**Fig. 6.** The process form of $B(m, n, k; s) * A(m, n, k)$

## 4   Experimental Evaluation

In this paper, based on LEO satellites, we design a satellite coverage model with hopping beam technology and have finished the simulation about the cells division with hopping beams under the cover of the single satellite, the total capacity demand distribution of users in each cell, and the comparison between beam hopping technology and fixed point beams technology. In this section, we provide the simulation results in order to show the advantages of beam hopping technology.

Figure 7 shows the user distribution within each cell, where the distribution is random.

Figure 8 shows that in one of the cells, we divide the cell into 3 × 3 = 9 units, and each unit corresponds to having a total capacity demand of all the users in the unit.

We compare the performance between the beam hopping technology and Fig. 9 shows comparison results between the hopping beam and the fixed point beam scheme. As shown in Fig. 9, compared to the traditional beam fixed tech-

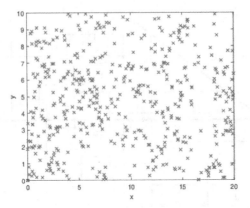

**Fig. 7.** The random distribution of users in one cell

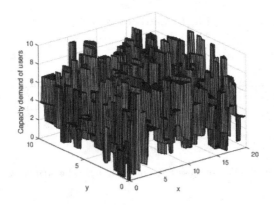

**Fig. 8.** Capacity demand distribution in each cell

nique, with the number of beams increasing, the beam hopping scheme truly has better performance in the total throughput of users in a cell.

Beam fixed technique has the randomness that once we choose the beams, they are fixed and unchanged. What might happen is that the chosen units are unfortunately the least capacity among all of the units in one cell, and then we may have the least total throughput of users in a cell.

In theory, beam hopping scheme should have more than the outstanding performance of total throughput of users in a cell. According to the flexibility of beam hopping, when the user distribution is extremely uneven, compared with the fixed beam technique, beam hopping scheme has its own prominent advantages.

In order to make the comparison much clearer we measure the user distribution by variance, which represents the degree of dispersion, and the comparison results between hopping beam and fixed point beam with different user distribution variance are shown in Fig. 10. As a result, we can see that with different

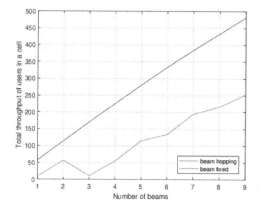

**Fig. 9.** Comparison results between the hopping beam and the fixed point beam scheme

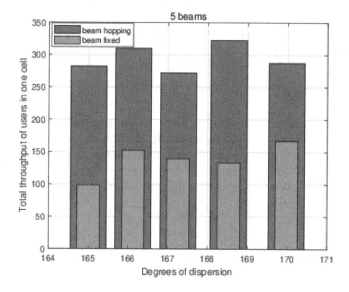

**Fig. 10.** The throughput of the hopping beam and fixed point beam techniques with different degrees of dispersion

degree of dispersion, beam hopping method always has more throughput than fixed point beam technique.

## 5  Ongoing Research Efforts

For the traditional fixed multi-beam satellite communication system, the beam hopping based wireless resource management policy usually only involves the frequency domain and time domain, and seldom considers user delay and quality of service (QoS). QoS is the comprehensive effect of service performance, which determines the users degree of satisfaction with the communication services [14]. In most cases, the QoS guarantee is usually measured by parameters such as bandwidth, time delay and accuracy. The key to QoS guarantee is that the different service types have different QoS requirements, therefore there are different service levels. For example, voice services need low bandwidth requirement but have strict requirements for maximum transmission delay. Another example is about the data services, which usually allows not too obvious QoS delay while the E-mail and short messages are typically of low bandwidth but file transfer needs significantly higher bandwidth. Video services not only have the high bandwidth requirements, but also ask for the strict requirements for maximum transmission delay.

Previous research content is focused on finding optimal throughput to select target, but considering the next generation satellite network, in order to meet the needs of service differentiation, we need to consider time delay, priorities and band as a hopping beam switching to selected target. This section highlights research efforts we consider of particular importance for using the beam hopping technology in the practice, especially in these aspects: QoS, flexibility and complexity.

## 6    Conclusion

This paper proposed a beam hopping (BH) model which performs better than traditional fixed beams method theoretically. As proved in this work, such BH model brings flexibility in the LEO satellite and the simulation results in this paper also proved the improvement on throughout performance of the fast moving LEO satellite modes. The service differentiation of BH technology will be considered as our future work.

**Acknowledgments.** This work is supported by Science and Technology Commission of Shanghai Municipality (No. 17DZ1100700), Shanghai Sailing Program (No. 18YF1422100), and National Natural Science Foundation of China (No. 61601295, No. 2017YFB0502902).

## References

1. http://www.oneweb.world. Accessed June 2018
2. www.spacex.com. Accessed June 2018
3. Angeletti, P., Prim, D.F., Rinaldo, R.: Beam hopping in multi-beam broadband satellite systems: System performance and payload architecture analysis. In: 24th AIAA International Communications Satellite Systems Conference, pp. 53–76 (2006)
4. Mokhtar, A., Azizoglu, M.: Downlink capacity of a packet-switched broadband LEO satellite network with hopping beams. In: 1999 Global Telecommunications Conference, GLOBECOM 1999, vol. 2, pp. 1505–1510. IEEE (1999)
5. Mokhtar, A., Azizoglu, M.: On the downlink throughput of a broadband lEO satellite network with hopping beams. IEEE Commun. Lett. 4(12), 390–393 (2000)

6. Whitefield, D., Gopal, R., Arnold, S.: Spaceway now and in the future: on-board IP packet switching satellite communication network. In: 2006 IEEE Military Communications Conference, MILCOM 2006. pp. 1–7. IEEE (2006)
7. http://www.satixfy.com/beam-hopping-make-possible-part-1. Accessed June 2018
8. Jacomb-Hood, A.W., Dentinger, A.M., Maalouf, K.J.: Apparatus, method, and computer program products for cell-hopping satellite communications. US Patent 6,522,643. 18 February 2003
9. Cooper, S.A., Jue, R., Yousefi, E., Wright, D.A., Linsky, S.T., Bever, M.E.: Downlink beam hopping waveform. US Patent 6,992,992. 31 January 2006
10. Pecorella, T., Fantacci, R., Lasagni, C., Rosati, L., Todorova, P.: Study and implementation of switching and beam-hopping techniques in satellites with on board processing. In: 2007 International Workshop on Satellite and Space Communications, IWSSC 2007, pp. 206–210. IEEE (2007)
11. Anzalchi, J., Couchman, A., Gabellini, P., Gallinaro, G., D'agristina, L., Alagha, N., Angeletti, P.: Beam hopping in multi-beam broadband satellite systems: system simulation and performance comparison with nonhopped systems. In: 2010 5th Advanced Satellite Multimedia Systems Conference (ASMA) and the 11th Signal Processing for Space Communications Workshop (SPSC), pp. 248–255. IEEE (2010)
12. Fonseca, N.J.G., Sombrin, J.: Multi-beam reflector antenna system combining beam hopping and size reduction of effectively used spots. IEEE Antennas Propag. Mag. **54**(2), 88–99 (2012)
13. Sharma, S.K., Chatzinotas, S., Ottersten, B.: Cognitive beamhopping for spectral coexistence of multibeam satellites. Int. J. Satell. Commun. Network. **33**(1), 69–91 (2015)
14. Altman, E., Jimenez, T.: Lecture notes on ns simulator for beginners. Jae Chung and Mark Claypool, NS by Example (2003)

# Delay-Constrained Load Balancing in the SDN

Ziyi Ma[2], Xiaoqiang Di[1(✉)], Yuming Jiang[2], Huilin Jiang[2],
and Huamin Yang[2]

[1] Changchun University of Science and Technology,
No.7186, Weixing Road, Changchun, Jilin, China
dixiaoqiang@cust.edu.cn
[2] Changchun, China

**Abstract.** In the low earth orbit (LEO) satellite networks, a single satellite may cover areas with various population quantity, economic conditions and time zones. In this case, networks have time-varying traffic load and may face with unbalanced load distribution. Moreover, software defined networking (SDN) has dynamic monitoring function that can be implemented in the satellite network to observe the real-time status of satellite links and nodes, and quickly update routing tables. However, high link utilization is likely to cause local network congestion, resulting in increased delay. To solve this problem, we propose a load balancing algorithm under the delay constraint. The experimental results show that our proposed scheme can reasonably allocate link bandwidth under the delay requirement and achieve lower end-to-end delay and higher system throughput.

**Keywords:** LEO satellite network · Load balancing ·
Delay constraint · SDN

## 1 Introduction

Satellite networks use wide-area coverage of satellites to provide mobile communication services. This is an important means of achieving communication globalization and personalization. Compared with medium earth orbit (MEO) satellite networks and geostationary earth orbit (GEO) satellite networks, low earth orbit (LEO) [1] satellite networks are close to the ground and have advantages in terms of delay and loss. At the same time, its low transmission loss is very advantageous for the broadband service and the miniaturization terminal. Therefore, LEO satellite is very suitable for future mobile communication system. In the LEO network, the area that a single satellite covers has different population and different status of economic development. Besides, it is also affected by time zones, horoscopes, and the rotation of the Earth. Therefore, the distribution of satellite network load is uneven and has time-varying characteristics. Unbalanced load probably makes the high utilization rate of links, causes congestion and delay instability, which affects the overall efficiency of the network. However, the low utilization rate of links is not selected, which is clearly unreasonable.

Software Defined Networking (SDN) is a new network architecture defined by the Open Networking Foundation [2]. The SDN controller arranges network resources in a rational and flexible manner, and further optimizes network performance. Therefore,

© Springer Nature Singapore Pte Ltd. 2019
Q. Yu (Ed.): SINC 2018, CCIS 972, pp. 124–134, 2019.
https://doi.org/10.1007/978-981-13-5937-8_14

SDN has been accepted as a key technology to be implemented on satellite networks. The main characteristic of SDN is to separate the control plane from the data plane [3]. We focus on using SDN to dynamically control traffic and then ensure the QoS requirements for each user. The control plane and data plane should be analyzed jointly.

In this paper, to complete the dynamic traffic control and path analysis, we propose a systematic design method to provide deterministic QoS guaranteed in LEO satellite network, which considers different delay demand for diverse user requests. In the data plane, we apply Hierarchical Token Bucket (HTB) [4] to control various priorities of data flows. Through scheduling, classifying and controlling transmission rate of packages, HTB is used to reduce the network traffic burst. We also utilize the Deterministic Network Calculus (DNC) to calculate the delay and estimate the deterministic delay bounds of traffic. In the control plane, we propose a routing algorithm to achieve load balancing under the delay constraints. The controller can dynamically forward or reject traffic to balancing the network traffic. Delay bound is used to determine whether a new arrival flow meets the delay requirement and the switch can forward this flow. Finally, the forwarding decisions and the optimal paths for different user requests can be determined.

The rest of the paper is organized as follows. Section 2 introduces the research status of HTB queue discipline, network calculus, and the load balancing strategies. Section 3 describes the concept of DNC in analyzing data flow delay performance. Section 4 provides a delay-constrained load balancing routing algorithm under SDN architecture. Section 5 shows the experimental results by the Open Virtual Switch (OVS) and Ryu controller on the Mininet platform [19]. Finally, Sect. 6 concludes this paper.

## 2 Related Work

### 2.1 HTB Queue Discipline

HTB is a class-based queuing discipline that arranges packets in order. HTB combines leaky bucket with token to provide more efficient control of network traffic. HTB system is shown in Fig. 1. The classification work is suitable to divide a fixed amount of bandwidth for different destination flows, providing bandwidth guarantees, and

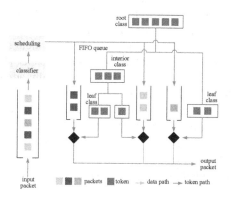

**Fig. 1.** Hierarchical token bucket model [7]

specifying the amount of bandwidth that can be borrowed [5]. In the leaf class, upper flows must be classified by the filter and put into the leaf class [6]. Filter can distinguish between different types of traffic, services, IP addresses, and priorities. HTB uses tokens and buckets to control link bandwidth. It outputs packets from the bucket only if there are available tokens.

## 2.2   Network Calculus in SDN

Network calculus establishes deterministic protocols for performance metrics such as delay, backlog, and queue length. We can analyze the performance of network traffic. Applying the mathematic model on the performance analysis of OpenFlow-based SDN has a great research value of the subject. In the case of a single switch node, there is already the M/M/1 queue to configure packet buffer time and decrease the loss rate of packets. However, when multiple nodes are involved, the end-to-end real-time service of SDN is used to flexibly control each forwarding element. Reference [8] uses network calculus to choose an optimal path for each flow in the above scene. Compared with traditional QoS reservation path methods, the average utilization of link in [8] is better. To reduce the data packet loss, paper [9] compares the delay performance of the multi-hop model with the threshold model. It is proved that the flow has a strict end-to-end delay bound. The Delay cannot be ignored in the SDN architecture. SDN provides a centralized control that can be used to monitor the real-time network topology for network traffic. Reference [10] solves the serious handoff delay when mobile users hand off to another base station. A delay analysis model based on network calculus is proposed to evaluate the handover delay bounds of SDN switches and controllers. For large-scale traffic, Huang [11] proposes a flow aggregation admission control model in SDN to achieve QoS guarantee, which requires bandwidth and buffer space for the flow aggregation in order to satisfy the performance requirements. We use network calculus to analyze the delay performance of different packets, and aim to achieve load balancing in SDN.

## 2.3   Load Balancing in Satellite Network

Load balancing is mainly used to implement a series of traffic control schemes to avoid local congestion. To achieve better traffic distribution, [12] proposes an explicit load balancing (ELB) scheme. Neighbor satellites can exchange their congestion information about their links. Since ELB does not consider individual queue, link congestion cannot be effectively prevented. To solve this problem, paper [13] proposes a traffic-light-based intelligent routing strategy. Packets dynamically adjust the route based on the real-time traffic lights at each node. This method reduces the packet loss and improves the throughput, but the end-to-end delay is not stable. Considering the end-to-end delay, paper [14] designs a state-aware and load-balancing routing model for LEO satellite networks, with the objective to reduce end-to-end delay in the terms of load balancing. Considering the real-time updates of validated routing tables, we aim to guarantee load balancing under delay constraints.

## 3 Deterministic Network Calculus Model of Static Priority Scheduling

Network calculus (NC) is a systematic theory, which is implemented in computer networks [15], including stochastic network calculus and deterministic network calculus. Deterministic Network Calculus (DNC) identifies appropriate boundary value of network performance. We want to provide deterministic QoS to the LEO satellite network, so we use the DNC and provide some basic definitions for NC.

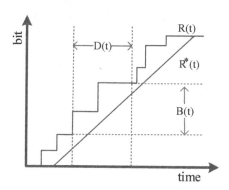

**Fig. 2.** Delay and backlog performance of input and output function

**Definition 1** (Input Function): $R(t)$ is a cumulative input function and indicates a wide-sense increasing function in interval $[0, t]$, $R(t) = 0$ and $R(t_1) < R(t_2)$ if $t_1 \leq t_2$.

**Definition 2** (Output Function): For the input function $R(t)$, $R^*(t)$ represents the total number of output packets in time slot $1, 2, \ldots, t$. $R^*(t)$ is also a wide-sense increasing function.

**Definition 3** (Arrival Curve): The upper bound of the $R(t)$ is the arrival curve $\alpha$, or $R(t)$ is constrained by $\alpha$, $R(t) - R(s) \leq \alpha(t - s)$, if $0 \leq s \leq t$.

**Definition 4** (Service Curve): System S considers $R(t)$ and $R^*(t)$, and offers a service curve $\beta$ with $\beta(0) = 0$ and $R^*(t) \geq \inf_{s \leq t}[R(s) + \beta(t - s)]$.

As shown in Fig. 2, the vertical distance between the arrival curve and the service curve represents the backlog and reflects the buffered data flow waiting to be processed at S. The horizontal distance between the arrival curve and service curve is the packet delay, which reflects the worst-case response time of a packet.

**Definition 5** (Delay Bound): Suppose a data flow is constrained by $\alpha$ and S provides a service cure $\beta$, the delay bound $D(t)$ must satisfy the Eq. 1.

$$D(t) \leq h(\alpha, \beta) = \sup_{s \geq 0}\{\inf[T \geq 0 : \alpha(s) \leq \beta(s + T)]\} \tag{1}$$

NC can be represented by the concept of min-plus algebra, max-plus algebra, and matrix [16]. In min-plus algebra, convolution operator $\otimes$ is defined as $f \otimes g(t) = \inf_{0 \leq s \leq t} \{f(t-s) - g(s)\}$. The relation between $R(t)$, $R^*(t)$ and $\beta$ is $R^*(t) \geq R(t) \otimes \beta(t)$, $t \geq 0$.

Assuming $\beta(t)$ is the service curve of a network node, the service curve of aggregated flow is $\beta_c(t) = [\beta(t) - l_{max}]^+$, $l_{max}$ is the maximum length of the arriving packets, $[x]^+$ is $\max[0.x]$. Data flows are divided into two kinds of priorities $P_1$ and $P_2$. Network node deals with two aggregated flows $Q_1(t)$ and $Q_2(t)$ in two queues. $Q_1(t)$ and $Q_2(t)$ represent the accumulated function of packets and $Q_1^*(t) * Q_2^*(t)$ is their output flows respectively. Define $\beta(t-s) = S(t) - S(s)$, then $Q_1^*(t) - Q_1(s) \geq S(t) - S(s)$, where s is a starting point of arrival flow. $\beta(t)$ is service curve to flow $R_1(t)$.

$$Q_1^*(t) \geq Q_1(s) + \beta(t-s) = (Q_1 \otimes \beta)(t) \tag{2}$$

Supposing a new flow $Q_2(t)$ arrives, network node identifies whether it is capable to forward this flow. If the flow can be forwarded, based on $\beta_c(t)$, the service curve of this flow is,

$$\beta_1^*(t) = \left[\beta(t) - A_1(t) - \alpha_{N,p_N}(t)\right]^+$$
$$= \left[\beta(t) - \sum_{p_i \in p} R(t) - R_N(t)\right] \left[t - \frac{l_{max} + \sum_{p_i \in p} b_i + b_N}{\beta(t) - \sum_{p_i \in p} R(t) - R_N(t)}\right]^+ \tag{3}$$

From Eq. 3, the service rate and delay of a new data flow is calculated as follows.

$$R(t) = \beta(t) - \sum_{p_i \in p} R(t) - R_N(t) \tag{4}$$

$$d(t) = \frac{l_{max} + \sum_{p_i \in p} b_i + b_N}{\beta(t) - \sum_{p_i \in p} R(t) - R_N(t)} \tag{5}$$

If $R(t) > 0$, the switch is capable to forward this new flow.

## 4   Load Balancing in SDN

A load balancing routing algorithm based on the DNC model is implemented in this section. We will discuss how to apply the delay analysis and the service process rate of Sect. 3 to SDN. According to the Eq. 5, we compare the new flow delay and our delay threshold. If the value of the delay threshold is bigger, the forwarding path needs to be calculated. The Fig. 3 illustrates the proposed load-balancing system guaranteed by deterministic QoS. Firstly, the service user process is defined by the network function and the delay requirement is set by the user. Secondly, the system dynamically monitors the traffic load and CPU utilization rate of server of each link, which affects the delay performance. Then, we solve the routing problem through link and node load balancing algorithms. If there is no path that satisfies the delay, users must resend the

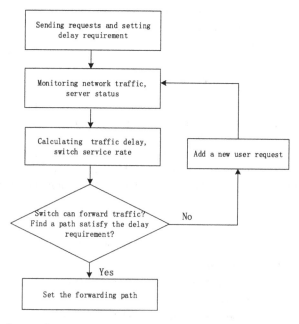

**Fig. 3.** System flow for providing deterministic QoS-guaranteed user service

---

**Algorithm 1.** Delay-constrained Load Balancing Algorithm

---

**Require:** host$_{src}$, switch$_{src}$, serverload, linkload

**Ensure:** server$_{dst}$ , switch$_{arr}$

    P←Path (switch$_{src}$; server$_{dst}$)

    **if**  (d(t) ≤ T$_{delayconstraint}$&&R(t) ≥ 0)  **then**

        **for** p$_i$ ∈ p **do**

            **for** eachswitch[v] adjacent to server[u] **do**

                **if** p$_i$ ≠ ∅ **then**

                switch[v] ← min(linkload $_{src\_switch[v]}$)

                server$_{dst}$ ← min(server_load[u])

                **end if**

            **end for**

        **end for**

        **return** server$_{dst}$ , switch$_{arr}$

    **end if**

---

requests. Finally, the controller updates the switch flow table. In the remaining parts of this section, two specific phases are introduced, namely the network status information collection and path selection.

### 4.1  Network Condition Collecting

In the first stage, the controller monitoring module collects network status information and network topology information. Network status information includes the CPU usage of each server and the remaining bandwidth resources of each link between the switch and servers. The network topology can be described as the link status through a table of host-port-switch and a matrix of switch link. Table 1 is an example to record how the host is connected to the switch. The switch link matrix shown in the Table 2 is used to record the status of interconnected switches.

**Table 1.** An example of host-port-switch table

| Host IP | Host MAC | Switch | Port number |
|---------|----------|--------|-------------|
| 10.0.0.1 | 00:00:00:00:00:01 | 00:00:00:00:00:01 | 1 |
| 10.0.0.2 | 00:00:00:00:00:02 | 00:00:00:00:00:04 | 3 |
| 10.0.0.3 | 00:00:00:00:00:03 | 00:00:00:00:00:04 | 4 |

**Table 2.** An example of switch-link table

|  | Switch 1 | Switch 2 | Switch 3 | Switch 4 |
|---|----------|----------|----------|----------|
| Switch 1 | x | 3 | 4 | x |
| Switch 2 | 1 | x | x | 2 |
| Switch 3 | 1 | x | x | 2 |
| Switch 4 | x | 1 | 2 | x |

### 4.2  Path Selecting

In the second stage, we firstly analyze the delay performance of host requests, and then determine the optimal path according to network status. The forwarding path of package is determined by the network request types, link status, and server load requested by the client. According to the OpenFlow [17] protocol, the switch forwards the header packet to the controller while receiving a new data flow. The controller obtains source or destination host address of the packet and evaluates the delay performance based on the network status. Then the best path is determined through the DCLB algorithm. The last step is updating information of flow tables. We need to periodically check the end-to-end delay performance to estimate whether delay is satisfactory. If the delay performance requested by the host violates the delay requirements, the optimal path needs to be recalculated.

## 5  Simulation and Analysis

We conducted a series of experiments to prove the effectiveness of the proposed delay-constrained load balancing (DCLB) algorithm. As is shown in Fig. 4, an SDN network is realized on the Mininet [18] simulation platform. Mininet can simulate the interconnected network of end hosts, switches, and controllers. We use the open source Ryu Controller and the OVS switch [19]. The OpenFlow protocol we used between them is version 1.3. Queue configurations are implemented through the OVS commands. We use the HTB in switch node. The queues are set up on the output ports of the switch. Switch outputs the flows by the priority. Different types of users have different requirements for bandwidth. Assuming there are three data flow types, the bandwidth demands are 60 kbps, 100 kbps, and 300 kbps respectively. In Mininet, iperf tool is used to simulate the host. The host cyclically sends three types of bandwidth requests to servers.

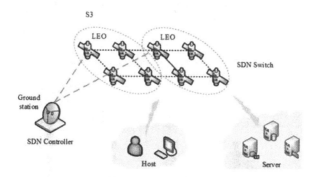

**Fig. 4.** Topology used in simulation

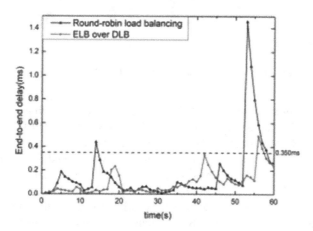

**Fig. 5.** Delay performance of two load balancing algorithms without delay requirement

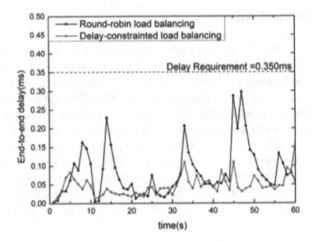

**Fig. 6.** Delay performance of two load balancing algorithms with delay requirement

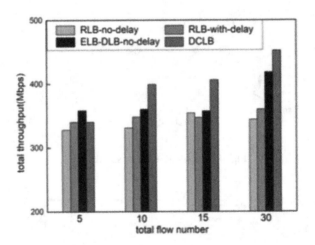

**Fig. 7.** Total throughput of different total flow number

For the Mininet simulation, we compare our proposed algorithm with the round-robin load balancing (RLB) algorithm [20] and the application of ELB over Dijkstra's Load Balancing (DLB) algorithm [12]. The RLB algorithm redirects every new request to a different server in a certain order. Figure 5 shows the end-to-end delay performance measured by two algorithms without adding delay bounds. The RLB algorithm may forward requests to congested links or loaded servers, resulting in increasing delay suddenly. In contrast, end-to-end delay is lower when we select the optimal path based on the load status of link and node. But both algorithms have the fluctuation of delay.

After adding the delay requirement, we measure the end-to-end delay of both routing algorithms. As is shown in the Fig. 6, the overall delay performance tends to be flattened after adding bounds. Compared with Fig. 5, the maximum delay is reduced. The simulation result of total throughput for each algorithm is shown in Fig. 7. With the increase of total flow number, all throughputs of these algorithms' system increase respectively. This is because the utilization of link bandwidth increases with the increase of total flow number. However, when total flow number is high, the increase of RLB-no-delay algorithm is low as the flow number has already reach the limit of link bandwidth. Delay-constrained load balancing algorithm has a relatively higher total throughput than other algorithms. Therefore, it is important to consider the delay requirement and the status of entire network. Under the condition that the delay is guaranteed, links and server nodes are balanced to avoid the overload status.

## 6 Conclusion

In this work, we presented a delay-constrained load balancing algorithm for software defined LEO satellite network. We judged the new data flow forwarding and analyzed traffic service delay performance by using network calculus. We selected an optimal path to achieve better load balancing between network links and nodes. Experiments results show that the proposed algorithm can get good effects of delay and throughput.

## References

1. Rao, Y., Wang, R.-C.: Agent-based load balancing routing for LEO satellite networks. Comput. Netw. **54**(17), 3187–3195 (2010)
2. Open Networking Foundation: Software-defined networking: the new norm for networks. ONF White Pap. **2**, 2–6 (2012)
3. Yeganeh, S.H., Ganjali, Y.: Kandoo: a framework for efficient and scalable offloading of control applications. In: The Workshop on Hot Topics in Software Defined Networks, pp. 19–24 (2012)
4. Lee, C.H., Kim, Y.T.: QoS-aware hierarchical token bucket (QHTB) queuing disciplines for QoS-guaranteed DiffServ provisioning with optimized bandwidth utilization and priority-based preemption. In: International Conference on Information NETWORKING, pp. 351–358 (2013)
5. Maxwell, G., Mook, R.V., Oosterhout, M.V., Schroeder, P.B., Spaans, J.: Linux advanced routing and traffic control howto. Acta Medica Scandinavica **145**(S280), 1122 (2002)
6. Valenzuela, J.L., Monleon, A., San Esteban, I., Portoles, M.: A hierarchical token bucket algorithm to enhance QoS in IEEE 802.11: proposal, implementation and evaluation. In: Vehicular Technology Conference, VTC 2004-Fall, vol. 4, pp. 2659–2662. IEEE (2004)
7. Ren, S., Feng, Q., Wang, Y., Dou, W.: A service curve of hierarchical token bucket queue discipline on software defined networks based on deterministic network calculus: an analysis and simulation. J. Adv. Comput. Netw. **5**(1), (2017)
8. Guck, J.W., Kellerer, W.: Achieving end-to-end real-time quality of service with software defined networking. In: IEEE International Conference on Cloud Networking, pp. 70–76 (2014)

9. Guck, J.W., Bemten, A.V., Kellerer, W.: DetServ: network models for real-time QoS provisioning in SDN-based industrial environments. IEEE Trans. Netw. Serv. Manag. **PP**(99), 1 (2017)
10. Lin, C.R., Chen, Y.J., Wang, L.C.: Handoff delay analysis in SDN-enabled mobile networks: a network calculus approach. In: IEEE Vehicular Technology Conference, pp. 1–5 (2017)
11. Huang, J., He, Y., Duan, Q., Yang, Q., Wang, W.: Admission control with flow aggregation for QoS provisioning in software-defined network. In: Global Communications Conference, pp. 1182–1186 (2014)
12. Taleb, T., Mashimo, D., Jamalipour, A., Hashimoto, K.: SAT04-3: ELB: an explicit load balancing routing protocol for multi-hop NGEO satellite constellations. In: Global Telecommunications Conference, GLOBECOM 2006, pp. 1–5. IEEE (2007)
13. Song, G., Chao, M., Yang, B., Zheng, Y.: TLR: a traffic-lightbased intelligent routing strategy for NGEO satellite ip networks. IEEE Trans. Wirel. Commun. **13**(6), 3380–3393 (2014)
14. Li, X., Tang, F., Chen, L., et al.: A state-aware and load-balanced routing model for LEO satellite networks. In: 2017 IEEE Global Communications Conference, GLOBECOM 2017, pp. 1–6. IEEE (2017)
15. Le Boudec, J.-Y., Thiran, P. (eds.): Network Calculus - A Theory of Deterministic Queuing Systems for the Internet. LNCS, vol. 2050. Springer, Heidelberg (2001). https://doi.org/10.1007/3-540-45318-0
16. Fidler, M.: An end-to-end probabilistic network calculus with moment generating functions. In: IEEE International Workshop on Quality of Service, pp. 261–270 (2006)
17. Lara, A., Kolasani, A., Ramamurthy, B.: Network innovation using openflow: a survey. IEEE Commun. Surv. Tutor. **16**(1), 493–512 (2014)
18. Lantz, B., Heller, B., Mckeown, N.: A network in a laptop: rapid prototyping for software-defined networks. In: ACM Workshop on Hot Topics in Networks, HOTNETS 2010, Monterey, CA, USA, pp. 1–6, October 2010
19. Ryu controller. http://osrg.github.io/ryu/
20. Kaur, S., Kumar, K., Singh, J., Ghumman, N.S.: Round-robin based load balancing in software defined networking. In: 2015 2nd International Conference on Computing for Sustainable Global Development (INDIACom), pp. 2136–2139. IEEE (2015)

# Research on Handover Strategy of Low Orbit Spacecraft Based on Multi-beam GEO Communication Satellite

Yun Shi[⊠], Zijing Cheng, Qidi You, and Mian Liu

Beijing Institute of Satellite Information Engineering, Beijing 100086, China
shiyun3379@163.com

**Abstract.** After analysis on traditional data transmission mode of low-orbit spacecraft, this paper studies the problem of access and handover of low-orbit spacecraft based on GEO communication satellite. In conjunction with the location information of low-orbit spacecraft and the feature of predictable beam dwell time, we proposed a method based on SCPC\MF-TDMA hybrid access and centralized handover detection through comparative analysis of typical multiple access and beam handover mechanism of satellite communication system. The analysis and comparison of handover delay approved that the centralized handover detection of low-orbit spacecraft and resource reservation according to track prediction proposed in this paper can reduce handover delay effectively.

**Keywords:** Low-orbit spacecraft · Multi-layered satellite networks · Multiple access · Beam handover

## 1 Introduction

In order to solve with the global real-time information transmission problems, low-orbit satellites usually rely on inter-satellite links and global stations to transmit on-board information to the ground. It is constrained by many factors such as the storage capacity of satellite, the number of satellites, and the cost of the satellite constellation. And if we adopt the ground station transmission method, it will face the problem of ground station sit selection and the feasibility of establishing a global station. Therefore, it is necessary to expand the new effective transmission mode to solve the problem of real-time information transmission of low-orbit satellite. At the same time, the downlink information of the space station test can be transmitted through the TDRSS (Tracking and Data Relay Satellite System), but TDRSS is mainly used for the measurement and control of the medium and low-orbit spacecraft [1, 2], which is not suitable for the transmission of a large number of real-time test information of the space station.

To solve the above problems, this paper applies GEO communication satellites to solve the problem of low orbit spacecraft information transmission. Some scholars have proposed multi-layer satellite networks, including two-layer satellite networks (low-orbit satellite + medium-orbit satellite, medium-orbit satellite + high-orbit satellite), and

© Springer Nature Singapore Pte Ltd. 2019
Q. Yu (Ed.): SINC 2018, CCIS 972, pp. 135–145, 2019.
https://doi.org/10.1007/978-981-13-5937-8_15

three-layer satellite network (low-orbit satellite + medium-orbit satellite + high-orbit satellite, Low-orbit satellite + high-orbit satellite + high altitude platform stations) [3–6]. However, these studies mainly focus on inter-satellite routing between various layers of satellites and multi-layer satellite access strategy [7], there are no specific access methods and beam handover research for low-orbit spacecraft access to multi-beam GEO communication satellites.

Access and handover strategies are mainly concentrated in single-layer satellite networks (mainly concentrated in low-orbit satellite constellations). Several typical multi-star access strategies in single-layer satellite networks are distance priority, coverage time priority, and elevation weighted coverage time priority, etc. [7, 8]. Typical beam handover mechanisms in single-layer satellite networks are geometry based, tilt angle based, resident time based beam switching mechanisms, etc. [9, 10].

Based on the research of network architecture, this paper discussed the access methods and beam handover mechanisms of low orbit spacecraft based on multi-beam GEO communication satellites, and analyzed the technical feasibility through the analysis of handover delay.

## 2   Network Architecture

### 2.1   Application Scenarios

A typical application scenario of low-orbit spacecraft transmission based on GEO communication satellites is shown in Fig. 1. The space segment includes low-orbit spacecraft and communication satellites; the ground segment includes ground stations, terminals, and terrestrial networks. The low-orbit spacecraft can transmit information over two links: one is transmitted to the ground station via the GEO communications satellite; the other is transmitted directly to the terminals. In this scenario, the low-orbit spacecraft acts as a low-orbit node moving at high speed, and its link has a large space-time scale and high dynamic characteristics.

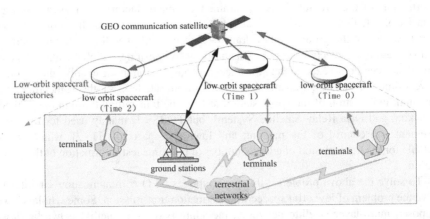

**Fig. 1.** Dynamic transmission system of low-orbit spacecraft based on GEO communications satellites

## 2.2  Channel Environments

Since different mobile terminals have different speed characteristics and channel environments, we will classify and analyze them in this section:

### LOS
LOS means Line-of-Sight. This channel environment refers to the state of line-of-sight transmission, or low-fading state for most of the time [11]. This channel condition can be approximated by the AWGN additive white Gaussian noise channel. According to the measured LOS transmission channel conditions, such mobile channels can be regarded as narrowband without memory. Since the multipath fading statistics are described by the Rice distribution, we can simulate the scene with a pure Rice channel with a high Rice factor. The Rice process with the LOS component added is as follow:

$$m(t) = m_1(t) + jm_2(t) = \rho_m \exp\left(j\left(2\pi f_\rho + \theta_m\right)\right) \tag{1}$$

In the above formula, $f_\rho$ is the Doppler Frequency. Since the LOS transmission state is very similar to the AWGN additive white Gaussian noise channel, the noise can be described by a zero-mean complex Gaussian process with a variance of $\sigma_0^2$:

$$k(t) = k_1(t) + jk_2(t) \tag{2}$$

The probability density function of the amplitude of the received signal obtained by summing the above equation and taking the absolute value is as follows:

$$p_X(x) = \frac{x}{\sigma_0^2} \exp\left(-\frac{x^2 + \rho^2}{2\sigma_0^2}\right) I_0\left(\frac{x\rho}{\sigma_0^2}\right) \tag{3}$$

Where $I_0()$ is the first-order zero-order modified Bessel function, and the K value (the ratio of the direct signal power to the multipath signal power) is $\frac{\rho_m^2}{2\sigma_0^2}$, which represents the influence of multipath phenomenon on signal distribution, the larger the K value, the smaller the influence of the multipath component.

### Non-LOS
Non-LOS means Non- line-of-sight. This kind of channel environment refers to the condition that the terminal is in the ground and the line-of-sight transmission condition is frequently affected by signal blocking and fading. Mobile terminals in such channel environment may encounter obstacles such as buildings, vegetation, bridges, tunnels, etc. The terminal will be blocked for a certain period of time, thus causing shadow effects and signal fading. This transmission channel condition can be simulated by a three-state Markov chain model, and the three states are LOS line-of-sight transmission state, shadow state, and blocking state, respectively. The channel conditions with shadows and shadows can be described by the Loo distribution. We assume that the multipath signal component is not affected by shadow fading, and only the direct signal

component is affected by shadow fading, therefore the Loo model is also called a partially shadow channel model, and the received signal is expressed as:

$$r(t) = [z(t) + d(t)]s(t) = R(t) \cdot s(t) \tag{4}$$

In the above formula, $z(t)$ is a direct signal component, $s(t)$ is a shadow fading component, and $d(t)$ is a multipath signal component. If only the multipath signal component exists in the received signal, the envelope of the multipath signal component obeys the Rayleigh distribution.

According to the above channel environment classification, the link channel environment between the low-orbit spacecraft and the GEO satellite depends on the environment in which the low-orbit spacecraft is located. Different from the ground mobile terminal, since the low-orbit spacecraft is within the range of 200–2000 km above the ground, there is no problem of shadowing, and the channel environment can be approximated to the LOS line-of-sight transmission environment, which represents the relatively stable physical channel conditions of the low-orbit spacecraft.

## 3   Research on Handover Mechanism

Since the coverage of each beam of the multi-beam GEO communication satellite is small, and the coverage diameter is usually only a few hundred kilometers, the single beam visible time of the low-orbit spacecraft and the multi-beam GEO communication satellite is usually less than 1 min. In order to make full use of satellite resources, it is important for the low-orbit spacecraft to quickly access to satellite communication systems, and transmit information of data at high speed. Therefore, the access mechanism and handover strategy of the system are very important, especially the timeliness of access and the delay of handover.

### 3.1   Analysis of Access Method

The basic multiple access methods in satellite communication systems mainly include: Frequency Division Multiple Access (FDMA), Time Division Multiple Access (TDMA), Code Division Multiple Access (CDMA), and Space Division Multiple Access (SDMA). With the development of technology and application requirements, a variety of basic multiple access methods (such as MF-TDMA, PCMA, etc.) can be combined to achieve more flexible access of user terminals through hybrid multiple access [12].

The analysis and comparison of mainstream multiple access methods [12] are as follows:

FDMA: The SCPC/DAMA method commonly used in FDMA is mainly applied to a thin routing system with a large amount of traffic, a single type, and a small number of terminals. This method has the advantages of reliable network operation and simple management.

CDMA: The CDMA method not only has to overcome the influence of system noise, but also solves the problem of mutual interference between users by increasing the transmission power, it also bring higher requirements for small terminals. In addition, CDMA systems require strict power control. Especially for satellite systems in the Ka and above bands, the fading of large channels and long transmission delays make strict power control very difficult, which further reduces the capacity of CDMA systems.

TDMA: A simple high-speed TDMA system requires user terminals to have large EIRP and G/T values. In a broadband satellite communication system environment, most user terminal antennas have smaller apertures, and are used by terminals with smaller EIRP and G/T values. It is not realistic to implement a single-carrier high-speed TDMA system. In addition, achieving high-speed TDMA network synchronization and burst modulation and demodulation by a common user terminal are also very difficult.

MF-TDMA: MF-TDMA compensates for the shortcomings of TDMA to a certain extent, and can gradually increase the number of carriers as the traffic increases. This kind of method can allocate different carriers and timeslots according to the service requirements of the terminal, and flexible support for multiple rate requirements, which is usually used in the broadband satellite communication system. In addition, combined with multi-beam antenna technology, MF-TDMA and SDMA can be combined by frequency multiplexing to further increase the capacity of the system.

In summary, different multiple access methods have their own advantages and disadvantages, and are applicable to different application scenarios. It is necessary to comprehensively select appropriate access modes in combination with system network size, terminal type, and service characteristics [13] to improve system resource utilization and QoS levels.

## 3.2  Access Scheme

In terms of access mode, since the low-orbit spacecraft and the GEO communication satellite have a short visible time, if the access time is considered from the perspective of access time, it is suitable for SCPC access mode, but we need to consider the resource utilization rate of the entire satellite communication system at the same time. Therefore, considering the regular trajectory of the low-orbit spacecraft, it is suitable for SCPC and MF-TDMA hybrid access mode.

We use Fig. 2 as an example to illustrate the low-orbit spacecraft access strategy based on multi-beam GEO communication satellites. The network control center derives the sequence of beams that are sequentially experienced by the low-orbit spacecraft based on its predicted trajectory. We reserve logon timeslot 1, synchronization timeslot 1 and traffic timeslot 1 (can be adjusted to several) to the low-orbit spacecraft in each beam by pre-judging. The logon timeslot 2 is used for other terminals to access the system in a competitive manner, and the synchronization timeslot 2 is used for synchronization of other terminal cycles, and the traffic timeslot is dynamically allocated. When the traffic data of the low-orbit spacecraft is not too heavy, we maintain this MF-TDMA access method. When the traffic data of the low-orbit spacecraft increases (the low-orbit spacecraft requests traffic through the synchronization timeslot), the network control center sends a signal in the current beam to inform the low-orbit spacecraft to adopt the SCPC/DAMA mode in the next beam, transmit traffic data in carrier 5 in next beam, and reserve resources in subsequent beams. At the same time, when the low-orbit spacecraft switches to the next beam, the current beam resources are released in time.

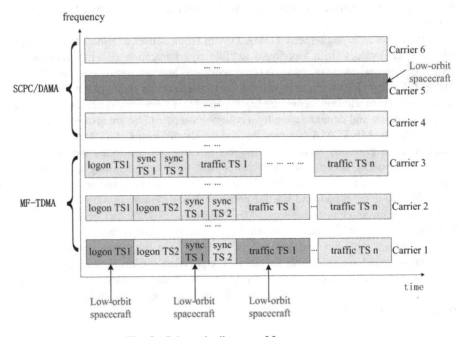

**Fig. 2.** Schematic diagram of frame structure

## 3.3    Analysis of Handover Strategy

Since the low-orbit spacecraft has a fast moving speed and the single-beam visible time is smaller under the coverage of the multi-beam GEO satellite, the system handover occurs more frequently. System handover includes beam handover, gateway handover, and satellite handover, where satellite handover causes gateway handover and beam handover; gateway handover causes beam handover. It will cause beam handover no matter what kind of handover, therefore beam handover is the key to the whole system handover. This paper will focus on beam handover strategies.

The handover mechanism in a single-layer satellite network is mainly geographical location based (including geographical geometric location based beam handover and tilt angle based beam handover), and handover based on resident time.

The handover process is divided into three phases: the handover detection phase, the handover decision phase, and the handover execution phase.

1. The handover detection phase mainly determines whether there is a need for handover by periodically detecting and collecting information. The parameters of the handover detection generally include the geographical location of the mobile terminal and channel conditions. The handover detection includes two methods: distributed detection and centralized detection. The distributed detection refers to the

mobile terminal trigger the handover according to the detection beam handover requirement, and submits the detection situation to the network control center; The centralized detection is performed by the network control center.
2. The handover decision phase is the core phase of beam handover. In the handover decision phase, the network control center analyzes the handover requirements, decides whether to handover according to the current system beam resources, load conditions, and handover timing. Whether the handover decision is executed in time and accurately will directly affect the handover delay and handover success rate of the mobile terminal.
3. The handover execution phase is a process of signaling between the network control center and the mobile terminal, during which the terminal access the target beam after disconnecting the current beam, logon and transmit traffic data according to the channel resource information sent by the network control center.

In terms of handover strategy, the network control center can predict the position information of the low-orbit spacecraft and the dwell time of each beam in advance, because the trajectory of the low-orbit spacecraft can be followed regularly. Therefore, we can make full use of this priori information, and the network control center initiates the handover instruction for the low-orbit spacecraft. In this way, we can reduce the complexity of the system and release the system resources in time, and effectively improve the quality of service of the low-orbit spacecraft while ensuring the resource utilization of the entire system.

## 3.4   Handover Scheme

In this paper, we designed a centralized handover detection method. The network control center gives the handover demand according to the trajectory of the low-orbit spacecraft. During the handover decision process, the network control center plans the system resources in advance by predicting the trajectory of the low-orbit spacecraft, reserve the beam resources and send the handover timing and target beam information to the low-orbit spacecraft in advance. Through the handover scheme of this paper, the time of low-orbit spacecraft access to system can be saved and the handover delay can be reduced, and the timeliness of information transmission of low-orbit spacecraft can be improved.

## 3.5   Summary

The low-orbit spacecraft handover strategy based on multi-beam GEO communication satellites is as follows:

1. The low-orbit spacecraft adopts a resource reservation method to complete the handover process and input the low-orbit spacecraft trajectory to the ground network control center in advance.
2. The network control center converts the trajectory information of the low-orbit spacecraft into geographic coverage information and converts it into beam-handover detection information. At the same time, the target beam information is sent to the low-orbit spacecraft in advance, and the target beam resources are reserved.

3. The access mode defaults to the MF-TDMA mode. When the low-orbit spacecraft has a large amount of traffic, the low-orbit spacecraft sends request information. After receiving the request, the network control center changes the low-orbit spacecraft to the SCPC/DAMA access mode in the next beam.

## 4  Analysis of Handover Delay

This section analyzes the handover delay according to the access handover strategy designed in this paper. Since the beam resources are calculated in advance, the time of handover detection and handover decision is saved. The handover delay is mainly the signaling interaction process after the beam handover instruction is sent [11]. The handover delay is shown in Fig. 3.

The network control center sends a beam handover command at time T0, and the low-orbit spacecraft completes the handover at time T3.

Handover delay $= (DN + DS) + D1 + D2 + D3 + D4 + (DS + DN) + D5 + (DN + DS) + D6 + (DS + DN) + D7 + (DN + DS) + D8$

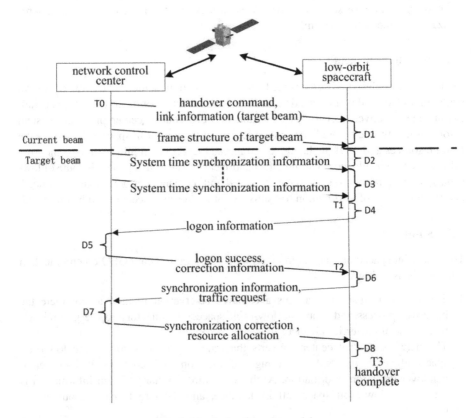

**Fig. 3.** Analysis of handover delay

In the above formula:

DN is the link delay between the communication satellite and the ground network control center, and DS is the link delay between the communication satellite and the low-orbit spacecraft.

D1 is the time required to analyze and store the forward and return link information (such as the frequency, polarization, modulation, coding, in the forward link, etc., and various types of ID information in the target beam, etc.) of the target beam, usually requires 2–3 superframe periods.

D2 is the time required to analyze and process the target beam frame structure information, and usually requires 2–3 superframe periods.

D3 is the time when the low-orbit spacecraft receiving transmitter is tuned to the new carrier, usually 500 ms–2 s, this time is uncertain, we assume it is 500 ms.

D4 is the time at which the logon information is generated, usually 1–2 superframe periods.

D5 is the time to analyze the logon information and correct the information such as frequency and time, usually 2–3 superframe periods.

D6 is the time to analyze the correction information, generate synchronization information, traffic request information, etc., usually 1–2 superframe periods.

D7 is the time of analyzing synchronous signaling, correcting information such as frequency and time, and resource allocation, usually 2–3 superframe periods.

D8 is the time to analyze synchronization correction information and resource allocation information, usually 1–2 superframe periods.

We assume DN = DS = 120 ms, and the superframe period is from 10 ms to 100 ms. The handover delay range is shown in Fig. 4.

If we adopt the conventional distributed beam detection method, the handover delay needs to increase the satellite transmission delay (about 240 ms) from the

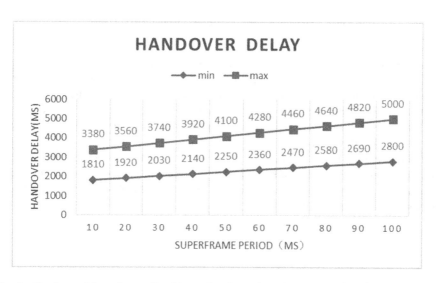

**Fig. 4.** Handover delay of centralized beam handover detection strategy based on SCPC\MF-TDMA hybrid access

low-orbit spacecraft to the network control center, the handover request analysis (about 1 superframe period) and target beam resource availability and selection (about 2 superframe periods) and other time. If we do not adopt the resource reservation method based on low-orbit spacecraft proposed in this paper, we will increase the logon time (logon time from T1 to T2 in Fig. 3). Since we adopts the competition mode of the slotted ALOHA, the number of logon is random, and the handover delay is continuously extended. We select the shortest time of D1 to D8, and comparing the handover delay under each strategy, we can figure out that under the same conditions of superframe period, the method proposed in this paper has the shortest handover delay according to Fig. 5.

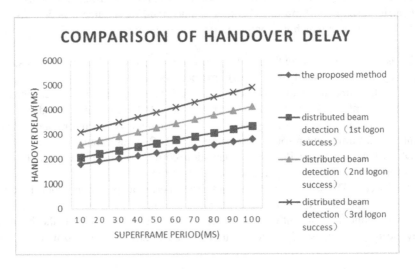

**Fig. 5.** Handover delay of different handover strategies

According to the channel environment analysis of Sect. 2.2, the low-orbit spacecraft is in the LOS transmission condition, so the above analysis results are obtained based on the relatively stable physical channel conditions. Fading changes in physical channel conditions may result in errors or loss of signaling, resulting in retransmissions that increase handover delay. This paper focuses on the optimization of the process to decrease the handover delay.

Therefore, from the above analysis, the number of handshakes between the network control center and the low-orbit spacecraft during beam handover is the main influencing factor of the beam handover delay. The method in this paper can effectively shorten the handover delay.

## 5   Conclusion

In this paper, we studied the access and handover techniques for the application of multi-beam GEO communication satellites to transmit low-orbit spacecraft information, and proposed a handover method based on SCPC\MF-TDMA hybrid access and centralized beam switching detection. We adopt centralized handover detection and resource reservation based on trajectory prediction for low-orbit spacecraft. The proposed method is superior to the conventional distributed beam detection method in handover delay, which can effectively shorten the handover delay.

## References

1. Wang, Z.: Challenges and opportunities facing TT&C and communication systems for China's manned space station program. Spacecraft TT&C Technol. **32**(4), 281–285 (2013). (in Chinese)
2. Liu, B., Wu, B.: Application of TDRSS in Chinese space TT&C. Spacecraft TT&C Technol. **31**(6), 1–5 (2012). (in Chinese)
3. Zhao, F.: Research on routing and switch technology for LEO satellite communication system. University of Electronic Science and Technology of China, Chengdu (2015). (in Chinese)
4. Kimura, K., Inagaki, K., Karasawa, Y.: Double-layered inclined orbit constellation for advanced satellite communications network. IEICE Trans. Commun. **80**(1), 93–102 (1997)
5. Akyildiz, I.F., Ekici, E., Bender, M.D.: MLSR: a novel routing algorithm for multilayered satellite IP networks. IEEE/ACM Trans. Networking (TON) **10**(3), 411–424 (2002)
6. Dash, D.S., Durresi, A., Jain, R.: Routing of VoIP traffic in multilayered satellite networks. In: Performance and Control of Next-Generation Communications Networks. International Society for Optics and Photonics, vol. 5244, pp. 65–76 (2003)
7. Zhang, H., Sun, F., Xu, F.: Studies on access strategy of layered satellite networks. Comput. Eng. Des. **26**(5), 1121–1124 (2005)
8. Huang, F.: Research on Access and Handover Strategy of Low Orbit Satellite. University of Electronic Science and Technology of China, Chengdu (2009)
9. Deng, Z., Long, B., Lin, W., et al.: GEO satellite communications system soft handover algorithm based on residence time. In: 2013 3rd International Conference on Computer Science and Network Technology (ICCSNT), pp. 834–838. IEEE (2013)
10. Lattanzi, F., Acar, G., Evans, B.: Performance study of a lightweight DVB-RCS handover scheme for vehicular GEO networks. In: IEEE International Workshop on Satellite and Space Communications, IWSSC 2008, pp. 216–220. IEEE (2008)
11. TR 102 768-V1.1.1 – Digital Video Broadcasting (DVB); Interaction Channel for Satellite Distribution Systems; Guidelines for the use of EN 301 790 in mobile scenarios (2009)
12. Feng, S., Lv, J., Zhang, G., et al.: Broadband multimedia satellite communication system of multiple access technology. Satell. Netw. (8), 66–68 (2010)
13. Tropea, M., Fazio, P., De Rango, F., et al.: Novel MF-TDMA/SCPC switching algorithm for DVB-RCS/RCS2 return link in railway scenario. IEEE Trans. Aerosp. Electron. Syst. **52**(1), 275–287 (2016)

# Resource Scheduling and Cooperative Management of Space Information Networks

Rui Wang, Xiaodong Han[⊠], Nuo Xu, Chao Wang, and Xi Zhou

Institute of Telecommunication Satellite,
China Academy of Space Technology, Beijing 100094, China
13426461933@163.com

**Abstract.** Along with the expansion of the range and space of space-based information networks, and the enhancement of network cognitive ability, real-time, reliability and security were needed to satisfy higher requirements. The demands or space-based information network designing referred to different platforms and users, random access in anytime, heterogeneous network architecture, cooperative management of different type of resource, and so on. Space-based network operation had the characteristic of high-dynamic, multi-type and big data. The realization of efficient resource management was discussed, and the analysis of multiple dimensions to objects in space information networks was realized, the design of dynamic space-based resource virtualization was further mentioned, scheduling and cooperative management was mentioned.

**Keywords:** Space information networks · Object analysis · Resource scheduling · Cooperative management

## 1 Introduction

The building of space-ground integrated information networks extend the ground system to space system, and expand the two-dimensional networks to three-dimensional networks. The structure of space-based networks makes the substantial increasing of links between satellites, satellite-ground and terminals. In future space information system, spacecrafts are more extensive and complex. Except in the large-scale mixed constellation space-based networks which constitute the space backbone networks, most of application spacecrafts become the basic unit of space information system, and the management of them far exceed the scope of equipment monitoring. Along with the improvement and scale expansion of future space-based information system, the management of space-based networks is more complex, and needs pointed resource scheduling and operation control for various space demands. For demanding and application of space mission, the QoS of service supplied by space-based networks is more focused, but not limited by the work parameters of communication devices. The faced space operation, system-level integrated network management is more significant for space information system [1–3].

**Foundation Items:** The National Natural Science Foundation of China (No. 61471360).

Q. Yu (Ed.): SINC 2018, CCIS 972, pp. 146–151, 2019.
https://doi.org/10.1007/978-981-13-5937-8_16

## 2  Analysis of Manage Objects in Space Information Networks

The typical work mode of space information networks demands on independently accessing to information acquisition satellites to supply task guarantee service; space-based information searching to multi-user spacecraft, information passing back and distribution to target spacecraft to supply multi-type, multisource information support; multitask cooperation and information pushing to different kinds of units in specific area to supply multitask cooperative guarantee service as navigation and communication.

The objects of management of space information networks are sources in networks. The expressive methods of resources are multi-dimensional and multi-standard, and the target is optimizing the partial or integral performance of networks. In management, all the useful information could be regarded as the resource of network, the programming of them improve the performance of networks. These resources are divided to hypostatic and functional, the standard of classification is existing definable entity or not.

1. Hypostatic resources mainly include weight, power, time, temperature, time delay, throughput, storage space, processing capacity, speed, topology, network density, and so on.
2. Functional resources are mainly the description of resources, include connectivity, congestion rate, stability, reliability, security, compatibility, priority, complexity (of calculation or network), expandability, and so on.

The resources could be classified as this table (Table 1).

**Table 1.** Classification of management objects

| Object | Hypostatic | Functional | Entity | Characteristic |
| --- | --- | --- | --- | --- |
| Calculate resource | Processing capacity | Stability, reliability, distributivity, complexity, expandability, autonomy, priority | Space-based management center | High-speed computation, multithread and distributive processing, fault-tolerant, ability of reshuffle |
| Communication resource | Throughput, frequency band, time slot, time delay | Stability, reliability, connectivity, congestion rate, security, priority | Space-based networks | High channel bandwidth, reliable data transmission |
| Storage resource | Storage space | Stability, reliability, security, expandability | Space-based management center, foundation management and control center | Bulk-storage memory |

*(continued)*

**Table 1.** (*continued*)

| Object | Hypostatic | Functional | Entity | Characteristic |
|---|---|---|---|---|
| Telemetry and telecontrol resource | Frequency band, time slot, precision | Reliability, fraction of coverage, synchronous rate | Space-based management center, foundation management and control center | High fraction of coverage and data rate, multiple target, precisely orbit determination |
| Navigation resource | Precision, location, speed, time | Sensitivity, synchronous rate | Space-based management center, navigational satellite | Persistent and high-precision location, ranging and time service |
| Program resource | Throughput, storage space, processing capacity, topology, network density | Congestion rate, distributivity, stability, security, compatibility, fraction of coverage, complexity, expandability | Space-based management center | State observation, network performance optimization, analytic logic, optimization algorithm |

Because of the space-based network need have the independent working ability, space-based management center and networks assume infinite proportion of function of resource management. The entity of network resource management is space information network.

## 3  Dynamic Space-Based Resource Virtualization

The content of space-based resources not only contains the essential equipment and capacity in information obtaining, calculating, storage and transmission, but also contains the invisible functional realization in these courses. There are constraint for different demands in space networks, and the independence of resources model built by different resources entities. It results in the heterogeneous in resource modeling, description and application, and lacks of uniform, integrated definition and expression among the entities in cooperation. And then, it leads to information deficiency in resource information exchanging, resource semantic confliction in resource information sharing, method incompatibility in resource information handling [4–6]. The cooperative management of distributed, heterogeneous, various space-based network resources is the precondition of resource efficiently sharing and well-organized cooperation in space information network entities.

Resource virtualization is the efficient path to solve this problem. Its essence is convert the bottom hypostatic resource and functional resource to abstract logical function unit by some kinds of mechanism, to realize efficient resource sharing, distribution and interoperating of entities. In the meanwhile of removing the isolation between resource entities and connotations, resource virtualization also supplies efficient implementation model to resource scheduling and cooperative management. The architecture of space-based resource virtualization could be divided to 4 layers: resource layer, monitoring layer, virtualization layer and application layer. The content and processing are as Fig. 1

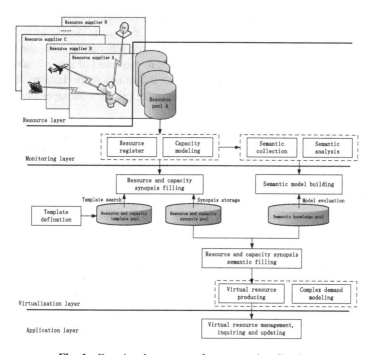

**Fig. 1.** Functional structure of resource virtualization

To explain multi-grained and multi-dimension resource functional characteristics and dynamic integrate them, the virtual resource space need to consider the focus of different 3 aspects: process, activity and property, and set appropriate resource aggregate function. They corresponding to 3 key elements in complex task disassembling: resource cooperation and combination, the grain distinction between resource functional characteristic and demanded functional characteristic, and the resource functional similarity [7, 8].

## 4   Space-Based Resource Scheduling and Cooperative Management

Virtual resource scheduling is the process of resource management based on the constraint mainly of time and task by space-based networks. With the characteristic of autonomy in satellite, real-time and efficient resource scheduling could save expenditure of calculation and storage, and improve the efficiency of data exchanging [9, 10].

For traditional satellite communication system, the link between ground and satellite have long time-delay and been influence by many kinds of natural factors. Meanwhile, building command sequence need high precision. It rigorously demands to satellite communication system, like the demands in task expenditure, task reliability, real-time communication and so on. Space-based networks could works by space-ground cooperative networking, and also have the capacity of independently networking and communicating based on satellite management center, to realize autonomous controlling and resource scheduling. At the same time, some complex conditions raise new challenging problems to resource scheduling, like: the constraint of task target and priority, the constraint of time, the constraint of space-based resource characteristic, and the constraint of information transmission mechanism. The architecture of task-oriented dynamic space-based network resource management is divided to 4 modules:

1. Module of initial task analysis: to receive the task requirement from application layer and initial analyze, its input comes from the proposed party of the task. And extract task factors; determine their characteristics and resolve tasks which need repeating to specific subtasks.
2. Module of task demand mapping: to receive the task factors and the states of network resources, map the task factors to the demand to available network resources.
3. Module of resource conflict analysis: get the state of available network resources, analyze the condition of conflict and represent them by time-varying conflict map.
4. Module of task programming: get the demand to resource from module of task demand mapping, and get the resource conflict model from module of resource conflict analysis, build the planning scheme of task programming by conflict disintegration and method as resource aggregation, transferring and exchanging (Fig. 2).

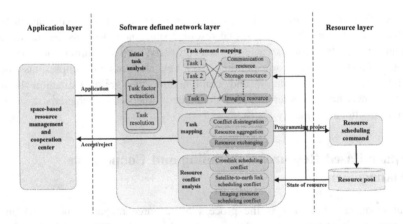

**Fig. 2.** Architecture of task-oriented dynamic space-based network resource management

Application file is needed to complete the task of space-based network resource scheduling. The file of resource virtualization model and resource scheduling task definition are contained in application file as the input of programming. And the output is consequence of programming.

## 5 Conclusion

The space information network is important part of the implementation scheme of future three-dimensional space networks. In network demand, Space-based network operation had the characteristic of high-dynamic, multi-type and big data. The real-time and efficient management is significant content of improving performance of data transmission and communication support. In this paper, we focus on resource scheduling in space-based networks, to make fine-grained and multi-dimensional analysis; based on the characteristic and focus of resources, researches the algorithm of virtual resource producing. Further mentioned the architecture of task-oriented resource dynamic management in space-based networks, researches the resource scheduling method based on different constraint.

## References

1. Shen, R.J.: Conception of space and earth integrated space internet in China. Chin. Eng. Sci. **8**(10), 19–30 (2006)
2. Yuan, X.K.: Architecture of space base synthetic information networks. Aerospace Shanghai **18**(1), 12–15 (2001)
3. Han, X., Liu, J., Xie, D., et al.: Robust $H_\infty$ guaranteed cost satisfactory fault-tolerant control for discrete-time systems with quadratic D stabilizability. J. Syst. Eng. Electron. **21**(3), 496–502 (2010)
4. Wu, L., Zhang, Y., Li, H.: Research on fault detection for satellite attitude control systems based on sliding mode observers. In: International Conference on Mechatronics and Automation, pp. 4408–4413 (2009)
5. Chen, C.C., Zhang, Y.X., Zhou, Y.Z., et al.: Lightweight virtual machine-based transparent computing system. Comput. Eng. **36**(11), 39–41 (2010)
6. Liu, N.: Key technology and application of virtualization of cloud manufacturing resources. Southeast University, Nanjing (2015)
7. Deng, G., Gong, Z.H., Wang, H., et al.: Analysis and survey of resource management on modern data center networks. J. Commun. **35**(2), 166–181 (2014)
8. Jing, C., Zhu, Y., Li, M.: SEED: solar energy-aware efficient scheduling on datacenters. Concurr. Comput. Pract. Exp. **26**(18), 2811–2835 (2015)
9. Fu, X., Zhu, X., Han, J.: QoS-aware replica placement for data intensive applications. J. China Univ. Posts Telecommun. **20**(3), 43–47 (2013)
10. Liu, N., Li, X., Shen, W.: Multi-granularity resource virtualization and sharing strategies in cloud manufacturing. J. Netw. Comput. Appl. **46**, 72–82 (2014)

# Research on Satellite-Ground Communication in Terahertz Massive Satellite Systems

Shuai Zhang, Siwei Zhang, Xiaolin Zhou, and Xin Wang[✉]

Key Laboratory of EMW Information,
Fudan University, Shanghai 200433, China
xwangll@fudan.edu.cn

**Abstract.** The explosive growth of the data traffic in future satellite communications can be leveraged by exploiting higher unlicensed spectrum band. In particular, Terahertz (THz) communication has been considered as a promising solution, since it can provide tens of GHz bandwidth. In addition, massive multiple input multiple output (MIMO) with a very large antenna array can be used in THz communications to provide large array gain to compensate for severe signal attenuation. To this end, this paper analyzes a terahertz MIMO channel modeling and simulation method for massive antenna array based satellite-ground communications. Taking into account the molecular absorption noise, transmission path loss, and molecular reradiation effects of the terahertz channels under a variety of typical weather models, we evaluate the bit error rates (BERs) for different frequencies, communication distances and signal strengths. Numerical results validate the feasibility of the proposed modeling approach.

**Keywords:** 5G · Terahertz · Massive MIMO ·
Satellite-ground communication · Channel model ·
System simulation · BER

## 1 Introduction

With the rapid development in mobile and telecommunication, the 5th generation (5G) of mobile communication system has become one of the main research fields in the world today. Up to the year 2020, all new 5G technologies expect to be put in use [1–4]. According to the development law of mobile communications, 5G will have much higher spectrum efficiency and energy efficiency when compared to 4G. In terms of transmission rate and resource utilization, it will also increase by one order of magnitude or even higher. In addition, the wireless coverage performance, transmission delay, system security and user experience will also be significantly improved [5–9]. The main development target of 5G mobile communication system is to link up with other wireless mobile communication technologies and provide ubiquitous basic service for the rapid development of mobile Internet. In 2016 Future ICT Summit, Yu Quan, academician from the Chinese Academy of Engineering, pointed out that in the present field of communication network, two of the most popular words are 5G and satellite communication, and the relationship between ground mobile communication represented by 5G and satellite communications is not mutual competition or

Q. Yu (Ed.): SINC 2018, CCIS 972, pp. 152–160, 2019.
https://doi.org/10.1007/978-981-13-5937-8_17

substitution, but mutual reinforcement, which will ultimately realize the integrated information network of the earth and the sky.

Ultra-high definition video, augmented reality, cloud storage, online games and all other services require higher wireless access bandwidth and lower latency for 5G networks [10]. In future wireless communications, the explosive growth of data services can be exploited by utilizing higher unauthorized spectrum. Terahertz (THz) communication is considered as a promising solution since it can provide tens of GHz bandwidth [11]. Because of its wide bandwidth, small antenna size and high directivity, terahertz band (0.1–10 THz) communication has drawn more and more attention. Similar to lower frequency communication systems, antenna arrays can be used to implement MIMO communication systems, which can increase communication distance by beamforming, or achieve considerable data rates by spatial multiplexing [12].

Large bandwidth is fatal for realizing the next generation of high-speed wireless communications. However, severe signal attenuation caused by the extremely high terahertz frequency is still a key problem. MIMO with very large scale of antenna arrays can be used in THz communications to provide sufficient array gain to compensate for this serious signal attenuation. In this case, a large antenna array with tens to hundreds of elements is used to improve spectral efficiency. In terahertz band the antenna becomes much smaller and thus more elements can be embedded within the same size. MIMO technology can not only improve data throughput, but also improve system reliability [13].

Terahertz wave reveals great advantages in space communications. Satellite space imaging and communication technology has become an important research area for many countries. In terms of information technology, the principle tests of terahertz wave transceiver have been carried out. The terahertz detector carried on satellite, which is also under study as a means of broadband wireless communication, has successfully mapped the temperature distribution of the ocean. In this paper, we analyze a terahertz MIMO channel modeling and simulation method for massive antenna array based satellite-ground communications. Taking into account the molecular absorption noise, transmission path loss, and molecular reradiation effects of the terahertz channels under a variety of typical weather models, we evaluate the bit error rates (BERs) for different frequencies, communication distances and signal strengths. Numerical results validate the feasibility of the proposed modeling approach.

## 2 Channel Model

### 2.1 Free Space Loss

The attenuation of radio signals at THz frequencies is due to the spreading effect and molecular absorption. The spreading effect attenuation is given by

$$A_{spread}(f, d) = \left(\frac{4\pi f d}{c}\right)^2 \tag{1}$$

where $c$ is the speed of light.

## 2.2   Molecular Absorption Coefficient

Calculation of molecular absorption spectrum is the key to terahertz channel modeling. Molecular absorption needs to study the vibration and rotation parameters of each molecule at different frequencies. Various countries have established databases for the radiation characteristics of atmospheric molecular absorption spectrum. At present, there are GEISA database in France, CDSD database in Russia, JPL database and HITRAN database in the United States. The well-known HITRAN database, developed by Harvard University and updated every four years till HITRAN 2016 now, contains spectral parameters of 47 atmospheric molecules and 120 isotopes, ranging from microwave to ultraviolet band.

The medium absorption coefficient is the weighted sum of the molecular absorption coefficient in frequency $f$ [14], which can be expressed as

$$k_{abs}(f) = \sum_{i=1}^{N} m_i k_i(f) \tag{2}$$

where $k_i(f)$, obtained from HITRAN database, is the molecular absorption coefficient of species $S_i$ on condition of temperature $T$ and pressure $P$.

## 2.3   Molecular Absorption Loss

Attenuation caused by molecular absorption is characterized as

$$A_{abs}(f, d) = e^{k_{abs}(f)d} \tag{3}$$

where $k_{abs}(f)$ is the absorption coefficient of the medium at frequency $f$.

In a nutshell, the received power at the receiver due to the spreading effect and molecular absorption can be formulated as

$$P_{r,LoS}(f, d) = P_t(f) \left( \frac{c}{4\pi f d} \right)^2 e^{-k_{abs}(f)d} \tag{4}$$

## 2.4   Molecular Re-radiation

The molecules in the communication medium can be excited by electromagnetic waves at specific frequencies. After the temporal excitement, the vibrational rotational energy level of the molecule will return to a stable state as the absorbed energy will be re-radiated at the same frequency. In [14], the re-radiation waves are considered noise. Because the resonance frequencies of various molecules are different, molecular absorption is not white noise and its power spectral density is uneven. Referring to

[14], the atmospheric noise $S_{N^B}$ and the self-induced $S_{N_m^X}$ noise contribute to the power spectral density of the molecular absorption noise, which affects the transmission by

$$S_{N_m}(f,d) = S_{N^B}(f,d) + S_{N_m^X}(f,d) \tag{5}$$

$$S_{N^B}(f) = \lim_{d \to \infty} k_B T_0 \left(1 - |H_{abs}(f,d)|^2\right) |H_{ant}^R(f)|^2 \tag{6}$$

$$S_{N_m^X}(f,d) = S_{X_m}(f) |H_{ant}^T(f)|^2 \left(1 - |H_{abs}(f,d)|^2\right) \cdot |H_{spread}(f,d)|^2 |H_{ant}^R(f)|^2 \tag{7}$$

## 2.5   Channel Transfer Function

In general, the channel transfer function of a single LoS channel is given by

$$\tilde{h}_{LoS}(f,d) = \left(\frac{c}{4\pi f d}\right) e^{-k(f)\frac{d}{2}} e^{j2\pi\frac{d}{\lambda}} \tag{8}$$

Considering the molecular re-radiation effect, the transfer function induced by molecular re-radiation is given by

$$\tilde{h}_a(f,d) = \sqrt{\left(1 - e^{-k(f)d}\right) \left(\frac{c}{4\pi f d}\right)^2} e^{j2\pi\beta_{random}} = \left(1 - e^{-k(f)d}\right)^{\frac{1}{2}} \left(\frac{c}{4\pi f d}\right) e^{j2\pi\beta_{random}} \tag{9}$$

Therefore, the total channel transfer function is the combination of the two parts of the channel transfer function above as

$$\tilde{h}(f,d) = \tilde{h}_{LoS}(f,d) + \tilde{h}_a(f,d) \tag{10}$$

$$\tilde{h}(f,d) = \left(\frac{c}{4\pi f d}\right) e^{-k(f)\frac{d}{2}} e^{j2\pi\frac{d}{\lambda}} + \left(1 - e^{-k(f)d}\right)^{\frac{1}{2}} \left(\frac{c}{4\pi f d}\right) e^{j2\pi\beta_{random}} \tag{11}$$

In this paper, we study a MIMO system consisting of $N_t$ transmitting antennas and $N_r$ receiving antennas in which the received signal vector $y$ of $N_r$ receiving antennas can be expressed as

$$y = \tilde{H}x + n \tag{12}$$

where $x$ is the transmit vector of $N_t$ transmitting antennas, $n$ is the $N_r \times 1$ independent noise vector with zero mean and variance $\sigma^2$. $\tilde{H}$ is the channel matrix, each of its elements $h_{ij}$ being a complex value of transfer coefficients associated with the $j$th transmitting antenna and the $i$th receiving antenna.

## 3  Simulation Analysis

### 3.1  Simulation Parameters

Both the transmitter and the receiver are 15-by-15 square antenna arrays, forming a 225-by-225 massive MIMO system. The internal distance of the antenna array is half of the wavelength. Antenna communication distance is 200–1500 km which is typical in low orbit satellite case. Transmit frequency is 0.1–1 THz, satellite elevation angle is 90°, and horizontal polarization angle is 0°. Here, we use QPSK modulation and MMSE detection method. Coding is not considered as we mainly address the channel model (Table 1).

**Table 1.**  Simulation parameters

| Category | Setup |
|---|---|
| Number of transmitter arrays | 225 |
| Number of receiver arrays | 225 |
| Distance | 200–1500 km |
| Transmission frequency | 0.1–1 THz |
| Satellite elevation angle | 90° |
| Horizontal polarization angle | 0° |
| Modulation mode | QPSK |
| Detection method | MMSE |
| Noise type | White Gaussian noise |

As mentioned above, we use the online browsing and mapping tools based on the HITRAN database to generate absorption coefficients for different single gases or some predefined standard marine atmospheric mixtures. Because water molecules play a major role in the normal atmospheric environment in the terahertz band, we select two typical models with the highest and lowest water molecular ratio, namely (i) USA model high latitude, winter, H = 0, and (ii) USA model, tropics, H = 0. The specific compositions of atmospheric standard gases under the two models are shown in the next table (Table 2).

**Table 2.**  Atmosphere standard gas mixture ratio in percentage for different climates

| Gas | USA model, high latitude, winter, H = 0 | USA model, tropics, H = 0 |
|---|---|---|
| $H_2O$ | 0.141000% | 2.590000% |
| $CO_2$ | 0.033000% | 0.033000% |
| $O_3$ | 0.000002% | 0.000003% |
| $N_2O$ | 0.000032% | 0.000032% |
| CO | 0.000015% | 0.000015% |
| $CH_4$ | 0.000170% | 0.000170% |
| $O_2$ | 20.900001% | 20.900001% |
| $N_2$ | 78.925780% | 76.476779% |

The ambient temperature is 273 K and the sea level pressure is 1 atm. We simulate the molecular absorption coefficients of two models. The relationship between absorption coefficient and frequency is shown in Fig. 1.

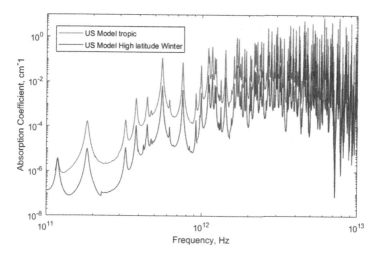

**Fig. 1.** Absorption coefficient

## 3.2  Simulation Results

### 3.2.1  Transmission Loss in a Typical Environment

Assume that the transmission distance is 200 km or 30000 km, and the signal frequencies are set to be 0.1–2 THz, respectively. We simulate the relationship between the two typical model frequencies and the path loss.

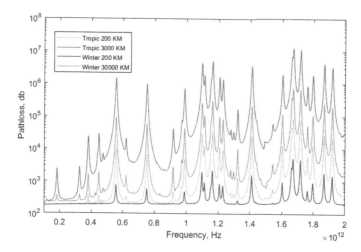

**Fig. 2.**  Distance = 200, 30000 km; frequency = 0.1–2 THz

As shown in Fig. 2, it can be observed that the losses corresponding to different models are different; namely, the loss of the tropical model is larger than that of the temperate winter, and the transmission loss has multiple frequency selective absorption peaks in the terahertz frequency band.

### 3.2.2 Transmission Loss in Typical Environments

When the frequency is 240 GHz and 500 GHz, the corresponding relationships between transmission loss and distance are investigated respectively. Figures 3 and 4 show the relationship curves for the two cases.

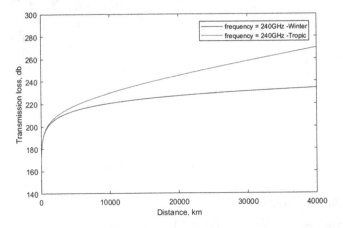

**Fig. 3.** Transmission loss, frequency = 240 GHz

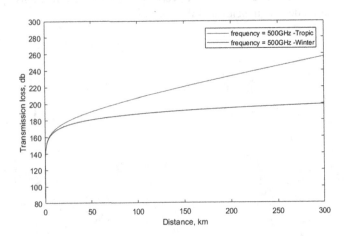

**Fig. 4.** Transmission loss, frequency = 500 GHz

It can be observed that transmission loss is increasing with the increase of transmission distance. In the tropical model, the transmission distance is 30 000 km at 240 GHz and the loss is up to 260 dB. Under the same loss, the transmission distance is only 300 km at 500 GHz.

### 3.2.3 BER in Typical Environments

In the next, the relationship between BER and transmission distance is addressed under the tropical model and the winter model respectively when the transmission frequency is 240 GHz.

As the transmission distance increases, the BER gradually increases. Moreover, Fig. 5 shows that the channel performance in the temperate winter scene is better than that in the tropical scene, and the main influencing factor is the difference in molecular absorption loss caused by the difference in water molecular ratio.

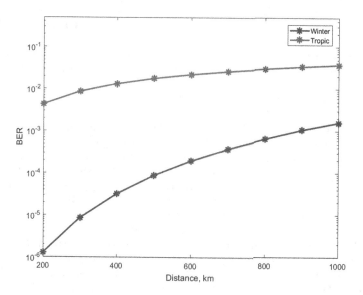

**Fig. 5.** BER in typical environments, frequency = 240 GHz

## 4   Conclusion

In this paper, we analyzed a method of modeling and simulation for satellite-ground communication in terahertz massive satellite systems. We simulated the channel model for the large-scale antenna satellite communications, where the combined effects of the molecular absorption noise, transmission path loss of the terahertz channel, and the molecular re-radiation are addressed. Based on a variety of typical environmental models in HITRAN, the BERs under different influences of frequency and communication distance are investigated and compared. Our simulations help understand the THz channel performance under different situations for the satellite-ground communications.

**Acknowledgement.** This work was supported by the National Natural Science Foundation of China under Grant No. 61571135 and No. 61671154.

# References

1. Boccardi, F., Heath, R.W., Lozano, A., et al.: Five disruptive technology directions for 5G. IEEE Commun. Mag. **52**(2), 74–80 (2014)
2. Gohil, A., Modi, H., Patel, S.K.: 5G technology of mobile communication: a survey. In: International Conference on Intelligent Systems and Signal Processing, pp. 288–292. IEEE (2013)
3. Rappaport, T.S., Sun, S., Mayzus, R., et al.: Millimeter wave mobile communications for 5G cellular: it will work! IEEE Access **1**(1), 335–349 (2013)
4. Roh, W., Seol, J.Y., Park, J., et al.: Millimeter-wave beamforming as an enabling technology for 5G cellular communications: theoretical feasibility and prototype results. Commun. Mag. IEEE **52**(2), 106–113 (2014)
5. Mitra, R.N., Agrawal, D.P.: 5G mobile technology: a survey. ICT Express **1**(3), 132–137 (2015)
6. Wang, C.X., Haider, F., Gao, X., et al.: Cellular architecture and key technologies for 5G wireless communication networks. J. Chongqing Univ. Posts Telecommun. **52**(2), 122–130 (2014)
7. Gupta, A., Jha, R.K.: A survey of 5G network: architecture and emerging technologies. IEEE Access **3**, 1206–1232 (2015)
8. Le, N.T., Hossain, M.A., Islam, A., et al.: Survey of promising technologies for 5G networks. Mobile Inf. Syst. **2016**, 25 (2016). Article ID 2676589
9. Jungnickel, V., Manolakis, K., Zirwas, W., et al.: The role of small cells, coordinated multipoint, and massive MIMO in 5G. IEEE Commun. Mag. **52**(5), 44–51 (2014)
10. Gao, X., Dai, L., Zhang, Y., et al.: Fast channel tracking for terahertz beamspace massive MIMO systems. IEEE Trans. Veh. Technol. **66**(7), 5689–5696 (2017)
11. Akyildiz, I.F., Jornet, J.M.: Realizing ultra-massive MIMO (1024 × 1024) communication in the (0.06–10) Terahertz band. Nano Commun. Netw. **8**, 46–54 (2016)
12. Khalid, N., Akan, O.B.: Experimental throughput analysis of low-THz MIMO communication channel in 5G wireless networks. IEEE Wirel. Commun. Lett. **PP**(99), 1 (2016)
13. Jornet, J.M., Akyildiz, I.F.: Femtosecond-Long pulse-based modulation for Terahertz band communication in nanonetworks. IEEE Trans. Commun. **62**(5), 1742–1754 (2014)
14. Hoseini, S.A., Ding, M., Hassan, M.: Massive MIMO performance comparison of beamforming and multiplexing in the Terahertz band. In: IEEE GLOBECOM Workshops, pp. 1–6. IEEE (2017)

# End-to-End Latency Optimization in Software Defined LEO Satellite Terrestrial Systems

Shaowen Zheng[1,2], Zhenxiang Gao[1], Xu Shan[1,2], Weihua Zhou[1(✉)], Yongming Wang[1,2], and Xiaohui Zhang[1,2]

[1] Institute of Information Engineering,
Chinese Academy of Sciences, Beijing 100049, China
{zhengshaowen,gaozhenxiang,zhouweihua,wangyongming,
zhangxiaohui}@iie.ac.cn
[2] School of Cyber Security, University of Chinese Academy of Sciences,
Beijing 100049, China

**Abstract.** Leveraging the concept of software-defined network (SDN), the integration of terrestrial and satellite networks improves the scalability and flexibility of networks. But resulting from the instability of satellite systems and ultra-high traffic volume of terrestrial networks, it is challenging to guarantee the end-to-end latency. Two major factors damage end-to-end latency are studied respectively in this paper. The first one is delay fluctuation due to limited resource and uneven traffic distribution of feeder. A load balancing algorithm based on the subset matching problem is proposed to mitigate the fluctuation. The second one is long forwarding latency due to excessive load in terrestrial networks, a resource allocation based on dynamic queue evaluation is proposed to decline the latency. Simulation results show the efficiency of our algorithm.

**Keywords:** LEO satellite networks · End-to-end latency · Load balancing · Resource allocation

## 1 Introduction

LEO (Low Earth Orbit) satellites, with advantages such as better signal quality and shorter propagation latency compared with MEO (Medium Earth Orbit) and GEO (Geostationary Earth Orbit), have attracted great attention [1, 2]. To achieve effective service delivery, data transmission and resource management on the traditional satellite networks, adopting Software-Defined Networking (SDN) [3] is a practice solution. The separation of control and data plan provides flexible and programmable management. Moreover, the regularity and predictability of satellite networks facilitate the real-time performance and efficient calculation of SDN [4].

However, the longer propagation latency and highly dynamic networks state of feeder impair the end-to-end (e2e) quality of service (QoS), especially the most intuitive QoS metric latency [1]. Thus, it is meaningful to take steps to handle the problems. Two major factors damage e2e latency are studied. First, delay fluctuation result from limited capacity (such as bandwidth and contract time) and uneven traffic distribution of feeder [5]. The fluctuation breaks load balancing even results in congestion

© Springer Nature Singapore Pte Ltd. 2019
Q. Yu (Ed.): SINC 2018, CCIS 972, pp. 161–173, 2019.
https://doi.org/10.1007/978-981-13-5937-8_18

in a partial link. Second, long forwarding latency in terrestrial networks with limited delay budget. Due to the excessive traffic load, the long forwarding latency is hard to meet the remaining delay budget of terrestrial networks.

For the fluctuation on the feeder, load balancing is one solution to the problem. Since the propagation latency is relatively constant and cannot be changed [6], the forwarding latency which is primarily affected by loads is of significance. Traditional load balancing algorithms forward latency-sensitive traffic to the neighboring least congested feeder link to prevent further increase of latency [7]. However, the forwarded traffic without considering the network situations may cause an additional network congestion at the neighboring LEO feeder links [8]. Therefore a load balancing algorithm that forwards the exact volume of traffic according to the network state is needed.

For the long forwarding latency in terrestrial networks, a valid resource allocation can greatly reduce the forwarding latency caused by congestion. Most previous works allocate transmitting resource according to the current or past arrivals [9–11]. This kind of resource allocation mechanism leads to serious latency resulting from the stochastic and burst arrivals. However, due to the long propagation latency introduced by satellites, the remaining latency budget is limited. A predictive resource allocation is a solution to meet the strict latency requirement and optimize the quality of service.

In this paper, two algorithms optimize the feeder and the terrestrial networks respectively to ensure e2e latency are proposed. First, Optimal Amount based Greedy Load Balancing (OAGLB) algorithm is put forward to optimize the latency distribution and achieve load balancing on feeder. The optimal transmission volume of each feeder link is calculated based on link state such as load and capacity. Routing tables are dynamically updated through a subset matching based greedy algorithm. Second, A Resource Allocation based on Prediction and Dynamic Queue (RAPDQ) is put forward to handle the long forwarding latency in terrestrial networks. With statistics of feeder collected from the controller, the queue evaluation based on prediction is then formulated for dynamic resource allocation.

The rest of this paper is structured as follows. Section 2 describes the system model. Section 3 describes a general latency model and the OAGLB. Section 4 elaborates the RAPDQ. Section 5 shows the simulation results. Finally, the conclusion of this paper is shown in Sect. 6.

## 2   System Model

As depicted in Fig. 1, it is an SDN-enabled integrated LEO-terrestrial networks architecture. The architecture is composed of two logical parts, i.e., the data plane and control plane. In the data plane, the LEO satellites send traffic to terrestrial networks through the ground station (GS) whose role is the gateway between satellites and terrestrial networks. The feeder links connect GS and satellites which are in the line-of-sight of the GS. The GS operates in a transparent way for the destination, while the data can be spread over the multiple under-laying paths [12]. The terrestrial network mainly relies upon fiber to establish connections among the SDN-enabled nodes. In the control plane, there are numbers of SDN controllers which are hosted on the physical nodes in the data plane, providing centralized control and management functions to both feeder, and core network. We consider a set of feeder links connect to the GS who are all under the SDN control. The capacity of feeders such as bandwidth, signal attenuation (e.g., scintillation and rain fading) and contact time (i.e., the time connecting to GS [13]) are known. The amount of traffic to be offloaded to the GS on feeder link $i$ is denoted by $x_i^t$. The sum traffic from feeder links at time $t$ is the arrival of the GS, denoted as $T(t)$.

Given a subset of feeder links, their capacity $\mu_i^t$ and traffic $x_i^t$ at time slot $t$, the first problem of our concern is to propose a load balancing algorithm to offload traffic from heavy loaded feeder links to those light loaded. In such way, the system latency is decreased, and feeders are load balanced. Secondly, with traffic arrival $T(t)$ at the GS, a predictive resource allocation scheme is needed to satisfy the limited remaining latency budget for terrestrial networks. The corresponding algorithms are further elaborated in the next two sections.

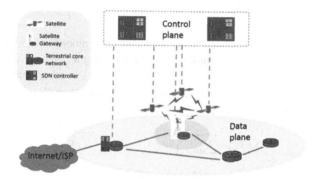

**Fig. 1.** System model

# 3 Feeder Load Balancing

## 3.1 Latency Model

Latency consists of propagation latency and forwarding latency [6]. The propagation latency is mainly determined by the distance between the source node and the destination node, therefore, can be formulated as

$$p_i^t = D_i/c, \tag{1}$$

where $D_i$ is the distance between the source node and destination node $i$, $c$ is the propagation speed. Considering the gigabit optical links among high-speed satellite communication networks [8], and the cooperation that allows satellites to forward traffic before they come to the contact with the GS [13], the latency on inter-satellite links can be omitted.

Since the distance between the source node and the destination node is relative constant [4], the forwarding latency fluctuates a lot is critical. Forwarding latency depending on the handled work and processor's performance fluctuates significantly with system load even if the same system handles the same work in multiple applications, especially for virtualized systems [14]. The forwarding latency can be estimated based on link load model $x_i^t/\mu_i^t$, where $x_i^t$ is the amount of traffic transmitted on a feeder link $i$ at time slot t, $\mu_i^t$ is the capacity of link $i$ at time slot $t$. Without loss of generality, the forwarding latency is exponentially related to load,

$$d_i^t = \exp(x_i^t/\mu_i^t). \tag{2}$$

The latency monotonically increasing with respect to the arriving traffic, monotonically decreasing with respect to the capacity. It has been widely discussed in the literature that forwarding latency is able to measure the average traffic load [19]. The latency consists of propagation latency $p_i^t$ and forwarding latency $d_i^t$ is modeled:

$$d\left(\mu_j^t, x_i^t\right) = p_i^t + d_i^t = \exp(x_i^t - \mu_i^t) + \frac{D_i}{c}. \tag{3}$$

An objective function is needed to decide the optimal amount of traffic transmit on each link. The purpose of the controller is to optimize the latency, which is a key performance indicator of QoS. It is noted that the latency is taken into the objective function instead of load model because the forwarding latency is closely related to load as mentioned before. The objective function is

$$\max_{x_i^t} U = \sum_{i=1}^n \left\{ \alpha_i * x_i^t - \gamma_i * d\left(\mu_j^t, x_i^t\right) \right\} \tag{4}$$

$$\text{s.t.} \sum_{i=1}^n x_i^t = \sum_{i=1}^n T_i^t, \tag{5}$$

where $d\left(\mu_i^t, x_i^t\right)$ is the latency when the arrival traffic is $x_i^t$ and load capacity is $\mu_i^t$ as (3), $\alpha_i, \gamma_i$ are the coefficient. $T_i^t$ is the traffic amount arrival at link $i$ after forwarding process, the constraint ensures that the forwarding process does not change the total amount of traffic. The sum traffic from feeder links at time $t$ is the arrival of the GS, denoted as

$$T(t) = \sum_{i=1}^n T_i^t. \tag{6}$$

The optimal amount of traffic $T_i^{t*}$ transmitted by link $i$ at time t is obtained by solving the following problem:

$$T_i^{t*} = \arg \max_x U. \tag{7}$$

That is:

$$T_i^{t*} = \max\left\{ \ln\left(\frac{\alpha_i + \lambda}{\gamma_i}\right) * \mu_i^t, \mu_i^t \right\}, \tag{8}$$

where $\lambda$ is the Lagrange Multiplier. The traffic beyond its capacity has to wait for the next contact time since it cannot be transmitted in this contact time without any forwarding. It results in an extremely large latency. Therefore, the optimal amount of data that is going to be offloaded in link $i$ is smaller than capacity, that is $\mu_i^t \geq x_i^t$.

Proof. The optimal amount of traffic $T_i^{t^*}$ transmitted by link $i$ is derived by introducing the Lagrange Multiplier $\lambda$. The Lagrange function is

$$L\left(x_i^t, \lambda\right) = \sum_{i=1}^{n} \left\{ \alpha_i * x_i^t - \gamma_i * d\left(\mu_j^t, x_i^t\right) \right\} + \lambda\left(\sum_{i=0}^{n} x_i^t - T(t)\right). \tag{9}$$

Checking the first derivative of $L\left(x_i^t, \lambda\right)$ with respect to $x_i^t$ and $\lambda$, respectively,

$$\frac{\partial L\left(x_i^t, \lambda\right)}{\partial x_i^t} = \alpha_i - \gamma_i * \exp\left(x_i^t / \mu_i^t\right) + \lambda = 0, \tag{10}$$

$$\frac{\partial L\left(x_i^t, \lambda\right)}{\partial \lambda} = \sum_{i=0}^{n} x_i^t - T(t) = 0, \tag{11}$$

$T_i^{t^*}$ and $\lambda$ can be got from the Eqs. (10) and (11), It is noted that being a linear equation with one known, the process of solving Eq. (11) does not require any iteration.

The second derivative of U with respect to $x_i^t$ is

$$\frac{\partial^2 U}{\partial x_i^2} = -\gamma_i * \exp\left(x_i^t / \mu_i^t\right) < 0. \tag{12}$$

The second order derivation is smaller than 0, which guarantees a global optimal of $U$. Since the utility of controller is a convex function of $x_i^t$, (8) is proved.

## 3.2 Load Scheduling Algorithm

After calculating the volume of traffic transmitted on each link, some links with more traffic arrival can be seen as source links, other links with less traffic can be seen as server link. The problem is to match the server links and source links then forward the excess part from sources to its corresponding servers. One source can have more than one server links, and one server link can server more than one source links. But the forwarding process increases the power consumption and introduces unknown errors. Therefore, less matching times is preferred. The problem is a subset matching problem with minimum matching times.

A greedy based scheduling algorithm OAGLB is proposed to forward the excess traffic from source link to its matched server links. The difference between the actual traffic arrival and optimal transmission volume of links are calculated, denoted as $S : \left\{s^1, s^2, \ldots, s^n\right\}$. When the difference is greater than zero, the link has excess traffic. The larger the difference, the more it exceeds. When the difference is less than zero, the link has enough capacity to help other links do the transmission job like a server. The smaller the difference, the more capacity it remains. The link with more excess traffic is more likely to be taken apart, resulting in an increase in the matching times. Therefore, the traffic on the link with the most excess traffic is going to be matched first. The excess data from source link with most difference is forward to the server link with least difference. Afterward, the remaining capacity and excess traffic on links are updated. Once one-time forwarding does not cover the whole excess traffic, the traffic left that has not been forwarded can be matched to other servers later after updating. Then repeating the processes above until $max(S) \leq 0$. The specific OAGLB steps are shown in the algorithm below.

After matching the source links and server links, the shortest path tree is got using the shortest routing algorithm such as Dijkstra. The time complexity of the OAGLB is $O(n^2)$. It is notable that we just redistributed the traffic and the traffic after OAGLB is unchanged as mentioned in Eq. (5). Therefore, the sum of $S$ equals to zero.

$$\sum\nolimits_{i=1}^{n} s^n = 0. \tag{13}$$

---

**Algorithm: OAGLB**

---

1. $T_i^{t^*} = max\left\{\ln\left(\frac{\alpha_i+\lambda}{\gamma_i}\right) * \mu_i^t, \mu_i^t\right\}$ /*Calculating optimal amount of offloading data at feeder $i$ */

2. $\Delta_i^t = x_i^t - T_i^{t^*}$ /*Calculating the difference between actual arrival traffic and optimal amount at feeder $i$ */

3. $C = 0$

4. While $max(S) > 0.001$ /* for satellite with excess traffic */

5.     $tmp = max(S) + min(S)$

6.     $S(first\ S == max(S)) = max(tmp, 0)$ /* update excess traffic*/

7.     $S(first\ S == min(S)) = min(tmp, 0)$ /* update remain resource */

8.     $C++$

9. End While

---

The subset sum problem can be regulated to a subset matching problem.

Proof: Subset matching: Given two sets: A $= (a_1, a_2, \ldots, a_n)$, B $= (b_1, b_2, \ldots, b_m)$, is there any partition $(A_1, A_2, \ldots, A_a)$ and $(B_1, B_2, \ldots, B_a)$ that satisfied for each partition $i \in (1, 2, \ldots, a)$, sum $(A_i) = $ sum$(B_i)$.

Step 1: It is obvious that the matching problem can be verified in polynomial time.
Step 2: subset sum instance: given subset S $= (s_1, s_2, \ldots, s_n)$, and integral k which is larger than sum(S). When set A equals set {S, k}, and set B equals {sum(S), k}, it is clear that the subset sum problem is an instance of subset matching problem, and it can be done in polynomial time. Therefore, the problem is NP-Complete.

## 4    Terrestrial Networks Resource Allocation

The transmission on terrestrial is mainly affected by processing and waiting process in servers. It can be well modeled by a dynamic queue. Moreover, it is convenient to take advantage of the traffic statistics to different application $T_j(t)$ with different latency budget $d_j^u$ to handle the limited remain latency budget and improve the resource efficiency. To avoid the latency due to the resource allocation only considering the current or past arrivals. A predictive scheduling [15] which can improve the system performance is proposed. Next, we introduce the predictive service mechanism.

### 4.1    Traffic Prediction

It is assumed that arrivals from the feeder of different applications are independent and identically distributes (i.i.d.) at different time slots, and the correlation can be not considered and ignored when analyzing [5]. We also assume that there exists max traffic upper bound such that $0 \leq T_j(t) \leq T^{max}$ for all $i$ and $t$.

Traffic prediction is an effective solution for the problems caused by congestion and traffic fluctuation. Due to the randomness of traffic from space, the time series models such as moving averages (MA), auto-regressions (AR), Autoregressive Integrated Moving Average Model (ARIMA), are too simple to model the complex patterns. What's more, it is hard to determine the order of those models, sometimes it even needs to be determined manually. Considering both the accuracy and computational complexity, Random Forest (RF) is a widely adopted prediction tool. RF is an ensemble learning method for regression, by constructing a multitude of decision trees at training time and outputting the result that is the mean prediction of the individual trees. An RF adopting randomness to control over-fitting, and uses averaging to improve the predictive accuracy.

We create a RF model for each application that is to be predicted (such as delay-sensitive applications). The training and predicting process are illustrated in Fig. 2. The input to train the RF model is the collection of observation windows organized as vectors of observed time series statistics. The prediction window starts right after the end of the observation window without delays.

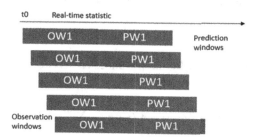

**Fig. 2.**  Average latency and load at each satellite

We tuned the hyper-parameters of the RF generation algorithm the following way. The number of trees is fixed to 50 per predicted application as suggested in [16]. The maximum number of split layers each decision tree can have (maximal depth) is set to the binary log of number of the whole set of types of applications.

As a result, given the arrival traffic $T_j(t)$, a series of predicted future traffic $A_j(t)$ using RF is got.

## 4.2   Resource Allocation

It is assumed that the controller at the ground station can predict and serve the future packet arrivals and allocate resource for applications with different latency budget. Let $D \geq 1$ be the prediction window size of GS. Then at each time slot t, the controller can predict arrival information of application $j$ in the look-ahead window $A_j(t) = A_j(t+1)$, $A_j(t+2), \ldots, A_j(t+D)$. At each time slot $t$, let $C_j(t+\tau)(\tau = 1, \ldots, D)$ denote the service capacity of application $j$ at time slot $(t+\tau)$, $C_j^\tau(t)$ denote the service capacity pre-allocated to application $j$ with packet arrivals $A(t+D)$,$C_j^0(t)$ denotes the service rate allocated for the arrival packets that are already in the queue. For each $C_j(t+\tau)$, there always has

$$\sum_{\tau=1}^{D} C_j^\tau(t) \leq C_j(t+\tau). \tag{14}$$

$A_j^\tau(t) = \left[A_j^1(t), A_j^2(t), \ldots, A_j^D(t)\right]$ are considered as the actual future arrivals after going through a series of predictive service, it is related to the pre-allocated capacity in previous time slots,

For $0 \leq \tau \leq D - 1$:

$$A_j^\tau(t) = max\left\{A_j^{\tau+1}(t) - C_j^{\tau+1}(t-\tau-1), 0\right\} \tag{15a}$$

For $\tau = D$:

$$A_j^\tau(t) = A_j(t+\tau). \tag{15b}$$

The queue length is denoted as $Q_n(t)$, the evolution of queue length at time $t+\tau$ is

$$Q_j(t+\tau) = \left[Q_j(t) + A_j(t+\tau) - C_j(t+\tau)\right]^+, \tag{16}$$

The future arrival is served by the pre-allocated service capacity $C^\tau(t)$, as mentioned in (15), then the queue length is

$$Q_j(t+\tau) = \left[Q_j(t) + A_j(t+\tau) - \sum_{\tau=1}^{D} C_j^\tau(t)\right]^+. \tag{17}$$

The predicted queue length at the future time t is

$$Q_j^\tau(t) = \left[ Q_j^{\tau-1}(t) + \sum_{\tau=1}^{D} A_j^\tau(t) - \sum_{\tau=1}^{D} C_j^\tau(t) \right]^+. \tag{18}$$

According to the Little's Law [17], the predicted average waiting time is

$$W_j^{av} = \frac{Q_j^{av}}{A_j^{av}} = \frac{\sum_{\tau=1}^{D} \left[ Q_j^{\tau-1}(t) + A_j^\tau(t) - C_j^\tau(t) \right]^+}{\sum_{\tau=1}^{D} A_j^\tau(t)}. \tag{19}$$

To handle the latency on the feeder, the average waiting time is limited to a threshold value. For an application j with upper latency budget $d_j^u$, and latency on feeder $d_i^t$, the remaining latency budget of packets may diverse. To make sure all packets latency of this application are within the latency budget, the minimum remaining latency budget $d_{rem}^{min} = \min\left\{ d_j^u - d_i^t \right\}$ is satisfied. That is: $0 < W_j^{av} < d_{rem}^{min}$. Then the resource allocated to each application is obtained.

## 5   Experimental Evaluation

For simulations, we consider a subset of feeder links established between LEO satellites at the altitude of 780 km and a GS. The number of feeder links in this subset is [8] in this simulation. The traffic needs to be offloaded to GS is the video file size from a dataset which was crawled on February 22nd, 2007 from YouTube [18]. Up/down bandwidth is 20 Mb/s. Each time slot is 50 ms (ms), and the whole simulation lasts 2.8 h. The prediction window is 1 s.

Figure 3 shows the results of OAGLB and WLB (without any load balanced forwarding process) on each link during the simulation. Figure 3(a) is the average latency, (b) is the average load. It is obvious that both the load distribution and latency distribution on feeder are very unbalanced without any forwarding strategy. And the

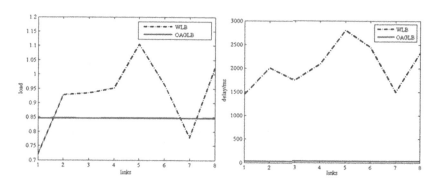

**Fig. 3.** Results of OAGLB and WLB at each link: (a) Average load at each satellite, (b) Average latency at each satellite

average latency is reduced from 2041 ms to 32 ms after using OAGLB. Figure 4 shows the load and latency changes on one link over time using WLB and OAGLB. They demonstrate that without any forwarding, the latency on feeder fluctuates a lot. Meanwhile, after adopting the OAGLB, both the mean latency and load are lower and more balanced.

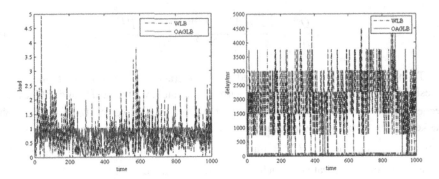

**Fig. 4.** Latency and load throughout simulation: (a) Load throughout simulation; (b) Load throughout simulation;

Figure 5 shows the results of Greedy Based Routing algorithm (GBR) who forwards the excess traffic to link with enough capacity without calculating the optimal forward amount. The graphs show the latency and load average results on each link. Compared with WLB shown in Fig. 4(b), the GBR reduces the average latency to 56 ms while OAGLB reduces more. Moreover, the load balancing of OAGLB is better than GBR.

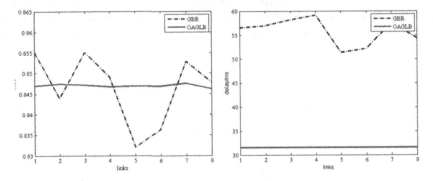

**Fig. 5.** Results of OAGLB and OBR at each link, (a) Average load at each link; (b) Average latency at each link

Then we show the simulation results on prediction based resource allocation. Figure 6 shows average queue latency using different resource allocation algorithms.

Performances of following resource allocation algorithms are compared: (1) QWP: resource allocation scheme adopting the queue evaluation without prediction, it allocates the resource to queue according to the historical statistics; (2) PWQ: resource allocation adopting prediction but without queue evaluation, it allocates the resource to queue according to the exact volume of predicted future arrival; (3) RAPDQ: our algorithm. It can be seen that, prediction helps to get a better resource allocation performance. However, without a good queue management, better resource allocation still cannot be achieved in spite of the traffic prediction is used. It is clear in sub Fig. 6 (a) that PWQ cannot even stabilize the queue. Figure 6(b) shows the detailed results on QWP and RAPDQ. Compared with QWP, RAPDQ reduces the average queue latency from 0.99 ms to 0.64 ms after the queue system becomes stable.

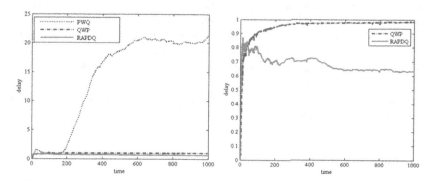

**Fig. 6.** Average queue latency using different resource allocation algorithms PWQ, QWP and RAPDQ: (a) Average queue latency; (b) Average queue latency

Figure 7 shows the results of RAPDQ with different latency budget. The average latency is used to indicate the state of queue. After the dynamic queue becomes stable, the average queue latency satisfied the budget. Obviously, the lower latency budget, the lower average latency. In a word, our algorithm is able to cope with service with

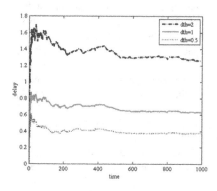

**Fig. 7.** Average queue latency with different latency budget

**Table 1.** The improvement of e2e latency on feeder

| Satelites | Feeder | |
|---|---|---|
| | Ave | Std |
| GBR+QWP/s | 0.55 | 0.48 |
| OAGLB+RAPDQ/s | 0.31 | 0.44 |
| Improvement/% | 0.43 | 0.09 |

various latency budget. Compared with e2e latency using GBR and QWP, the improvement of e2e latency on average and standard deviation of feeder after using OAGLB and RAPDQ can be seen in Table 1. The statistic shows that our algorithms reduce the average e2e latency by 43% and reduce the standard deviation by 9%.

## 6  Conclusion

In this paper, two algorithms optimize the e2e latency are proposed. OAGLB forwards the excess data to other links based on a subset matching problem. The optimal transmission amount on each feeder link is calculated according to its capacity. In such way, the load balancing is achieved and thereby the latency on the feeder is optimized. Subsequently, RAPDQ allocates the appropriate amount of resource according to the remaining latency budget with the help of a dynamic queue model and prediction. As a result, the long forwarding latency is avoided, the limited latency budget is satisfied and thereby guarantee the e2e delay. Extensive simulations have been conducted, and the results show that the e2e latency can be optimized by OAGLB and RAPDQ.

**Acknowledgment.** This work was supported by research project of shanghai science and technology commission (Grant No. 17DZ1100702) in China.

## References

1. 3GPP TR22.822: Study on using Satellite Access in 5G, V0.2.0, February 2018
2. 3GPP TR38.811: Study on New Radio (NR) to support non terrestrial networks, V0.3.0, December 2017
3. Kreutz, D., Ramos, F.M.V., Verissimo, P.E., et al.: Software-defined networking: a comprehensive survey. Proc. IEEE **103**(1), 14–76 (2015)
4. Liu, J., Shi, Y., Zhao, L., et al.: Joint placement of controllers and gateways in SDN-enabled 5G-satellite integrated network. IEEE J. Sel. Areas Commun. **36**(2), 221–232 (2018)
5. Alagoz, F., Korcak, O., Jamalipour, A.: Exploring the routing strategies in next-generation satellite networks. IEEE Wirel. Commun. **14**(3) (2007)
6. Li, F., Lam, K.Y., Liu, X., et al.: Joint pricing and power allocation for multibeam satellite systems with dynamic game model. IEEE Trans. Veh. Technol. **67**(3), 2398–2408 (2018)
7. Bayhan, S., Gür, G., Alagöz, F.: Performance of delay-sensitive traffic in multi-layered satellite IP networks with on-board processing capability. Int. J. Commun Syst. **20**(12), 1367–1389 (2007)
8. Nishiyama, H., Kudoh, D., Kato, N., et al.: Load balancing and QoS provisioning based on congestion prediction for GEO/LEO hybrid satellite networks. Proc. IEEE **99**(11), 1998–2007 (2011)
9. Yoon, M.S., Kamal, A.E.: NFV resource allocation using mixed queuing network model In: Global Communications Conference, pp. 1–6. IEEE (2016)
10. Teymoori, P., Sohraby, K., Kim, K.: A fair and efficient resource allocation scheme for multi-server distributed systems and networks. IEEE Trans. Mob. Comput. **15**(9), 2137–2150 (2016)
11. Hao, F., Kodialam, M., Lakshman, T.V., et al.: Online allocation of virtual machines in a distributed cloud. IEEE/ACM Trans. Netw. **25**(1), 238–249 (2017)

12. Bouttier, E., Dhaou, R., Arnal, F., et al.: Analysis of content size based routing schemes in hybrid satellite/terrestrial networks. In: IEEE Global Communications Conference, pp. 1–6 (2016)
13. Jia, X., Lv, T., He, F., et al.: Collaborative data downloading by using inter-satellite links in leo satellite networks. IEEE Trans. Wirel. Commun. **16**(3), 1523–1532 (2017)
14. Qu, X., Duan, Y., Liu, W., et al.: Dynamic load balancing for delay CDF α-percentile optimization with a global view. In: 2015 IEEE 26th Annual International Symposium on Personal, Indoor, and Mobile Radio Communications (PIMRC), pp. 1300–1304. IEEE (2015)
15. Huang, L., Zhang, S., Chen, M., et al.: When backpressure meets predictive scheduling. IEEE/ACM Trans. Netw. (TON) **24**(4), 2237–2250 (2016)
16. Perner, P. (ed.): Machine Learning and Data Mining in Pattern Recognition. LNCS (LNAI), vol. 6871. Springer, Heidelberg (2011). https://doi.org/10.1007/978-3-642-23199-5
17. Little, J.D.C., Graves, S.C.: Little's Law in Building Intuition, pp. 81–100. Springer, Boston (2008). https://doi.org/10.1007/978-0-387-73699-0_5
18. Cheng, X., Dale, C., Liu, J.: Statistics and social network of youtube videos. In: 2008 16th International Workshop on Quality of Service, IWQoS 2008, pp. 229–238. IEEE (2008)
19. Li, X., Tang, F., Chen, L., et al.: A state-aware and load-balanced routing model for LEO satellite networks. In: IEEE Global Communications Conference GLOBECOM 2017, pp. 1–6. IEEE (2017)

# Sparse Characterization and Fusion Processing

# A Link Selection Algorithm Based on EKF and Overlapping Coalition Formation Game for Hybrid Cooperative Positioning

Mingxing Ke[✉], Shiwei Tian, Chuang Wang, and Xudong Zhong

Army Engineering University of PLA, Nanjing 210007, China
lgdxkemingxing@163.com

**Abstract.** The cooperative localization as a satellite enhanced mean can extend the availability of positioning system and improve the accuracy of localization in some harsh environments, such as urban canyons, dense foliage, building block and so on. However, if there is a large amount of cooperative objectives in a densely deployed scenario, much connected links will cost a large number of time-frequency resources. The goal of this paper is to address the above question by a link selection algorithm based on an Extended Kalman Filter (EKF) and overlapping coalition formation (OCF) game. First, the EKF is used to obtain real-time state information updates. Then, a criterion is developed to determine whether users are well localized. If the criterion is satisfied, the efficient link selection problem is considered as an OCF game; otherwise, the user cooperates with others as many as possible to obtain accuracy state information. Numerical results show that the proposed algorithm can achieve performance improvement in localization accuracy compared to the no-cooperative approach, and achieve a much fewer link number at the cost of appropriate performance degradation.

**Keywords:** Cooperative localization · Link selection · EKF · Overlapping coalition formation game

## 1 Introduction

Generally, the Global Navigation Satellite System (GNSS) plays an important role for users to obtain their position in a global scale. However, when in the harsh environments, such as valley, forest and urban canyon, the GNSS does not operate very well or even be not available [1]. A practical way to address this need is hybrid cooperative positioning by leveraging the range measurements and sharing location information between neighboring terminals [2]. Naturally, to achieve higher localization accuracy, higher resource consumption is cost by more links added. However, considering that users are densely deployed, the cooperative localization requires a large amount of time-frequency resources and may cause network jam and packet collisions.

© Springer Nature Singapore Pte Ltd. 2019
Q. Yu (Ed.): SINC 2018, CCIS 972, pp. 177–188, 2019.
https://doi.org/10.1007/978-981-13-5937-8_19

To solve this problem, there are extensive researches to optimize the resource allocation in localization systems. In [3], the author proposed a cooperative game-theoretic measurement allocation algorithm for localization in unattended ground sensor networks. In [4], a coalitional game was proposed to optimize cooperative objectives for distributed estimation in wireless sensor network. In [5], two resource management games were formulated, Stackelberg game and link bargaining game, to obtain efficient link selection and power allocation. In [6], the opportunistic cooperative localization was proposed and overlapping coalition formation (OCF) game was employed to select efficient links.

While for the traditional cooperative link selection algorithms, there are some obvious limitations. Firstly, they didn't consider the dynamic scenarios. If the users are dynamic, the link relationships between users may be changeable. Secondly, they didn't consider the relink mechanism. It is necessary to reduce cooperative links when localization accuracy is satisfactory and require re-cooperating links when localization accuracy is unsatisfactory in multivariate environments.

To solve above questions, we first use an Extended Kalman Filter (EKF) to obtain users' real-time state information updates. Based on the estimated state information, a criterion is developed to determine whether users are well localized. If the criterion is satisfied, we then consider the efficient link selection problem. Otherwise, means that the user isn't well localized, so the users should cooperate with others without link selection to improve the localization accuracy and convergent rate. Last, an optimized link selection algorithm based on OCF game is proposed to select efficient cooperative links.

## 2    System Model

### 2.1    Scenario Formation

Consider a scenario with $M$ users and $S$ satellites like the one depicted in Fig. 1, denoted as $\mathcal{M} = \{1, 2, ..., M\}$ and $\mathcal{S} = \{1, 2, ..., S\}$, respectively. All users can move independently in the 2D space. Focusing on a particular user $m \in \mathcal{M}$, denote by $\mathcal{N}_m^{(k)}$ the subset of users it can communicate with and $\mathcal{S}_m^{(k)}$ the subset of satellites it can see at time $k$. The position of user $m$ is denoted by $\mathbf{p}_m^{(k)}$. We consider 2D positions expressed in the earth centered earth fixed (ECEF) frame, $\mathbf{p}_m^{(k)} = [x_m^{(k)} \ y_m^{(k)}]^T$, where the superscript T denotes transpose. The clock bias of user $m$ at time $k$ with respect to the GNSS time is denoted by $\delta_m^{(k)}$. Then the bias in meters can be expressed by $b_m^{(k)} = c \cdot \delta_m^{(k)}$ where $c$ is the speed of light. In our work, we consider dynamic users with very low and random accelerations so the users are considered as uniform motion with the respective velocity components $\tilde{\mathbf{p}}_m^{(k)} = [\tilde{x}_m^{(k)} \ \tilde{y}_m^{(k)}]^T$ and optionally the clock drift, $\tilde{b}_m^{(k)}$, expressed in meters per second.

In the considered scenario, there are two types of measurements: (i) pseudo-range measurements which are the distances from satellites to users:

$$\rho_{sm}^{(k)} = \|\mathbf{p}_s^{(k)} - \mathbf{p}_m^{(k)}\| + b_m^{(k)} + \xi_{sm}^{(k)}; \tag{1}$$

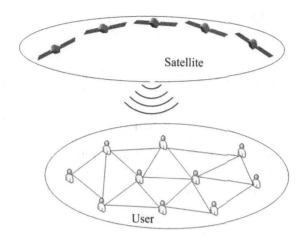

**Fig. 1.** Example of a hybrid cooperative network with satellites and users.

(ii) range measurements which are the distances between users:

$$r_{nm}^{(k)} = \|\mathbf{p}_n^{(k)} - \mathbf{p}_m^{(k)}\| + b_{nm}^{(k)} + \zeta_{nm}^{(k)}, \tag{2}$$

where $\| \cdot \|$ denotes the Euclidean distance, $m, n \in \mathcal{M}, s \in \mathcal{S}$, $\xi_{sm}^{(k)}$ and $\zeta_{nm}^{(k)}$ are noises for pseudorange measurement and range measurement, respectively. In addition, pseudorange measurements are affected by the bias $b_m^{(k)}$. While for range measurements, the round-trip time of arrival or received signal strength measurements are used to avoid the effect of bias with $b_{nm}^{(k)} = 0$.

## 2.2   State Transition Process

In this paper, the state transition process is modeled by [7]

$$\mathbf{x}_m^{(k)} = f(\mathbf{x}_m^{(k-1)}, \omega_m^{(k)}), \tag{3}$$

$$\omega_m^{(k)} \sim \mathcal{N}(0, \mathbf{Q}_m^{(k)}), \tag{4}$$

where $f(\cdot)$ is the state transition function (STF), which evolves the state of user $m$ in time given previous state $\mathbf{x}_m^{(k-1)}$. The process noise vector $\omega_m^{(k)}$ is accounted as non-linearities and perturbations on the system and it is modeled as a vector of random noise with zero mean and covariance matrix $\mathbf{Q}_m^{(k)}$. Then the corresponding STF and $\mathbf{Q}_m^{(k)}$ matrix in a dynamic scenario are given by

$$f(\mathbf{x}_m^{(k-1)}, \omega_m^{(k)}) = \begin{bmatrix} \mathbf{I} & \Delta k \mathbf{I} \\ \mathbf{0} & \mathbf{I} \end{bmatrix} \mathbf{x}_m^{(k-1)} + \begin{bmatrix} \frac{\Delta k^2}{2} \mathbf{I} \\ \Delta k \mathbf{I} \end{bmatrix} \omega_m^{(k)}, \tag{5}$$

$$\mathbf{Q}_m^{(k)} = \text{diag}\big([\sigma_{\ddot{x}_m}^{(k)^2} \ \sigma_{\ddot{y}_m}^{(k)^2} \ \sigma_{\ddot{b}_m}^{(k)^2}]\big), \tag{6}$$

where $\mathbf{0}$ is an all zeros element matrix and $\mathbf{I}$ is the identity matrix of size $2 \times 2$, and $\Delta k$ is the time elapsed between the previous $k-1$ and current time slot $k$. $\mathbf{Q}_m^{(k)}$ is the process noise covariance matrix.

## 2.3   Observation Model

The observation model can be expressed by

$$\mathbf{z}_m^{(k)} = h(\mathbf{x}_m^{(k)}, \mathbf{X}_{sm}^{(k)}, \mathbf{X}_{nm}^{(k)}, \mathbf{v}_m^{(k)}) = \begin{bmatrix} h_s(\mathbf{x}_m^{(k)}, \mathbf{X}_{sm}^{(k)}, \xi_{sm}^{(k)}) \\ h_n(\mathbf{x}_m^{(k)}, \mathbf{X}_{nm}^{(k)}, \varsigma_{nm}^{(k)}) \end{bmatrix} \tag{7}$$

$$\mathbf{v}_m^{(k)} \sim \mathcal{N}(0, \mathbf{R}_m^{(k)}), \tag{8}$$

where $h(\cdot)$ is the observation function, $\mathbf{X}_{sm}^{(k)}$ are positions for all available satellites $s \in \mathcal{S}_m^{(k)}$, $\mathbf{X}_{nm}^{(k)}$ are positions for all available neighboring users $n \in \mathcal{N}_m^{(k)}$, $\mathbf{v}_m^{(k)} = [\xi_{sm}^{(k)} \ \varsigma_{nm}^{(k)}]$ is the observation noise vector with zero mean and covariance matrix

$$\mathbf{R}_m^{(k)} = \begin{bmatrix} \mathbf{R}_{sm}^{(k)} & 0 \\ 0 & \mathbf{R}_{nm}^{(k)} \end{bmatrix}. \tag{9}$$

For the pseudorange measurements, we have the observation function as (7). Then the Jacobian matrix can be obtained by the partial derivatives of this model:

$$\mathbf{H}_{\mathbf{x}_m}^s = [\frac{\partial h_s}{\partial x_m} \ \frac{\partial h_s}{\partial y_m} \ \frac{\partial h_s}{\partial b_m} \ \frac{\partial h_s}{\partial \hat{x}_m} \ \frac{\partial h_s}{\partial \hat{y}_m} \ \frac{\partial h_s}{\partial \hat{b}_m}] \tag{10}$$

The Jacobian matrices $\mathbf{H}_{\mathbf{x}_m}^n$ are exactly the same found for range measurements.

## 2.4   Extended Kalman Filter

The EKF mainly consists by two phases: predict and update [8].

(1) Predict Phase

When obtaining the previous a posteriori estimates in $k-1$, a prior state and covariance at time $k$ can be predicted by

$$\tilde{\mathbf{x}}_m^{(k|k-1)} = f(\tilde{\mathbf{x}}_m^{(k-1)}), \tag{11}$$

$$\tilde{\mathbf{P}}_m^{(k|k-1)} = \mathbf{F}^{(k)} \mathbf{P}_m^{(k-1)} \mathbf{F}^{(k)^T} + \mathbf{Q}_m^{(k)}, \tag{12}$$

where

$$\mathbf{F}^{(t)} = \frac{\partial f}{\partial \mathbf{x}_m} \Big|_{\tilde{\mathbf{x}}_m^{(k|k-1)}}, \tag{13}$$

are the Jacobian matrices of the state transition function with respect to the state.

(2) Update Step

The measurement residuals are given by

$$\Delta \mathbf{z}^{(k)} = \mathbf{z}_m^{(k)} - h(\tilde{\mathbf{x}}_m^{(k|k-1)}, \mathbf{X}_{sm}^{(k)}, \tilde{\mathbf{X}}_{nm}^{(k)}), \tag{14}$$

$$\mathbf{S}_m^{(k)} = \mathbf{H}^{(k)} \mathbf{P}_m^{(k|k-1)} \mathbf{H}^{(k)^T} + \mathbf{R}_m^{(k)}, \tag{15}$$

where

$$\mathbf{H}^{(t)} = \frac{\partial h}{\partial \mathbf{x}_m}\Big|_{\tilde{\mathbf{x}}_m^{(k|k-1)}},\tag{16}$$

are the Jacobian matrices of the observation function with respect to the state. Then the cross covariance and Kalman gain are computed by

$$\mathbf{P}_{x|z}^{(k)} = \mathbf{P}_m^{(k|k-1)}\mathbf{H}^{(k)^T},\tag{17}$$

$$\mathbf{K}^{(k)} = \mathbf{P}_{x|z}^{(k)}\mathbf{S}^{(k)^{(-1)}}.\tag{18}$$

The measurement residuals are used to correct the state estimate with Kalman gain by

$$\tilde{\mathbf{x}}_m^{(k)} = \tilde{\mathbf{x}}_m^{(k|k-1)} + K^{(k)}\Delta\mathbf{z}^{(k)},\tag{19}$$

and update the prior covariance by

$$\tilde{\mathbf{P}}_m^{(k)} = \tilde{\mathbf{P}}_m^{(k|k-1)} - K^{(k)}\mathbf{S}^{(k)}K^{(k)^T}.\tag{20}$$

## 3   Problem Formulation for Link Selection

Cooperating with neighbors, users not only can increase the position accuracy but also improve the localizability. However, when users are densely deployed, the multi-neighbors will requires a large amount of time-frequency resources and may cause network jam and packet collisions. For example, if there are 10 users to construct a cooperative network and it is a full connect network. Then the total link number is 90. In particular, part of the cooperative links makes limited contribution to localization accuracy while it may not compensate for the cost of resource consumption. So it is necessary to select part cooperative link to reduce the load of cooperative network.

First, a coalition $\mathcal{I}_m$ is defined as $\mathcal{I}_m = m\bigcup\mathcal{C}_m$, where user $m$ is the core user and $\mathcal{C}_m$ is the cooperative neighbors which can provide localization information to cooperatively localize user $m$. The cooperation between users will bring benefit on the localization accuracy of the core user. On the other side, the cooperative link number is in direct proportion to resource consumption. So the link number is recognized as the cost of a coalition. Therefor, when to formulate a coalition, the localization accuracy and link number should be considered simultaneously.

The localization accuracy can be quantified by the mean squared error (MSE) of position estimation and it satisfies following inequation [9]

$$\mathbb{E}\{\|\hat{\mathbf{p}}_m - \mathbf{p}_m\|^2\} \geq tr\{\mathbf{J}_m^{-1}\},\tag{21}$$

where the $\mathbf{J}_m^{-1}$ is the $2 \times 2$ individual EFIM for user which is determined by following lemma.

Lemma 1: For round-trip TOA ranging in an asynchronous network, the individual EFIM $\mathbf{J}_m^{-1}$ for user $m$ can be given by

$$\mathbf{J}_m = \mathbf{J}_m^0 + \mathbf{J}_m^c,\tag{22}$$

$$\mathbf{J}_m^c = \sum_{n \in \mathcal{N}(m)} \lambda_{nm} J_r(\phi_{nm}), \tag{23}$$

where $\mathbf{J}_m^0$ is the localization information from satellites and $\mathbf{J}_m^c$ correspond to the localization information from cooperation, $\lambda_{nm}$ is a nonnegative number called the ranging information intensity (RII) [5], $\phi_{nm}$ is the angel between $n$ and $m$, $J_r(\phi_{nm})$ in called ranging direction matrix (RDM) with following structure [10]:

$$J_r(\phi_{nm}) \triangleq \begin{bmatrix} cos^2\phi_{nm} & cos\phi_{nm}sin\phi_{nm} \\ cos\phi_{nm}sin\phi_{nm} & sin^2\phi_{nm} \end{bmatrix}, \tag{24}$$

Based on reference [6], we define the cost function as

$$cost(|\mathcal{C}_m^{(k)}|) = -log\left[1 - \left(\frac{|\mathcal{C}_m^{(k)}| - \Delta}{N_m}\right)^2\right], \tag{25}$$

where $|\mathcal{C}_m^{(k)}|$ is the link number of user $m$ at time $k$, $N_m$ is the number of users within the communication range of user $m$, $\Delta$ is introduced to avoid an infinite value of the cost function when $|\mathcal{C}_m^{(k)}| = N_m$, here we set $\Delta = 0.1$. Note that there are two important characteristics about cost function: (i) It increase monotonically with respect to link number $|\mathcal{C}_m^{(k)}|$; (ii) The slop of cost function is steeper with more links, i.e., larger value of $|\mathcal{C}_m^{(k)}|$. In summary, the utility of each coalition can be defined as

$$U(m) = \frac{1}{tr\{(\mathbf{J}_m^c)^{-1}\}} - \beta \cdot cost|\mathcal{C}_m|. \tag{26}$$

The first term in the right side represents the benefit of user $m$ obtained from the coalition $\mathcal{C}_m$. The second term in the right side in the coalition represents the cost of the coalition. In addition, to balance the benefit and cost, the second term is endowed with a balance factor, i.e., $\beta$. These balance factor should be predefined according to the practical scenarios. Then the optimization objective for the total network can be formulated as:

$$max \sum_{m \in \mathcal{M}} U(m) \tag{27}$$

$$s.t. \ \ \mathcal{C}_m \in \mathcal{N}_m \tag{28}$$

## 4   Link Selection Algorithm

### 4.1   Game Formulation

First, the definition of OCF is given as follows.

**Definition 1 (OCF game):** An OCF game is defined as $G = (\mathcal{M}, U, \mathcal{CS})$, where $\mathcal{M}$ is the set of players (users), $U$ is the utility function, and $\mathcal{CS}$ is the overlapping coalitional structure. The structure of OCF game is defined as a set $\mathcal{CS} = \{\mathcal{I}_1, ..., \mathcal{I}_M\}$.

Due to the overlapping characteristic, $\exists \mathcal{I}_m^{(k)}, \mathcal{I}_n^{(k)} \in \mathcal{CS}^{(k)}, m \neq n$, such that $\mathcal{I}_m^{(k)} \cap \mathcal{I}_n^{(k)} \neq \emptyset$. The utility of a coalition $\mathcal{I}_m^{(k)}$ can be defined according to the optimization objective in (26). If an user $m$ cooperates with all neighbors at iteration $k$, we call this type of coalition as *full coalition*. Besides, if an user has no cooperative object or the cost is too expensive to cooperate, then the coalition $\mathcal{I}_m^{(k)}$ only contains the user $m$ itself. We call this coalition as *single coalition* and define its utility $U(\mathcal{I}_m^{(k)}) = 0$.

### 4.2   Criterion for Localization Judgement

Although the link selection algorithm is to reduce the computation complexity and resources consumption, the localization performance still be the main purpose. So before the link selection algorithm, a initial process should be completed to obtain the convergent state estimations by EKF. Then a criterion is proposed to determine whether they are well localized.

**Criterion 1:** For an user $m$ at time $k$, we will recognize that it is well localized if the following condition is satisfied:

$$var(|\mathbf{x}_m^{(k)} - \mathbf{x}_m^{(k|k-1)}|) < T_m, k \in [T - \Delta T, T], \tag{29}$$

where $\mathbf{x}_m^{(k)}$ is the estimated state in the correction step of EKF, $\mathbf{x}_m^{(k|k-1)}$ is the predicted state in the predict phase of EKF. Actually, we can find in equation (19) that $\mathbf{x}_m^{(k)} - \mathbf{x}_m^{(k|k-1)} = K^{(k)} \Delta \mathbf{z}^{(k)}$ where $\Delta \mathbf{z}^{(k)}$ is the measurement residuals and $K^{(k)}$ is the Kalman Gain. $var(\cdot)$ represents the covariance of $|\mathbf{x}_m^{(k)} - \mathbf{x}_m^{(k|k-1)}|$ during $k \in [T - \Delta T, T]$, where $T$ is the current iteration and $\Delta T$ is the judgement interval. $T_m$ is the threshold value.

Intuitively, if the state of an user is well estimated, the measurement residuals will be small, then the covariance must be small, and vice versa. At the same time, the judgement interval is introduced to avoid the influence of stochastic error. On the other hand, we can determine whether the state has changed according to the *criterion 1*. For a dynamic user $m$, its state may be instantaneous and changeful. When it does not satisfies *criterion 1*, it means that the user $m$ does not well localized or its state has changed. So all the neighboring users help to localize user $m$ unconditionally. This is also meaningful to rebuild link connection in multivariate environments.

### 4.3   OCF Based Link Selection Algorithm

To achieve the trade-off between localization accuracy and link selection, two switching orders are defined at first.

Consider a coalition structure as $\mathcal{CS}_P = \{\mathcal{I}_1, ..., \mathcal{I}_m, ..., \mathcal{I}_n, ..., \mathcal{I}_M\}$, where user $m$ is within the communication range of user $n$ but doesn't provide location information to user $n$.

**Definition 2 (Merge Order)** [6]: If user $m$ provides location information to user $n$ to form a new coalition $\mathcal{I}_n^*$. At the same time, the coalition $\mathcal{I}_m$

becomes $\mathcal{I}_n^*$ and a new coalition structure is formed from $\mathcal{CS}_P$ to $\mathcal{CS}_Q = \{\mathcal{I}_1, ..., \mathcal{I}_m^*, ..., \mathcal{I}_n^*, ..., \mathcal{I}_M\}$. Then, the *Merge Order* $\triangleright_M$ means that $\mathcal{CS}_Q$ prefers to $\mathcal{CS}_P$, which is defined as

$$\mathcal{CS}_P \triangleright_M \mathcal{CS}_Q \Leftrightarrow \begin{cases} U(\mathcal{I}_m^*) > U(\mathcal{I}_m) \\ U(\mathcal{I}_n^*) \geq U(\mathcal{I}_n) \end{cases}. \tag{30}$$

According to above definition, the *Merge Order* $\triangleright_M$ implies that only if the utility of new forming coalition $\mathcal{I}_n^*$ surpass the previous one and the utility of new forming coalition $\mathcal{I}_m^*$ is not less than previous one, then link $m \rightarrow n$ establishes.

Corresponding to *Merge Order*, the definition of *Split order* is given as follows. Considering a coalition structure as $\mathcal{CS}_P = \{\mathcal{I}_1, ..., \mathcal{I}_m, ..., \mathcal{I}_q, ..., \mathcal{I}_M\}$, where user $m$ provides location information to user $q$.

**Definition 3 (Split Order)** [6]: If user $m$ doesn't provide location information to user $q$, the coalition $\mathcal{I}_q$ changes to $\mathcal{I}_q^\dagger$. Besides, the coalition $\mathcal{I}_m$ becomes $\mathcal{I}_m^\dagger$ and the new coalition structure switches from $\mathcal{CS}_P$ to $\mathcal{CS}_W = \{\mathcal{I}_1, ..., \mathcal{I}_m^\dagger, ..., \mathcal{I}_q^\dagger, ..., \mathcal{I}_M\}$. Then, the *Split Order* $\triangleright_S$ means that $\mathcal{CS}_M$ prefers to $\mathcal{CS}_P$, which is defined as

$$\mathcal{CS}_P \triangleright_S \mathcal{CS}_W \Leftrightarrow \begin{cases} U(\mathcal{I}_m^\dagger) > U(\mathcal{I}_m) \\ U(\mathcal{I}_q^\dagger) \geq U(\mathcal{I}_q) \end{cases}. \tag{31}$$

Similarly, only when the utility of new forming coalition $\mathcal{I}_m^\dagger$ surpass the previous one and the utility of new forming coalition $\mathcal{I}_q^\dagger$ is not less than previous one, the user $n$ will split from previous coalition.

To summarize, the EKF-based OCF game algorithm for hybrid cooperative positioning can be described explicitly in Algorithm 1. Initially, each user constructs a full coalition. The next stage is the EKF filter to obtain real-time state. Then if criterion 1 is satisfied, each user can make its own decision to select suitable cooperative set by *Merge* and *Split* operations. If criterion 1 isn't satisfied, the user should cooperate with others as much as possible to obtain convergent estimation.

## 5   Simulation Results

In this section, the performance of proposed algorithm is evaluated. We consider that five fixed satellites can be visible by each user. Tables 1 and 2 give the initial state of each user and satellites' positions, respectively. Realistic biases are generated uniformly in the interval $\pm 0.5$ milliseconds of clock misalignment and we neglect the clock drift. Pseudorange and P2P range measurements are corrupted by additive white Gaussian noise with standard deviation $\sigma_{sm} = 5\,\text{m}$ and $\sigma_{nm} = 20\,\text{cm}$. The communication range of user is 100 m which means this is a fully connected network.

To obtain the SPEB of each user, the ranging signals is considered with carrier frequency $f_c = 2.1\,\text{GHz}$ and band-with $W = 40\,\text{MHz}$. The noise power

---

**Algorithm 1.** Link selection algorithm based on EKF and OCF game for cooperative positioning

---

1: Initially Stage: Set $n = 1$ and give estimates $\tilde{\mathbf{x}}_m^{(0)}$, $\tilde{\mathbf{P}}_m^{(0)}$, $\forall m \in \mathcal{M}$, threshold value $T_m$, judgement interval $\Delta T$, coalition structure $\mathcal{CS}^{(0)}$.

2: Every user communicates with its all neighbors.

3: All users in parallel do.

4: Compute position predictions $\tilde{\mathbf{x}}_m^{(k|k-1)}$ and $\tilde{\mathbf{P}}_m^{(k|k-1)}$;
   Compute Jacobian matrix $\mathbf{H}_m^{(k)}$;
   Compute the innovation vector $\Delta z^{(k)}$, covariance $\mathbf{S}^{(k)}$, Kalman gain $\mathbf{K}^{(k)}$ and a posteriori estimates $\tilde{\mathbf{x}}_m^{(k)}$ and $\tilde{\mathbf{P}}_m^{(t)}$.

5: If criterion 1 is satisfied, go to step 6; otherwise, go to step 7 and $\mathcal{CS}_m^{(k+1)} = \mathcal{M}_m$.

6: Compute the utility of each coalition $U(\mathcal{I}_m^{(k)})$ and update coalition structure according to the *Merge Order* and *Split Order*, till converge to a stable coalitional structure $\mathcal{CS}_{opt}$ and $\mathcal{CS}_m^{(k+1)} = \mathcal{CS}_{opt}$.

7: If reach the maximum time K, stop; else, go to step 2.

---

density is $-168$ dBm/Hz. The WINNER channel model is adopted as the ranging signal propagation:

$$Pathloss[dB] = A + B\log_{10}d[m] + 20\log_{10}\frac{f_c[GHz]}{5.0} + X, \qquad (32)$$

where $X \sim N(0, \sigma_s^2)$ accounts for the shadow fading. We choose parameters as $A = 41.0$, $B = 23.8$, and $\sigma = 4$, respectively [11]. For the utility function in (26), we set $\beta = 1000$. The judgement threshold value $T_m = 30$, judgement interval $\Delta T = 3$.

Here we consider two states of users. At first, all the users move with the initial states in Table 2. Then after 30 iterations, the velocity of each user becomes $0$ m/s. In other words, the state of swarm transforms from uniform speed to static. We also compare the performance of different approaches:

- *Proposed game*: The state of each user is obtained by the proposed game algorithm.
- *Full coalition*: Each user cooperates with all neighbors without link selection algorithm, i.e., $\forall k, \mathcal{CS}_m^k = \mathcal{N}_m^k$.
- *No cooperation*: Each user only depends on satellites to estimate its state, i.e., $\forall k, \mathcal{CS}_m^k = \emptyset$.

Figure 2 shows the link relationship at a iteration 20 by proposed OCF game algorithm. Figure 3 demonstrates the link number of proposed game algorithm and full coalition approach. We can see the link number is substantially reduced to about 30 in proposed algorithm, one-third of the link number of full coalition approach. It is clearly that the link number of OCF game algorithm is suddenly increased after iteration 31. This is caused by the change of users' states and the judgement of criterion 1 is unsatisfied, users will rebuild cooperative links to improve localization performance.

**Table 1.** Satellite' positions in ENU at initial time (origin at 45.06° lat., 7.66° long., 311.96 m height)

| Sat | 1 | 2 | 3 | 4 | 5 |
|---|---|---|---|---|---|
| $E(10^6\,m)$ | −11.67 | −22.30 | 7.56 | 6.33 | −2.44 |
| $N(10^6\,m)$ | 19.05 | 10.34 | 10.98 | 3.48 | 14.02 |
| $U(10^6\,m)$ | −12.41 | −11.57 | −1.03 | 13.67 | 8.26 |

**Table 2.** User' states in ENU at initial time

| User | 1 | 2 | 3 | 4 | 5 | 6 | 7 | 8 | 9 | 10 |
|---|---|---|---|---|---|---|---|---|---|---|
| $x(m)$ | 10 | 30 | 50 | 0 | 20 | 40 | 60 | 10 | 30 | 50 |
| $y(m)$ | 0 | 0 | 0 | 20 | 20 | 20 | 20 | 40 | 40 | 40 |
| $z(m)$ | 30 | 30 | 30 | 30 | 30 | 30 | 30 | 30 | 30 | 30 |
| $v_x(m/s)$ | 5 | 5 | 5 | 5 | 5 | 5 | 5 | 5 | 5 | 5 |
| $v_y(m/s)$ | 0 | 0 | 0 | 0 | 0 | 0 | 0 | 0 | 0 | 0 |
| $v_z(m/s)$ | 0 | 0 | 0 | 0 | 0 | 0 | 0 | 0 | 0 | 0 |

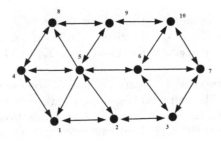

**Fig. 2.** The links after link selection Algorithm 1.

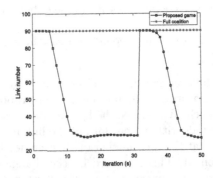

**Fig. 3.** The link number of OCF game and full coalition with respect to iteration.

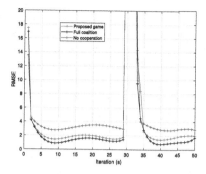

**Fig. 4.** The localization error of different approaches with respect to iteration.

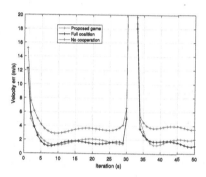

**Fig. 5.** The velocity error of different approaches with respect to iteration.

In Figs. 4 and 5, we compare the root mean square error (RMSE) of localization error and velocity error under different algorithms. First, for cooperative positioning approaches, the localization accuracy is better than no cooperation approach. We can see the average localization error is about 3.5 m for no cooperation approach after 10 iterations. Whereas the same error can reach about 1.5 m and 1.8 m for full coalition and OCF game based, respectively. Second, we can see that the performances of velocity estimation for cooperation obviously outperform than no cooperation approach. Generally speaking, more cooperative uses, higher localization accuracy can be achieved and more resource consumption consequently. However, in proposed OCF game link selection algorithm, a considerable number of formerly connected links are abandoned and the cost is lower accuracy.

## 6   Conclusion

Motivated by increasing the resource efficiency utilized for cooperation among densely deployed users, an EKF based OCF game were formulated to achieve a link selection scheme. At the same time, a criterion is used to determine whether users are well localized in the estimation process. If the criterion is satisfied, the OCF game is employed to construct a stable coalition as the cooperative set. Otherwise, all neighbors should cooperate to obtain satisfactory localization accuracy. Simulation result show that the cooperative positioning can achieve performance improvement in localization accuracy and velocity estimation compared to the no cooperation approach, and the proposed OCF game link selection approach can achieve a much fewer link number at the cost of appropriate performance degradation. We will consider the link selection problem for more complicated scenarios in the next step.

# References

1. Spilker Jr., J.J.: GPS signal structure and performance characteristics. Navigation **25**(2), 121–146 (1978)
2. Caceres, M.A., Penna, F., Wymeersch, H., et al.: Hybrid cooperative positioning based on distributed belief propagation. IEEE J. Sel. Areas Commun. **29**(10), 1948–1958 (2011)
3. Ghassemi, F., Krishnamurthy, V.: A cooperative game-theoretic measurement allocation algorithm for localization in unattended ground sensor networks. In: International Conference on Information Fusion, pp. 1–7. IEEE (2008)
4. He, H., Subramanian, A., Shen, X., et al.: A coalitional game for distributed estimation in wireless sensor networks. In: IEEE International Conference on Acoustics, Speech and Signal Processing, pp. 4574–4578. IEEE (2013)
5. Chen, J., Dai, W., Shen, Y., et al.: Resource management games for distributed network localization. IEEE J. Sel. Areas Commun. **35**(2), 317–329 (2017)
6. Zhang, R., Zhao, Z., Cheng, X., et al.: Overlapping coalition formation game based opportunistic cooperative localization scheme for wireless networks. IEEE Trans. Commun. **PP**(99), 1 (2017)
7. Sottile, F., Wymeersch, H., Caceres, M.A., et al.: Hybrid GNSS-terrestrial cooperative positioning based on particle filter. In: Global Telecommunications Conference, pp. 1–5. IEEE (2011)
8. Caceres, M.A., Sottile, F., Garello, R., et al.: Hybrid GNSS-ToA localization and tracking via cooperative unscented Kalman filter. In: International Symposium on Personal, Indoor and Mobile Radio Communications Workshops, pp. 272–276. IEEE Xplore (2010)
9. Shen, Y.: Fundamental limits of wideband localization. Massachusetts Institute of Technology (2008)
10. Chen, J., Dai, W., Shen, Y., et al.: Power management for cooperative localization: a game theoretical approach. IEEE Trans. Sig. Process. **64**(24), 6517–6532 (2016)
11. Dai, W., Shen, Y., Win, M.Z.: Distributed power allocation for cooperative wireless network localization. IEEE J. Sel. Areas Commun. **33**(1), 28–40 (2015)

# Robust Control of Distributed SAR Beam Synchronization Based on Inverse Optimal Method

Kai Li[1,2(✉)], Xibin Cao[1], Ming Liu[1], and Sentang Wu[2]

[1] Research Center of Satellite Technology,
Harbin Institute of Technology, Harbin, China
likai_1030@163.com
[2] School of Automation Science and Electrical Engineering,
Beihang University, Beijing, China

**Abstract.** Distributed SAR satellite formation has been widely studied and applied because of its unique advantages, and beam synchronization is the prerequisite for achieving its function. An inverse optimal control method is proposed for the ideal nominal system in this paper, which is based on two beam synchronization strategies of Doppler guidance and beam pointing synchronization. And on this basis, considering the influence of satellite communication delay, external disturbance and system model uncertainty, an integral sliding mode robust control method based on inverse optimal control is designed. The simulation results show that the control method has high control accuracy and good robustness.

**Keywords:** Distributed SAR · Beam synchronization ·
Inverse optimal control · Robust control

## 1 Introduction

Synthetic Aperture Radar (SAR) is widely used in satellite observation because of its high resolution, strong penetration into clouds, low requirement for working environment and wide working time [1]. Compared with optical remote sensors, it is completely immune to weather and illumination conditions and can observe all-day and all-weather. In a distributed SAR system with multiple transmitters and receivers, the beam coverage of master and slave satellites must exceed a certain proportion of overlap, so that the advantages of distributed SAR can be fully utilized to effectively improve the observation resolution and accuracy. Therefore, reasonable attitude planning and control of spacecraft should be carried out.

In the current study of beam synchronization control, six control strategies based on beam pointing synchronization were given in [2], and the requirements of beam synchronization on spacecraft attitude in several different flight control strategies was analyzed systematically in [3]. the accuracy requirements of beam control in distributed SAR was analyzed in [4]. Because of the relative velocity between spacecraft and ground targets, Doppler effect will be generated by radar waves. Therefore, the

© Springer Nature Singapore Pte Ltd. 2019
Q. Yu (Ed.): SINC 2018, CCIS 972, pp. 189–204, 2019.
https://doi.org/10.1007/978-981-13-5937-8_20

compensation of Doppler center frequency should be considered in beam synchronization control. Considering the yaw guidance of the master satellite, an attitude control strategy of beam coverage synchronization was given in [5] and has good control effect. Based on the control strategy in [5], an attitude planning scheme of slave satellite, using two-dimensional pitching guidance, was proposed in [6]. The beam synchronization of tethered SAR satellite was studied in [7], in which the tethered tension was used to control the attitude of the satellite and had good control effects.

In this paper, the beam synchronization control of distributed SAR is taken as the mission requirement, and the effects of communication delay between satellites, external disturbance and system model uncertainty are considered. Due to the insufficient consideration of the beam synchronization interference factors in current methods, a robust control method based on inverse optimal control is proposed in this paper. And the simulation results show that this method can achieve good beam synchronization in distributed SAR system under the above conditions.

## 2    Model Description

The attitude dynamics and kinematics equations of spacecraft are described as [7]

$$J\dot{\omega} = -\omega^\times J\omega + \tau + \tau_d \tag{1}$$

$$\dot{Q} = \frac{1}{2}\begin{bmatrix} -q^T \\ q^\times + q_0 I \end{bmatrix}\omega \tag{2}$$

where $J \in \mathbb{R}^{3\times3}$ denotes the inertia of the spacecraft, $\omega \in \mathbb{R}^3$ denotes the angular velocity, $Q = [q_0 \ \ q]^T = [q_0 \ \ q_1 \ \ q_2 \ \ q_3]^T$ denotes the attitude quaternion, $\tau \in \mathbb{R}^3$ denotes the control torque, $\tau_d \in \mathbb{R}^3$ denotes the disturbance torque, and $(\cdot)^\times$ is defined as

$$a^\times = \begin{bmatrix} 0 & -a_3 & a_2 \\ a_3 & 0 & -a_1 \\ -a_2 & a_1 & 0 \end{bmatrix}$$

The target attitude of spacecraft is set to $Q_d$, $\omega_d$, then the quaternion error can be expressed as

$$Q_e = \begin{bmatrix} q_{e0} \\ q_e \end{bmatrix} = Q^{-1} \otimes Q_d = \begin{bmatrix} q_0 \\ -q \end{bmatrix} \otimes Q_d \tag{3}$$

where "$\otimes$" is defined as

$$Q_i \otimes Q_j = \begin{bmatrix} q_{i0}q_{j0} - q_i^T q_j \\ q_{i0}q_j + q_{j0}q_i + q_i^\times q_j \end{bmatrix}$$

And the angular velocity error is

$$\omega_e = \omega - T(Q_e)\omega_d \tag{4}$$

where $T(Q_e)$ denotes the transfer matrix from the body frame of "target spacecraft" to the body frame of "real spacecraft".

$$T(Q_e) = (q_{e0}^2 - q_e^T q_e)I_3 + 2q_e q_e^T - 2q_{e0}q_e^\times \tag{5}$$

in which $I_3$ is a 3-order unit matrix. And the transfer matrix $T(Q_e)$ has the following properties

$$\|T(Q_e)\| = 1 \tag{6}$$

$$\dot{T}(Q_e) = -\omega_e^\times T(Q_e) \tag{7}$$

where $\|\cdot\|$ represents the 2-norm of the matrix, and if not specified, the following is the same.

In fact, besides the influence of external disturbance, the uncertainty of the inertia also affects the control accuracy of the spacecraft.

In the attitude motion model, let

$$\tilde{J} = J + \delta J \tag{8}$$

where $\tilde{J}$ represents the actual inertia of the spacecraft, $J$ represents the nominal inertia, and $\delta J$ represents the error of inertia.

The equation of attitude motion of spacecraft can be obtained by substituting Eqs. (3)–(8) into Eqs. (1)–(2),

$$\begin{cases} J\dot{\omega}_e = -\omega^\times J\omega + J\omega_e^\times T(Q_e)\omega_d + \tau + \tau_d \\ \dot{Q}_e = \frac{1}{2}\begin{bmatrix} -q_e^T \\ q_e^\times + q_{e0}I_3 \end{bmatrix}\omega_e \end{cases} \tag{9}$$

where $\tau_d = \tilde{\tau}_d - \delta J\,\dot{\omega}_e - \omega^\times \delta J\omega + \delta J\omega_e^\times T(Q_e)\omega_d - JT(Q_e)\dot{\omega}_d$ represents the sum of the system uncertainties and the disturbance torque.

## 3  Beam Synchronization Strategy

In actual work, there is a great relative velocity between the antenna of satellite and ground target, which will produce Doppler effect. And the Doppler effect will reduce the imaging quality and image synthesis quality enormously. The intermediate frequency of satellite antenna azimuth spectrum is called Doppler center frequency. Doppler center frequency should be compensated in order to reduce the impact on image quality. And this method is called Doppler guidance. If both master and slave satellites adopt beam pointing synchronization strategy, the system may produce a large

Doppler center frequency and poor imaging quality. If both master and slave satellites adopt Doppler guidance, the beam coverage will be reduced, and the system function will also be reduced. Especially in a multi-slave system, the beam coverage of slave satellites may not overlap.

In this section, a new synchronization strategy is proposed by combining the above two synchronization strategies: The master satellite uses Doppler guidance to reduce the Doppler center frequency, and the slave satellite carries out beam pointing synchronization according to the antenna pointing of the master satellite.

### 3.1 Doppler Guidance

Suppose that in a distributed SAR system with one master and multiple receivers, the master has dual functions of sending and receiving. The Doppler center frequency of the master is [8]

$$f_{DC} = \frac{2}{\lambda} \cdot \frac{v_{rt} \cdot r_{rt}}{\|r_{rt}\|} = \frac{2}{\lambda} \cdot v_{rt} \cdot \hat{r}_{rt} \tag{10}$$

where $\lambda$ denotes the radar wavelength, $r_{rt}$ and $v_{rt}$ denote the relative position and velocity between the master satellite and the ground target respectively in the inertial frame, and $\hat{r}_{rt}$ denotes the direction of the satellite antenna.

Let $R_T$ and $R_r$ represent the position vector of the ground target and the master satellite in inertial frame respectively, then

$$\begin{cases} r_{rt} = R_T - R_r \\ v_{rt} = \dot{r}_{rt} = \dot{R}_T - \dot{R}_r \end{cases} \tag{11}$$

Assuming that there is a ground target. For most of the distributed SAR satellites are in low orbit, $r_{rt}$ is far less than $R_r$, so

$$\dot{R}_T = w_E \times R_T = w_E \times (R_r + r_{st}) \approx w_E \times R_r \tag{12}$$

where $\omega_E$ denotes the rotation angular velocity of the earth. Substituting (11) and (12) into (10) yields

$$f_{DC} = \frac{2}{\lambda} \left( w_E \times R_r - \dot{R}_r \right) \cdot \hat{r}_{rt} = \frac{2}{\lambda} v_{eq} \cdot \hat{r}_{rt} \tag{13}$$

The equivalent relative velocity $v_{eq}$ of satellite and ground target is a constant at any time, if the satellite is not in orbit maneuver. In this case, adjusting the satellite attitude to make the antenna pointing $\hat{r}_{rt}$ perpendicular to $v_{eq}$, then the Doppler center frequency can be eliminated. Assuming that the earth is an ideal sphere, after the antenna pointing is solved by Eq. (13), a three-dimensional quadratic equation is needed to obtain the coordinates of the ground beam center (ground target) $R_T$, and then the attitudes of slave satellites are planned. However, when the master satellite is in circular orbit, the equivalent relative velocity $v_{eq}$ is perpendicular to the vector radius $R_r$ of master satellite. That is, when the antenna of master satellite is looking down, the Doppler guidance effect can be achieved, and the solution process of the ground beam center is simplified. At this time, the ground beam center $R_T$ can be indicated as

$$R_T = R_E \hat{R}_r \tag{14}$$

where $R_E$ denotes the mean radius of the earth, and $\hat{R}_r$ denotes the position vector of the master satellite.

## 3.2 Beam Pointing Synchronization

In the earth-centered inertial coordinate, the beam direction of the master satellite after Doppler guidance is recorded as $\hat{r}_{rt}$. According to Eq. (14), the position vector $R_T$ of ground target is obtained, and the expected position of the target relative to the slave antenna is

$$r_{ct} = R_T - R_c \tag{15}$$

where $R_c$ denotes the position of slave satellite.

At the initial time, the body coordinate of satellite is coincided with the inertial coordinate. The antenna is connected with the body coordinate, and its pointing is $\rho_b$. Then, the beam pointing of slave satellite at the initial time is represented as $\rho = \rho_b$ in the inertial coordinate. Suppose that the beam pointing can be coincided with the expected direction, after the slave satellite rotating $\phi$ around $\hat{e}$, then

$$\begin{cases} \hat{e} = \frac{\rho \times r_{ct}}{\|\rho \times r_{ct}\|} \\ \phi = ar\cos\left(\frac{\rho \cdot r_{ct}}{\|\rho\| \cdot \|r_{ct}\|}\right) \end{cases} \tag{16}$$

Since the body coordinate of slave satellite is coincided with the inertial coordinate at the initial time, the desired attitude of the satellite can be obtained from the definition of quaternion

$$Q_d = \begin{bmatrix} cos(\phi/2) \\ \hat{e}\ sin(\phi/2) \end{bmatrix} \tag{17}$$

The desired attitude and angular velocity of the satellite should be satisfied with the attitude dynamic equation shown in Eq. (2). Thus, the desired angular velocity of slave satellite is

$$\omega_d = 2\begin{bmatrix} -q^T \\ q^\times + q_0 I \end{bmatrix}^T \dot{Q}_d \tag{18}$$

where $\dot{Q}_d$ can be obtained by difference.

## 4 Cooperative Controller Design

### 4.1 Inverse Optimal Control of Beam Synchronization

Consider a nonlinear system

$$\dot{x} = f(x) + g(x)u \tag{19}$$

where $x \in \mathbb{R}^n$ denotes the system state, $f : \mathbb{R}^n \to \mathbb{R}^n$ and $g : \mathbb{R}^n \to \mathbb{R}^{n \times m}$ are smooth functions and $f(0) = 0$, and $u \in \mathbb{R}^m$ denotes control vector.

For $x \neq 0$, if the Lyapunov function $V(x)$ satisfies

$$L_g V(x) = 0 \Rightarrow L_f V(x) < 0 \tag{20}$$

then $V(x)$ is called control Lyapunov function (CLF) of the system [9], where $L_h V(x) = \frac{\partial V(x)}{\partial x} h(x)$ is called the Lie derivative of $V(x)$ about $h(x)$.

**Lemma 1** [10]. For the system in (19), if the controller

$$u^* = \kappa^*(x) := -R^{-1}(x) \cdot L_g V(x)^T \tag{21}$$

can be proved to make the system globally asymptotically stable through the Lyapunov function $V(x)$, then

$$u = \kappa(x) := -\beta R^{-1}(x) \cdot L_g V(x)^T, \beta \geq 2 \tag{22}$$

is an optimal controller of system (19) about the index function

$$I = \int_0^\infty \left[ l(x) + u^T R^{-1}(x) u \right] dt \tag{23}$$

where $R : \mathbb{R}^n \to \mathbb{R}^{m \times m}$ is a positive-definite and symmetric matrix.

The attitude dynamics and kinematics equations of satellite $i$ can be written in the form of (19), only considering the ideal dynamic environment without disturbance

$$\dot{x}_i = f(x_i) + g(x_i)\tau_i \tag{24}$$

Where $x_i = \begin{bmatrix} q_{i0e} \\ q_{ie} \\ w_{ie} \end{bmatrix}$, $f(x_i) = \begin{bmatrix} -\frac{1}{2} q_{ie}^T w_{ie} \\ \frac{1}{2} (q_{i0e} I_3 + q_{ie}^\times) w_{ie} \\ -J_i^{-1} w_i^\times J_i w_i + w_{ie}^\times T(Q_{ie}) w_{id} \end{bmatrix}$, $g(x_i) = \begin{bmatrix} 0 \\ 0_3 \\ J_i^{-1} \end{bmatrix}$,

$\tau_i = \begin{bmatrix} \tau_{ix} \\ \tau_{iy} \\ \tau_{iz} \end{bmatrix}$.

It is assumed that all satellites in the system can cooperate with each other through information interaction. There is a communication delay $T_{ij}$ between $i$ and $j$, and $|\dot{T}_{ij}| < 1$. Then the CLF of satellite $i$ can be set as

$$
\begin{aligned}
V(\boldsymbol{x}_i) &= k_{1i}(q_{i0e} - 1)^2 + k_{1i}\boldsymbol{q}_{ie}^T\boldsymbol{q}_{ie} + k_{2i}\boldsymbol{q}_{ie}^T\boldsymbol{w}_{ie} + k_{3i}\boldsymbol{w}_{ie}^T\boldsymbol{w}_{ie} + \sum_{j\in N_i}\int_{t-T_{ij}}^t \boldsymbol{z}_j^T\boldsymbol{z}_j dt \\
&= k_{1i}(q_{i0e} - 1)^2 + \begin{bmatrix} \boldsymbol{q}_{ie} \\ \boldsymbol{w}_{ie} \end{bmatrix}^T \begin{bmatrix} k_{1i} & \frac{k_{2i}}{2} \\ \frac{k_{2i}}{2} & k_{3i} \end{bmatrix} \begin{bmatrix} \boldsymbol{q}_{ie} \\ \boldsymbol{w}_{ie} \end{bmatrix} + \sum_{j\in N_i}\int_{t-T_{ij}}^t \boldsymbol{z}_j^T\boldsymbol{z}_j dt
\end{aligned}
\tag{25}
$$

where $\boldsymbol{z}_j = \boldsymbol{q}_{je} + c_j\boldsymbol{w}_{je}$, $c_j > 0$. In order to guarantee the positive definiteness of $V(\boldsymbol{x}_i)$, $\begin{bmatrix} k_{1i} & \frac{k_{2i}}{2} \\ \frac{k_{2i}}{2} & k_{3i} \end{bmatrix}$ is needed to be positive-definite only, that is $4k_{1i}k_{3i} > k_{2i}^2$. And in this case,

$$
\begin{aligned}
L_f V(\boldsymbol{x}_i) &= \frac{\partial V_i}{\partial \boldsymbol{x}_i}f(\boldsymbol{x}_i) = -k_{1i}(q_{i0e} - 1)\boldsymbol{q}_{ie}^T\boldsymbol{w}_{ie} + k_{1i}\boldsymbol{q}_{ie}^T(q_{i0e}\boldsymbol{I}_3 + \boldsymbol{q}_{ie}^\times)\boldsymbol{w}_{ie} \\
&\quad + \frac{k_{2i}}{2}\boldsymbol{w}_{ie}^T(q_{i0e}\boldsymbol{I}_3 + \boldsymbol{q}_{ie}^\times)\boldsymbol{w}_{ie} - k_{2i}\boldsymbol{q}_{ie}^T\boldsymbol{J}_i^{-1}\boldsymbol{w}_i^\times\boldsymbol{J}_i\boldsymbol{w}_i + k_{2i}\boldsymbol{q}_{ie}^T\boldsymbol{w}_{ie}^\times T(\boldsymbol{Q}_{ie})\boldsymbol{w}_{id} \\
&\quad - 2k_{3i}\boldsymbol{w}_{ie}^T\boldsymbol{J}_i^{-1}\boldsymbol{w}_i^\times\boldsymbol{J}_i\boldsymbol{w}_i + 2k_{3i}\boldsymbol{w}_{ie}^T\boldsymbol{w}_{ie}^\times T(\boldsymbol{Q}_{ie})\boldsymbol{w}_{id} \\
&= k_{1i}\boldsymbol{q}_{ie}^T\boldsymbol{w}_{ie} + \frac{k_{2i}}{2}\boldsymbol{w}_{ie}^T\boldsymbol{J}_i(q_{i0e}\boldsymbol{I}_3 + \boldsymbol{q}_{ie}^\times)\boldsymbol{w}_{ie} + k_{2i}\boldsymbol{q}_{ie}^T\boldsymbol{J}_i^{-1}\boldsymbol{w}_{ie}^\times T(\boldsymbol{Q}_{ie})\boldsymbol{w}_{id} \\
&\quad - k_{2i}\boldsymbol{q}_{ie}^T\boldsymbol{w}_i^\times\boldsymbol{J}_i\boldsymbol{w}_i - 2k_{3i}\boldsymbol{w}_{ie}^T\boldsymbol{w}_i^\times\boldsymbol{J}_i\boldsymbol{w}_i + 2k_{3i}\boldsymbol{w}_{ie}^T\boldsymbol{J}_i^{-1}\boldsymbol{w}_{ie}^\times T(\boldsymbol{Q}_{ie})\boldsymbol{w}_{id}
\end{aligned}
\tag{26}
$$

$$
L_g V(\boldsymbol{x}_i) = \frac{\partial V_i}{\partial \boldsymbol{x}_i}g(\boldsymbol{x}_i) = \left[ 2k_{3i}\boldsymbol{w}_{ie}^T + k_{2i}\boldsymbol{q}_{ie}^T \right]\boldsymbol{J}_i^{-1}
\tag{27}
$$

When $L_g V(\boldsymbol{x}_i) = 0$, $\boldsymbol{w}_{ie} = -\frac{k_{2i}}{2k_{3i}}\boldsymbol{q}_{ie}$ is obtained. Thus,

$$
\begin{aligned}
L_f V_i &= k_{1i}\boldsymbol{q}_{ie}^T\left(-\frac{k_{2i}}{2k_{3i}}\boldsymbol{q}_{ie}\right) + \frac{k_{2i}}{2}\left(-\frac{k_{2i}}{2k_{3i}}\boldsymbol{q}_{ie}^T\right)(q_{i0e}\boldsymbol{I}_3 + \boldsymbol{q}_{ie}^\times)\left(-\frac{k_{2i}}{2k_{3i}}\boldsymbol{q}_{ie}\right) \\
&= -\frac{k_{1i}k_{2i}}{2k_{3i}}\|\boldsymbol{q}_{ie}\|^2 + \frac{k_{2i}^3}{8k_{3i}^2}q_{i0e}\boldsymbol{q}_{ie}^T\boldsymbol{q}_{ie} \leq -\frac{k_{1i}k_{2i}}{2k_{3i}}\|\boldsymbol{q}_{ie}\|^2 + \frac{k_{2i}^3}{8k_{3i}^2}\boldsymbol{q}_{ie}^T\boldsymbol{q}_{ie} \\
&\leq -\frac{k_{2i}}{2k_{3i}}\left(k_{1i} - \frac{k_{2i}^2}{4k_{3i}}\right)\|\boldsymbol{q}_{ie}\|^2
\end{aligned}
$$

According to the positive-definite condition $4k_{1i}k_{3i} > k_{2i}^2$ of $V(\boldsymbol{x}_i)$,

$$
L_f V_i \leq -\frac{k_{2i}}{2k_{3i}}\left(k_{1i} - \frac{k_{2i}^2}{4k_{3i}}\right)\|\boldsymbol{q}_{ie}\|^2 < 0
$$

That is, the constrained condition $4k_{1i}k_{3i} > k_{2i}^2$ guarantees the positive definiteness of Lyapunov function $V(x_i)$ and makes it a CLF for the system (24). Thus, the CLF of system (24) has been found, and the design of inverse optimal controller is carried out below.

**Theorem 1.** According to Lemma 1, inverse optimal controller

$$\tau_{i1} = -\beta_i R^{-1}(x_i) \cdot L_g V(x_i)^T \tag{28}$$

can make the error of system (24) converge to $x_i = [1 \quad 0 \quad 0 \quad 0 \quad 0 \quad 0 \quad 0]^T$, where

$$R^{-1}(x_i) = \frac{1}{\beta_i L_g V_i \cdot L_g V_i^T} \sum_{j \in N_i} \left( \alpha_i z_i - \alpha_j z_j (t - T_{ij}) \right)^T \left( \alpha_i z_i - \alpha_j z_j (t - T_{ij}) \right),$$

$$+ \frac{1}{\beta_i L_g V_i \cdot L_g V_i^T} \left( L_f V_i + \gamma_i \sqrt{L_f V_i^2 + \left( L_g V_i \cdot L_g V_i^T \right)^2} \right)$$

$\beta_i \geq 2$, and $R(x)$ is positive-definite obviously.

**Proof.** According to the Lyapunov function $V(x_i)$ in (25), we can get the derivative of $V(x_i)$ about $x$

$$\dot{V}_i = \frac{\partial V_i}{\partial x_i} \dot{x}_i = \frac{\partial V_i}{\partial x_i} (f(x_i) + g(x_i)\tau_{i1})$$

Substitute the controller (28) into the derivative of $V(x_i)$, then

$$\dot{V}_i = L_f V_i + L_g V_i \cdot \left( -\beta_i R(x_i)^{-1} L_g V_i^T \right)$$

$$= L_f V_i - L_g V_i \frac{L_f V_i + \gamma_i \sqrt{L_f V_i^2 + \left( L_g V_i \cdot L_g V_i^T \right)^2}}{L_g V_i \cdot L_g V_i^T} L_g V_i^T$$

$$- L_g V_i \frac{\sum\limits_{j \in N_i} \left( \alpha_i z_i - \alpha_j z_j (t - T_{ij}) \right)^T \left( \alpha_i z_i - \alpha_j z_j (t - T_{ij}) \right)}{L_g V_i \cdot L_g V_i^T} L_g V_i^T$$

$$= -\gamma_i \sqrt{L_f V_i^2 + \left( L_g V_i \cdot L_g V_i^T \right)^2} - \sum_{j \in N_i} \left( \alpha_i z_i - \alpha_j z_j (t - T_{ij}) \right)^T \left( \alpha_i z_i - \alpha_j z_j (t - T_{ij}) \right)$$

For any $x_i \neq 0$, there is $\dot{V}_i < 0$. Therefore, the error of system (24) is globally asymptotically stable under the controller (28). ∎

## 4.2   Integral Sliding Mode Robust Control

Adding uncertainties and disturbance items on the basis of (24), then the dynamics of system is

$$\dot{x}_i = f(x_i) + g(x_i)\tau_i + g(x_i)\tau_{di} \tag{29}$$

Consider the controller

$$\tau_i = \tau_{i1} + \tau_{i2} \tag{30}$$

Where $\tau_{i1}$ denotes the inverse optimal controller (28), and $\tau_{i2}$ denotes the sliding mode robust controller.

The integral sliding manifold is designed as

$$\sigma_i = (x_i - x_i(0)) - \int_0^t (f(x_i) + g(x_i)\tau_{i1})dt \tag{31}$$

It is obviously that $\sigma_i = 0$ when $t = 0$. However, $\dot{\sigma}_i \neq 0$ due to the disturbance torque at the initial moment, and the system state will deviate from the sliding manifold. In this case, a sliding mode controller is needed to make $\lim_{x \to \infty} \sigma_i = \lim_{x \to \infty} \dot{\sigma}_i = 0$.

**Lemma 2**  [11]. The Super-Twisting algorithm (STA) can speed up its convergence by adding linear items. The form of fast Super-Twisting algorithm is as follows

$$\begin{cases} u = -\alpha|\sigma|^{\frac{1}{2}}sign(\sigma) - k_P\sigma + v \\ v = -\gamma sign(\sigma) - k_I\sigma \end{cases} \tag{32}$$

where $u$ denotes the control vector, $\sigma$ denotes the sliding manifold, $\alpha$, $\gamma$, $k_P$ and $k_I$ denote the controller gain.

**Theorem 2.** When the parameter in fast Super-Twisting algorithm satisfy $\alpha = \gamma = 0$, the controller

$$\begin{cases} \tau_{i2} = -k_{Pi}\sigma_i + v_i \\ v_i = -k_{Ii}\sigma_i \end{cases} \tag{33}$$

is a sliding mode robust PI controller which can converge the state error of the system (24) and stabilize it on the sliding manifold, that is $\sigma_i = 0$ and $\dot{\sigma}_i = 0$.

**Proof.** The derivative of sliding manifold is

$$\begin{aligned} \dot{\sigma}_i &= \dot{x}_i - (f(x_i) + g(x_i)\tau_{i1}) \\ &= (f(x_i) + g(x_i)\tau_i + g(x_i)\tau_{di}) - (f(x_i) + g(x_i)\tau_{i1}) \\ &= g(x_i) \cdot (\tau_{i2} + \tau_{di}) \end{aligned} \tag{34}$$

Substitute controller (33) into (34) and perform Laplace transform, then

$$sL(\sigma_i) = -k_{Pi}g(x_i)L(\sigma_i) - \frac{1}{s}k_{Ii}g(x_i)L(\sigma_i) + g(x_i)L(\tau_{di})$$

$$L(\sigma_i) = \frac{s \cdot g(x_i)L(\tau_{di})}{s^2 + s \cdot g(x_i)k_{Pi} + g(x_i)k_{Ii}}$$

It is known that $g(x_i)$, $k_{Pi}$ and $k_{Ii}$ are constants and $\tau_{di}$ is bounded. According to the final value theorem, it can be obtained that

$$\lim_{t \to \infty} \sigma_i = \lim_{s \to 0} sL(\sigma_i) = \lim_{s \to 0} \frac{s^2 \cdot g(x_i)L(\tau_{di})}{s^2 + s \cdot g(x_i)k_{Pi} + g(x_i)k_{Ii}} = 0$$

$$\lim_{t \to \infty} \dot{\sigma}_i = \lim_{s \to 0} sL(\dot{\sigma}_i) = \lim_{s \to 0} s^2 L(\sigma_i) = 0$$

Thus, it can be proved that the controller (33) can make the system state converge to the sliding manifold, when the system state deviates from the sliding manifold under the influence of disturbance and uncertainties.    ■

**Theorem 3.** For system (29), the controller

$$\tau_i = \tau_{i1} + \tau_{i2} \tag{35}$$

can make the system state error converge to $x_i = [1 \ \ 0 \ \ 0 \ \ 0 \ \ 0 \ \ 0 \ \ 0]^T$ under the influence of system uncertainties and external disturbance torque, where $\tau_{i1}$ is the inverse optimal controller (28), and $\tau_{i2}$ is the sliding mode robust controller (33).

**Proof.** It's shown in Theorem 2 that the controller $\tau_{i2}$ can make the system state converge to $\sigma_i = \dot{\sigma}_i = 0$ and stabilize on the sliding manifold when $\sigma_i \neq 0$.

When the system state slips on the sliding manifold, $\sigma_i = \dot{\sigma}_i = 0$, it can be derived from (34) that $\tau_{i2} = -\tau_{di}$. Substitute it into (29), then

$$\dot{x}_i = f(x_i) + g(x_i)\tau_i + g(x_i)\tau_{di}$$
$$= f(x_i) + g(x_i)\tau_{i1}$$

That is, the integral sliding mode controller can completely compensate the uncertainties and disturbances of the system, and make the system an ideal model as shown in (24). And according to Theorem 1, the inverse optimal controller $\tau_{i1}$ can converge the system error $x_i$ to the expected value for the ideal model (24).

Therefore, a robust controller $\tau_{i2}$ based on the inverse optimal controller $\tau_{i1}$ can effectively compensate for the influence of uncertainties and external disturbances, without affecting the stability of the original controller.    ■

## 5 Simulation Results

In this section, the effectiveness of the proposed sliding mode robust controller based on inverse optimal control is verified by numerical simulation.

Set the orbit of master satellite is a circular orbit, and the orbital elements is $[a \quad e \quad i \quad \Omega \quad \omega \quad M] = [7000\,\text{km} \quad 0 \quad 60° \quad 180° \quad 90° \quad 0°]$, which satisfies the simplified conditions for solving ground targets in (14). Therefore, the attitude of the master satellite and the fixed form of the antenna are no longer considered in this simulation, only considering that the antenna is looking downward. At the same time, it is assumed that the master has independent control system without cooperating with slaves, and its controller can guarantee the master to be stable in the desired attitude.

Since orbital control is not involved in this paper, it is assumed that each slave star can move in the desired relative orbit. The configuration parameters of the satellite formation are $[p \quad s \quad \theta_i \quad \alpha \quad l] = [550\,\text{m} \quad 100\,\text{m} \quad i \cdot 90° \quad 0° \quad 589\,\text{m}]$, where $i$ denotes the number of salve $(i = 1, 2, 3, 4)$. At the initial time, the body coordinates of each satellite coincide with the inertial coordinate, that is, the initial quaternion is $Q_i = [1 \quad 0 \quad 0 \quad 0]^T$, and the initial angular velocities of each satellite are $\omega_1 = [-0.07 \quad 0.05 \quad -0.03]^T \text{rad/s}$, $\omega_2 = [0.06 \quad -0.03 \quad 0.04]^T \text{rad/s}$, $\omega_3 = [-0.03 \quad 0.04 \quad 0.03]^T \text{rad/s}$ and $\omega_1 = [0.03 \quad -0.05 \quad 0.04]^T \text{rad/s}$ respectively.

In the distributed system, each slave satellite has the same specification and the same nominal inertia. Also, for the convenience of research, it is assumed that all slaves have the same inertia error

$$J_i = \begin{bmatrix} 7.5 & 0 & 0 \\ 0 & 8.5 & 0 \\ 0 & 0 & 8 \end{bmatrix} \text{kg} \cdot \text{m}^2, \delta J_i = \begin{bmatrix} 0.21 & 0.18 & 0.16 \\ 0.18 & -0.11 & 0.19 \\ 0.16 & 0.19 & 0.21 \end{bmatrix} \text{kg} \cdot \text{m}^2$$

The external disturbance torque of each slave satellite is

$$\tilde{\tau}_{di} = 10^{-4} \left[ \sin\left(\tfrac{\pi i}{10}t\right) \quad \cos\left(\tfrac{\pi i}{10}t\right) \quad \sin\left(\tfrac{\pi i}{10}t\right) \right]^T N \cdot m$$

In the distributed formation system, any satellite can communicate with the other, and the communication delay is

$$T = \begin{bmatrix} 0 & 1+0.5\cos(t) & 0.5+0.1\sin(t) & 1+0.1\sin(t) \\ 1+0.5\cos(t) & 0 & 1-0.1\sin(t) & 0.5+0.5\cos(t) \\ 0.5+0.1\sin(t) & 1-0.1\sin(t) & 0 & 1+0.5\sin(t) \\ 1+0.1\sin(t) & 0.5+0.5\cos(t) & 1+0.5\sin(t) & 0 \end{bmatrix} (s)$$

The parameters in the controller are $c_i = 1$, $\beta = 2$, $k_{1i} = 5$, $k_{2i} = 2$, $k_{3i} = 5$, $k_{Pi} = 10$, $k_{Ii} = 5$, $\gamma_i = 3$, $\alpha_i = 0.8$, $\alpha_j = 0.1$.

Since the state changes of each slave in distributed system are similar, this paper only the satellite 1 is taken as an example to illustrate the effect of the controller. And the control accuracy of other satellites will be given in the form of a list.

As can be seen from Figs. 1 and 2, the attitude quaternion error and the attitude angular velocity error can converge to the expected value within 80 s under the action of the attitude controller in this paper. However, due to the existence of external disturbance and the uncertainty of inertia, the state of the satellite will not strictly converge to expectations. Even so, the control precision is enough to satisfy the requirements of beam synchronization, in which the quaternion control precision is $1.98 \times 10^{-6}$ and the attitude angular velocity precision is $9.26 \times 10^{-7}$ rad/s.

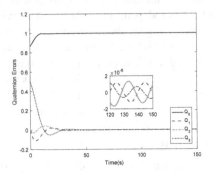

**Fig. 1.** Trajectories of quaternion errors

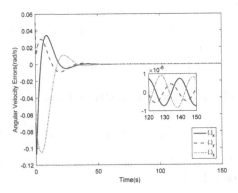

**Fig. 2.** Trajectories of angular velocity errors

Figures 3 and 4 are the actual attitude change curve of the satellite 1. It's shown in the picture that a large range of attitude adjustment appeared in the early simulation due to the large initial error. And after about 80 s, the attitude error is tended to be stable. The quaternion and attitude angular velocity of satellite appear to be stable to a certain value in the picture, but in fact, they have slow changes. The period of the attitude change is equal to the orbit period of the master, but the simulation time is far less than the orbit period. Hence, it is difficult to see the change of satellite in picture.

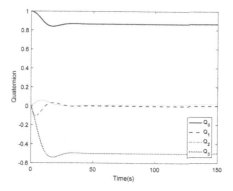

**Fig. 3.** Trajectories of quaternion

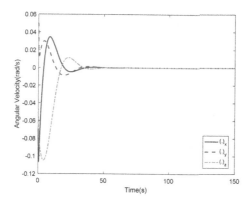

**Fig. 4.** Trajectories of angular velocity

The change curve of sliding manifold $\sigma_1$ of satellite is shown in Fig. 5. According to the properties of integral sliding mode, the state of satellite is on the sliding surface at the initial time, that is $\sigma_1 = 0$. However, the disturbance and the system uncertainty make $\dot{\sigma}_1 \neq 0$, so the system state departs from the sliding surface at the beginning of the simulation. Under the action of the sliding mode robust controller, $\sigma_1$ approaches the sliding mode surface again and oscillates with the sliding mode surface as the center.

The attitude control torque of the controller is shown in Figs. 6, 7 and 8. Due to the large initial attitude error, there is large control output in the early simulation. Since the nominal control system is a deterministic and undisturbed ideal model, the nominal system controller $\tau_{11}$ almost no longer outputs when the attitude of satellite reaches the desired value. But the robust controller $\tau_{12}$ continues to compensate the disturbance torque caused by external disturbances and system uncertainties to maintain the stability of the system. It can be seen from the picture that $\tau_{12}$ are of the same order of magnitude with the disturbance, which is consistent with the actual situation.

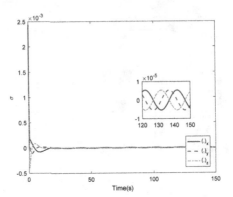

**Fig. 5.** The sliding manifold $\sigma_1$

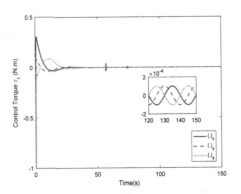

**Fig. 6.** The total control torque $\tau_1$

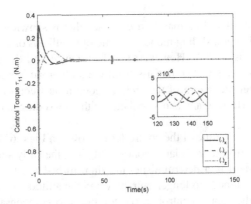

**Fig. 7.** The inverse optimal control torque $\tau_{11}$

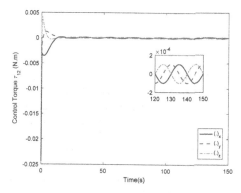

**Fig. 8.** The robust control torque $\tau_{12}$

The state error curves of the other satellites are no longer given in this paper, but only the steady-state errors shown in Table 1.

**Table 1.** The steady-state errors of slave satellites

| $i$ | Quaternion | Angular velocity (rad/s) |
|---|---|---|
| 1 | $1.98 \times 10^{-6}$ | $9.26 \times 10^{-7}$ |
| 2 | $3.26 \times 10^{-6}$ | $2.89 \times 10^{-6}$ |
| 3 | $3.35 \times 10^{-6}$ | $2.59 \times 10^{-6}$ |
| 4 | $3.10 \times 10^{-6}$ | $2.72 \times 10^{-6}$ |

# 6   Conclusion

The problem of beam synchronization in distributed SAR systems is studied in this paper. Two kinds of beam synchronization methods, Doppler guidance and beam pointing synchronization, are introduced. The desired attitudes of satellites are deduced by using Doppler guidance for master and beam pointing synchronization for slaves. Then an integral sliding mode robust control method based on inverse optimal control is proposed, which consists of inverse optimal controller and sliding mode robust controller. Simulation results show that the proposed integral sliding mode robust controller based on inverse optimal method can achieve beam synchronization under the influence of external disturbances and system uncertainty, and has high control accuracy and good beam synchronization effect.

**Acknowledgements.** This work is supported by the National Natural Science Foundation of China (91438202, 61473096, 61690212, 61333003), the Natural Science Foundation of Heilongjiang Province of China (Grant No. QC2012C082), the Open Fund of National Defense Key Discipline Laboratory of Micro-Spacecraft Technology (No. HIT.KLOF.MST.201701).

# References

1. Li, C.S., Wang, W.J., Wang, P.B., et al.: Current situation and development trends of spaceborne SAR technology. J. Electron. Inf. Technol. **38**(01), 229–240 (2016)
2. Huang, H.F., Liang, D.N.: Beam synchronization design strategies of noncooperative spaceborne bistatic radar. J. Astronaut. **26**(5), 606–611 (2005)
3. Knedlik, S., Loffeld, O., Gebhardt, U.: On position and attitude determination requirements for future bistatic SAR experiments. In: IEEE International Conference on Geoscience and Remote Sensing Symposium (IGARSS), pp. 1216–1219 (2006)
4. D'Errico, M., Moccia, A.: Attitude and antenna pointing design of bistatic radar formations. IEEE Trans. Aerosp. Electron. Syst. **39**(3), 949–960 (2003)
5. He, D.L., Cao, X.B.: Beam synchronization strategy for distributed InSAR satellites formation. J. Astronaut. **30**(5), 2031–2036 (2009)
6. Huai, C., Wang, W.Y.: Attitude strategy of beam synchronization for InSAR satellites formation. Aerosp. Shanghai **32**(2), 22–27 (2015)
7. Zhang, J.X., Zhang, Z.G., Wu, B.L.: Decentralized adaptive sliding mode control for beam synchronization of tethered InSAR system. Acta Astronaut. **127**, 57–66 (2016)
8. Pukdeboon, C.: Anti-disturbance inverse optimal control for spacecraft position and attitude maneuvers with input saturation. Adv. Mech. Eng. **8**(5) (2016)
9. Pukdeboon, C., Kumam, P.: Robust optimal sliding mode control for spacecraft position and attitude maneuvers. Aerosp. Sci. Technol. **43**, 329–342 (2015)
10. Sepulchre, D.R., Janković, D.M., Kokotović, P.V.: Constructive Nonlinear Control. Springer, London (1997). https://doi.org/10.1007/978-1-4471-0967-9
11. Yuri, S., Mohammed, T., Franck, P.: A novel adaptive-gain super-twisting sliding mode controller: methodology and application. Automatica **48**(5) (2012)

# Hyper-spectral Images Classification Based on 3D Convolution Neural Networks for Remote Sensing

Zhiming Mei$^{(\boxtimes)}$, Long Wang, and Cen Guo

ShanghaiTech University, Shanghai, China
`18047180798@163.com`

**Abstract.** With the rapid development of hyper-spectral imaging techniques, hyper-spectral image classification has been applied to many tasks such as monitoring, astronomy and substance exploration. Hyper-spectral Images with rich spatial and spectral content is more difficult to be classified than common images with RGB channels. Many deep learning methods have ignored the context between spectral features when extracting spectral-spatial features of hyper-spectral images. So we implemented a 3D Convolution Neural Network model to extract correlated and effective features and improve the performance for Hyper-spectral Images classification. The hyper-spectral data set we use is the University of Pavia which has less training samples. So we exploited dropout and cross validation methods in the training process to avoid over fitting and we have extended the training samples by some transformation. The results of our experiments have shown that our model can generally get better results than some of the state-of-the-art methods.

**Keywords:** Hyper-spectral image classification ·
Convolution Neural Network · Remote sensing · Deep learning

## 1 Introduction

Hyper-spectral image analysis has been widely used in a variety of fields, such as agriculture, monitoring, astronomy and substance exploration. In the majority of these fields, hyper-spectral image classification was used to accelerate and improve the hyper-spectral image analysis and process. Hence, hyper-spectral image classification is recently a hot research direction in remote sensing. Hyper-spectral Image has more than 200 spectral-spatial channels, which can provide more information for us to analyze the different objects in it. With the advance of the spectral sensor technology, the spatial resolution of hyper-spectral image was higher than before, which made it possible to catch little spatial objects and improve hyper-spectral image classification accuracy.

The existing approaches for hyper-spectral image classification such as support vector machine (SVM) [1] and K nearest neighbor classifiers can not deal

© Springer Nature Singapore Pte Ltd. 2019
Q. Yu (Ed.): SINC 2018, CCIS 972, pp. 205–214, 2019.
https://doi.org/10.1007/978-981-13-5937-8_21

well with the high dimension disaster. And Krishnapuram et al. [2] proposed an approach to reduce the dimension and applied multinomial logistic regression to improve image classification performance. However, these methods only consider how to reduce the dimension of the spectral features but ignore the noise of the maps. Then a variety of models based on deep features of the spectral have been proposed. These approaches also worked with spatial context information to produce pixel-wise classifiers. The extended morphological profiles (EMP) [3], multiple kernels learning (MKL) [4] and sparse representation (SR) [5] exploit both spectral and spatial information to improve the accuracy of hyper-spectral image classification. Convolution Neural Network has made a great breakthrough in conventional image feature extraction and classification. Then many methods have been proposed to apply Convolution Neural Network to Hyper-spectral Image Classification, some of these Convolution Neural Network are very famous such as AlexNet [6], GoogleNet [7], ResNet [8] and VGGNet [9]. Although these Convolution Neural Network have achieved great success in common image classification, they would not work the same well on hyper-spectral images. Hyper-spectral image classification requires extracting both spectral and spatial features at the same time. What's more, many feature layers have close relationship with each other [10], which should be taken into consideration by the model.

In our paper, we designed a 3D Convolution Neural Network (3D CNN) model for effective spectral and spatial features extraction and hyper-spectral image classification. Our model has extracted the spectral, spatial and spectral-spatial features simultaneously at each layer, which leads to better classification performance. Generally, the training images in computer vision tasks are very vast because a deep learning model always needs abundant training samples. So, hyper-spectral images with more complex data structure and limited image samples are difficult to be classified by deep learning approaches. We used a sample enhanced method to expand the training datasets when only a limited number of training samples are available in each class. The main contribution of this paper is that we extract deep and correlated spectral-spatial features for hyper-spectral image classification and exploit some methods to avoid the model getting into the trouble of over-fitting.

The rest of this paper are organized as follows: Introduce feature extraction based on Convolution Neural Network (CNN) in Sect. 2. The experiment results are shown in Sect. 3. The last part of the paper is conclusion and expectation.

## 2    CNN in Hyper-spectral Images Classification

**Related Works.** The key point in image classification and pattern recognition is the valid features which are extracted from the original images through a series of mapping. Conventional feature extraction methods are designed manually and they can extract effective features which may be as good as human. However, deep learning method aimed to learn an end-to-end model which extracting features automatically. Deep learning methods use a network as the tool to extract features and map these features to its labels. Generally the network has at least three layers which are able to learn complicated data. Although the architecture of deep convolution neural network is simple, the parameters are very vast. These parameters can be learned by some convex optimization and machine learning methods.

Convolution neural network processes input data such as image, voice and text by multiple layers, which would extract low level features in the front layers and correspond high level at the back of the network. So the high level features which are abstract and invariant are mapped from the low level features. The weights in the network are usually initialized randomly and will be assigned iteratively by the Stochastic Gradient Descent (SGD) algorithm. These characteristics of Convolution neural network make it an end-to-end learning approach, which has an advantage over conventional machine learning methods in a variety of applications such as image classification and object detection. Convolution neural network usually includes convolution layers, pooling layers and fully connection layers as shown in Fig. 1. Convolution Neural Network was first proposed by Le-Cun et al. [11,12] in 1996. The CNN model has achieved a great performance in hand-written digit recognition with the Stochastic Gradient Descent (SGD) and the back-propagation (BP) algorithm. However, this method was not widely used by academic and industrial circles in that time period. With the development of Internet and big data, CNN has been proposed again and has been improved by the latest deep learning techniques. Researchers proposed the neural network method inspired by the biological visual systems because it can accomplish classification, detection and recognition tasks efficiently and with high quality.

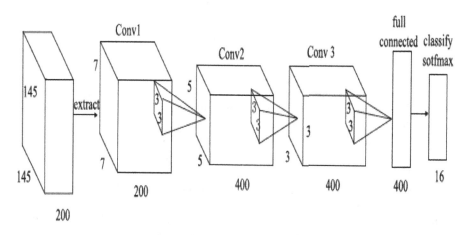

**Fig. 1.** The construct of Convolution Neural Network sample.

There are two special aspects in the architecture of CNN, namely local connection and shared weights. CNN exploit the local correlation using local connectivity between the neurons of the near layers. Some connections between neurons in CNN are replicated across the entire layer, which share the same weights and biases. Using these two special aspects CNN can extract deep effective features in the computer vision tasks. The architecture of 3D CNN when extracting features in hyper-spectral images is shown in Fig. 2.

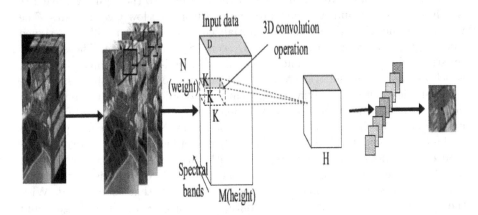

**Fig. 2.** Architecture of 3D CNN with spectral features extraction of hyper-spectral image.

Generally a 2D CNN layer includes a convolution layer and a pooling layer. The value of a nerve cell node at position $(x, y)$ of the $jth$ feature map in the $ith$ layer is denoted in Formula (1).

$$v_{ij}^{xy} = g(b_{ij} + \sum_m \sum_{p=0}^{P_i-1} \sum_{q=0}^{Q_i-1} w_{ijm}^{pq} v_{(i-1)m}^{(x+p)(y+q)}) \tag{1}$$

where $m$ is the number of feature maps in the $(i-1)$th layer connected to the current $(jth)$ feature map, $w_{ijm}^{pq}$ is the weight of position $(p, q)$ connected to the $m$th feature map, $P_i$ and $Q_i$ are the height and the width of the spatial convolution kernel, and $b_{ij}$ is the bias of the $jth$ feature map in the $ith$ layer. Pooling is carried out at the end of each layer which combines a small $n \times n$ patch of the convolution layer.

Recently many 3D CNN approaches have been proposed to extract the spatial and spectral features of hyper-spectral data simultaneously [13–17]. These methods have achieved great performance on the classification of the hyperspectral images based on the similar theory and architecture.

## 2.1 The Proposed 3D CNN

Based on the above theory we get that CNN extracts spectral features and the 2D CNN extracts the local spatial features of each pixel. We designed a 3D

CNN model to learn both spatial and spectral features of hyper-spectral images. Figures 3 and 4 show spatial features and both spatial and spectral features respectively.

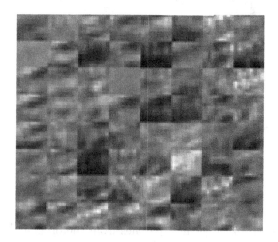

**Fig. 3.** The spatial features after three convolution layers on asphalt sample

The value of a nerve cell node at position $(x, y, z)$ of the $jth$ feature map in the $ith$ layer is denoted in Formulas (2) and (3).

$$z = b_{ij} + \sum_m \sum_{p=0}^{P_i-1} \sum_{q=0}^{Q_i-1} \sum_{r=0}^{R_i-1} w_{ijm}^{pqr} v_{(i-1)m}^{(x+p)(y+q)(z+r)} \tag{2}$$

$$v_{ij}^{xyz} = g(z) \tag{3}$$

where $m$ is the number of feature maps in the $(i-1)$th layer connected to the current $(jth)$ feature map, $P_i$ and $Q_i$ are the height and the width of the spatial convolution kernel. $R_i$ is the size of the kernel along toward spectral dimension, $w_{ijm}^{pqr}$ is the value of position $(p, q, r)$ connected to the $m$th feature map, and $b_{ij}$ is the bias of the $j$th feature map in the $i$th layer.

Although CNN has just a few layers, it needs to train a great number of weights. These weights are assigned randomly at the beginning which will cause the loss function to be caught in a local minimum. Then the training is not end up with the optimal case. In order to learn proper weights, a mass of samples are required in the training process. In fact the samples in the training data set are obtained by manually labeling a small number of pixels in an image. So obtaining enough training samples is expensive and time consuming. In remote sensing area the number of available training images is usually limited, which is a bottleneck in hyper-spectral images classification. To address this problem, we have extended the training samples by a series of transformation.

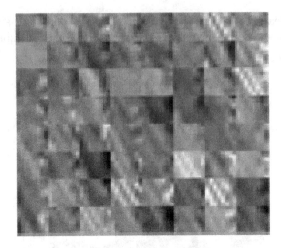

**Fig. 4.** Spatial-spectral features after three convolution layers on asphalt sample.

Our model is aimed to get new patches from the original training samples. While we processing the images we found that objects of the same class show different characteristics in different location. Because light is very complex in large scene. Hence we can generate a patch by multiplying a random factor to a training sample and adding random noise. What's more we can generate a patch from two original patches with proper ratios. These transformation methods can generate plentiful independent identically distributed samples with the original samples, which is very useful to the training step of the hyper-spectral images classification. The transformation Formulas are (4) and (5).

$$y_g = \mu_o x_o + \nu n \tag{4}$$

$$y_m = \frac{\theta_i x_i + \theta_j x_j}{\theta_i + \theta_j} + \vartheta n \tag{5}$$

New samples yn is obtained by multiplying a random factor and adding random noise to a training samples xm, because of the principle of objects of the same class in different locations are affected by different radiation. Hyperspectral imaging usually contains a large scene and new samples can be obtained by combination with different spatial patches with the same spectral patches. Consequently, the original training samples and the generated samples are used together as training samples to get the proper weights in the network. We have intended to use Generative Adversarial Network (GAN) to generate samples from the original samples. However, that work is still in progress. In a word, Changing radiation and mixture-based methods are simple yet effective ways. The above mentioned is the theory of our 3D CNN model. The architecture and parameters of our model as well as the datasets are presented minutely in the next section.

# 3   The Experiment Results

## 3.1   Data Set

The hyper-spectral data we use is an urban site over the city of Pavia, Italy which is mainly the area of university of Pavia. With 610 pixels × 340 pixels and 115 bands in the range of $[0.43, 0.86]um$, this hyper-spectral image was widely used and acquired by a sensor known as the Reflective Optics System Imaging Spectrometer over the city of Pavia, Italy. The high spatial resolution of 1.3 m/pixel aims to avoid a high percentage of mixed pixels. In the experiment, noisy bands have been removed and the remaining 103 channels were used for classification. Nine land-cover classes were selected, which are shown in Fig. 5 and the number of samples for each class are given in Table 1 During the image process, we split the labeled samples into two subsets namely training sets and test sets. We used 90% of the training samples to learn weights and biases of each neuron and the remaining 10% of the training samples was used to guide the design of proper architectures. The classification results of the remaining 10% training samples namely the validation sets is an important performance index of the network. We used the test set to assess the final classification performance.

 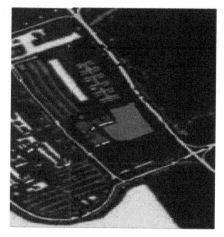

**Fig. 5.** University of Pavia data set (Left) False color composite (*bands* 10, 27, 46) and (right) representing nine land-cover classes. (Color figure online)

In our design process, we firstly extracted the deep spectral features of the hyper-spectral images. Then we test this features and changed our network parameters to investigate the effectiveness of the deep spectral and spatial features. At last we extended the samples and start to train our model.

**Table 1.** The classes of the university of Pavia data sets

| Class | | Samples | |
|---|---|---|---|
| No. | Name | Train | Test |
| 1 | Asphalt | 548 | 5472 |
| 2 | Meadows | 540 | 13750 |
| 3 | Gravel | 392 | 1331 |
| 4 | Trees | 542 | 2573 |
| 5 | Metal sheets | 256 | 1122 |
| 6 | Bare soil | 532 | 4572 |
| 7 | Bitumen | 375 | 981 |
| 8 | Bricks | 514 | 3363 |
| 9 | Shadow | 231 | 776 |
| Total | | 3930 | 33940 |

## 3.2   Model Parameters

After determining the architecture of our 3D Convolution Neural Network, we used $27 \times 27 \times 103$ neighbors of each pixel as the input 3D images. The input images are normalized into $[-0.5, 0.5]$ and the detailed information of the parameters are given in Table 2. Because of the quantitative comparison, we adopt the objective metrics, including the overall accuracy (OA), Average accuracy (AA) and k coefficient and class accuracies (CA), to evaluate the classification performance.

**Table 2.** The structure parameters of the 3D CNN.

| No. | Convolution | ReLU | Pooling | Dropout |
|---|---|---|---|---|
| 1 | $3 \times 3 \times 64 \times 64$ | Yes | $2 \times 2$ | no |
| 2 | $5 \times 5 \times 64 \times 128$ | Yes | $2 \times 2$ | 50% |
| 3 | $5 \times 5 \times 64 \times 256$ | Yes | No | 50% |

From the class-by-class accuracies shown in Table 3, it can be seen that the introduced 3D CNN method has better performance in classifying the majority of classes. The results of OA, AA and K indexes of 3D CNN have shown that our model outperformed the compared approaches [15–17], which owed to the spectral and spatial features extracted from the hyper-spectral images.

**Table 3.** Result comparison, all the accuracies are in percentage

| Class | SVM | RBF | MFL | 2D CNN | 3D CNN(LR) | R3DCNN | 3DCNN |
|---|---|---|---|---|---|---|---|
| 1 | 93.15 | 94.35 | 100 | 91.65 | 99.37 | 100 | 99.37 |
| 2 | 93.57 | 96.87 | 99.93 | 99.45 | 99.52 | 100 | 99.52 |
| 3 | 97.56 | 94.76 | 93.64 | 92.09 | 99.69 | 100 | 99.69 |
| 4 | 96.93 | 98.72 | 98.59 | 87.26 | 99.73 | 99.89 | 99.73 |
| 5 | 98.23 | 99.02 | 99.50 | 91.05 | 99.95 | 100 | 99.95 |
| 6 | 92.25 | 94.85 | 99.67 | 98.61 | 99.96 | 100 | 99.96 |
| 7 | 94.82 | 100.00 | 99.75 | 90.72 | 100.00 | 100 | 100.00 |
| 8 | 95.50 | 96.63 | 99.10 | 93.57 | 99.65 | 100 | 99.65 |
| 9 | 98.11 | 99.33 | 100 | 86.62 | 99.58 | 98.94 | 99.58 |
| OA | 96.05 | 97.72 | 99.42 | 95.46 | 99.54 | 99.97 | 99.54 |
| AA | 95.73 | 97.17 | 98.91 | 98.78 | 99.66 | 99.87 | 99.66 |
| $\kappa$ | 95.33 | 95.21 | 96.53 | 94.25 | 99.41 |  | 99.41 |

## 4   Conclusion and Expectation

The fine spatial resolution of recently operated sensors makes the analysis of small spatial structures in images possible. The aforementioned advances make the hyper-spectral data a useful tool for a wide variety of applications such as agriculture, monitoring, astronomy and substance exploration. In this paper, we used a 3D CNN to extract deep features of the hyper-spectral images and exploit it to complete the classification. Thus we built an accurate pixel-wise classifier for remote sensing images. This method has been proposed by some papers before but we designed different parameters and structures from them. The results of our experiments have shown that our model can obtain better performance in some indexes. In addition, many latest deep learning methods have not been reproduced in the classification of hyper-spectral images. In the future, we will use the Generative Adversarial Networks to extend the training samples and bring latest deep learning methods to this task.

## References

1. Scholkopf, B., Smola, A.J.: Learning With Kernels: Support Vector Machines, Regularization, Optimization, and Beyond. MIT Press, Cambridge (2001)
2. Krishnapuram, B., Carin, L., Figueiredo, M.A.T., Hartemink, A.J.: Sparse multinomial logistic regression: fast algorithms and generalization bounds. IEEE Trans. Pattern Anal. Mach. Intell. **27**(6), 957–968 (2005)
3. Benediktsson, J.A., Palmason, J.A., Sveinsson, J.R.: Classification of hyperspectral data from urban areas based on extended morphological profiles. IEEE Trans. Geosci. Remote Sens. **43**(3), 480–491 (2005)

4. Camps-Valls, G., Gomez-Chova, L., Muoz-Mar, J., Vila-Francs, J.: Composite kernels for hyperspectral image classification. IEEE Geosci. Remote Sens. Lett. **3**(1), 93–97 (2006)
5. Chen, Y., Nasrabadi, N.M., Tran, T.D.: Hyperspectral image classification using dictionary based sparse representation. IEEE Trans. Geosci. Remote Sens. **49**(10), 3973–3985 (2011)
6. Krizhevsky, A., Sutskever, I., Hinton, G.E.: ImageNet classification with deep convolutional neural networks. In: Proceedings Advances in Neural Information Processing Systems, pp. 1907–1105 (2012)
7. Szegedy, C., et al.: Going deeper with convolutions. In: Proceedings IEEE Conference Computer Vision and Pattern Recognition, pp. 1–9, June 2015
8. He, K., Zhang, X., Ren, S., Sun, J.: Deep residual learning for image recognition. In: Proceedings IEEE Conference Computer Vision and Pattern Recognition, pp. 770–778, June 2016
9. Simonyan, K., Zisserman, A.: Very deep convolutional networks for large-scale image recognition. https://arxiv.org/abs/1409.1556 (2014)
10. Li, J., et al.: Multiple feature learning for hyperspectral image classification. IEEE Trans. Geosci. Remote Sens. **53**(3), 1592–1606 (2015)
11. Le Cun, Y., et al.: Handwritten digit recognition with a backpropagation network. In: Proceedings Advances in Neural Information Processing Systems, pp. 396–404 (1990)
12. LeCun, Y., et al.: Backpropagation applied to handwritten zip code recognition. Neural Comput. **1**(4), 541–551 (1989)
13. Li, Y., Zhang, H., Shen, Q.: Spectral-spatial classification of hyperspectral imagery with 3D convolutional neural network. Remote Sens. **9**(1), 67 (2017)
14. Lee, H., Kwon, H.: Going deeper with contextual cnn for hyperspectral image classification. IEEE Trans. Image Process. **26**(10), 4843–4855 (2016)
15. Li, J., Plaza, A., Jia, X., Bioucas-Dias, J.M.: A discontinuity preserving relaxation scheme for spectral-spatial Hyperspectral image classification. IEEE J. Sel. Topics Appl. Earth Obs. Remote Sens. **9**(2), 625–639 (2016)
16. Chen, Y., Jiang, H., Li, C., et al.: Deep feature extraction and classification of hyperspectral images based on convolutional neural networks. IEEE Trans. Geosci. Remote Sens. **54**(10), 6232–6251 (2016)
17. Yang, X., Ye, Y., Li, X., et al.: Hyperspectral image classification with deep learning models. IEEE Trans. Geosci. Remote Sens. **PP**(99), 1–16 (2018)

# A Multi-sensor Target Recognition Information Fusion Approach Based on Improved Evidence Reasoning Rule

Xiaohan Zhang[1(✉)], Libo Yao[1], and Xiaohui Liu[2]

[1] Institute of Information Fusion of Naval
Aeronautical University, Yantai, China
15584175041@163.com, yirujiwang0511@gmail.com
[2] No. 91039 Navy of PLA, Beijing, China
lxh-3996@163.com

**Abstract.** The Evidence Reasoning (ER) rule extends traditional Dempster-Shafer evidence theory by establishing a new rule to combine multiple pieces of independent evidence with importance and reliability weights. The importance and reliability weight of an evidence source is usually decided by fusion system designers which is subjective. Aiming at solving the evaluation problem of evidence importance and reliability weight in ER rule, a new method is proposed in this paper under the application background of multi-sensor marine target recognition information fusion. The importance weight of evidence source is calculated based on the accuracy of sensor recognition in history observation, while the reliability weight is calculated based on the improved normalized angle distance which measures the conflicting among pieces of evidence. Then the pieces of weighted evidence are combined under ER rule to draw recognition fusion conclusion. The proposed approach improves the ER rule by giving an objective method to measure the importance and reliability weight of evidence. Simulation experiments are conducted, demonstrating that this approach can combine conflicting evidence more effectively. Moreover, compared with other methods, the improved ER rule shares good convergence performance and has higher computational efficiency, which is beneficial for engineering implementation.

**Keywords:** Evidence theory · Evidence Reasoning rule · Target recognition · Information fusion · Evidence weight

## 1 Introduction

In the fields of ocean targets surveillance, multi-sensors including pulse radar, sonar, infrared detector, photoelectric detector, spectrograph and SAR on satellite and plane platforms are widely used [1]. Considering that each sensor could be affected by its working condition, noises and outside interference during the observation, obtained information may be uncertain. Joint multi-sensor observation can obtain multi-dimensional information of targets from different levels and different aspects, which shares great advantages compared with single sensor observation.

© Springer Nature Singapore Pte Ltd. 2019
Q. Yu (Ed.): SINC 2018, CCIS 972, pp. 215–228, 2019.
https://doi.org/10.1007/978-981-13-5937-8_22

Dempster-Shafer evidence theory [2] is an effective way for multi-sensor recognition information fusion. In D-S evidence theory, each sensor is seen as one source of evidence, and pieces of evidence are combined through the Dempster's rule to get the fusion result [3]. It has been widely used in practice. Under the background of multi-sensor target recognition, this paper mainly studies the information fusion method base on D-S evidence theory. Firstly, in Sect. 2, the principle and deficiency of D-S evidence theory are analyzed, and the improvement schemes of scholars are reviewed. Then the concept of importance and reliability of evidence source in ER rule is introduced in Sect. 3. Next the practical significance of these two kinds of weights is analyzed and objective measure method is given. After these pretreatments, pieces of evidence are combined based on ER rules. Finally, the simulation experiment is carried out to verify the effectiveness of the proposed method in Sect. 5.

## 2  D-S Evidence Theory

### 2.1  Dempster's Rule

The D-S evidence theory scheme is based on a frame of discernment composed of a set of propositions that are mutually exclusive and collectively exhaustive. It uses the Basic Probability Assignment (BPA) instead of probability value of Bayes system as measure function. The BPA functions from different two or more pieces of evidence are fused under the Dempster's rule. Suppose $U = \{U_1, U_2, \cdots, U_N\}$ is a set of mutually exclusive and collectively exhaustive propositions, U is referred to as a frame of discernment, $U_i \cap U_j = \phi$, $i, j \in \{1, 2, \cdots, N\}$ and $i \neq j$. Then BPA function m: $2^U \to [0, 1]$ satisfies:

(1)  $m(\phi) = 0$
(2)  $\sum_{A \in U} m(A) = 1$

For $\forall A \subset U$, when $m(A) \neq 0$, A is referred to as a focal element, and $m(A)$ is referred to as basic probability of focal element $A$, which indicates the level of support for $A$ in this piece of evidence.

Two pieces of independent evidence represented by two BPAs: $m_1$ and $m_2$ with focal elements $B_i$ and $C_j$, can be combined by Dempster's combination rule:

$$m(A) = m_1 \oplus m_2 = \begin{cases} \frac{\sum_{B_i \cap C_j = A} m_1(B_i) m_2(C_j)}{1-K}, \forall A \in U, A \neq \phi \\ 0, A = \phi \end{cases} \quad (1)$$

$$K = \sum_{B_i \cap C_j = \Phi} m_1(B_i) m_2(C_j) \quad (2)$$

K is referred to as conflict index, and K should satisfy: $K \in (0, 1)$, for when $K = 0$ or 1, the two pieces of evidence could not be combined. Besides, the combination result $m(A)$ is also a BPA function.

## 2.2    Shafer's Rule

When a piece of evidence cannot be considered as fully credible, Shafer proposed a method to discount the evidence [5]. Suppose that there is only $1 - \alpha$ confidence level for the whole evidence, where $\alpha \in [0, 1]$ and $\alpha$ is called the discount rate. The Shafer's method is as follows:

$$\begin{cases} m^{\alpha}(A) = (1 - \alpha)m(A), \forall A \in U, A \neq \phi \\ m^{\alpha}(U) = (1 - \alpha)m(U) + \alpha \end{cases} \tag{3}$$

The essence of this method is to discount the evidence with certainty rate and then assign the remaining discount rate to the entire recognition framework, which is unknown. Then the discounted evidence is combined according to the Dempster's rules.

## 2.3    Inadequacy of D-S Evidence Theory

Although D-S evidence theory has been widely used in decision-level fusion, there may be some unreasonable results when the conflicting among evidence is very sharp. The inadequacy of D-S evidence theory are as follows:

(1)  Zadeh Paradox [6]

Suppose $U = \{A, B, C\}$ and there are 2 pieces of evidence $m_1$ and $m_2$. The value of BPA for evidence and the combination result is shown in Table 1.

**Table 1.**  BPA of evidence and the combination result

| Evidence | $A$ | $B$ | $C$ |
|---|---|---|---|
| $m_1$ | 0.99 | 0.01 | 0 |
| $m_2$ | 0 | 0.01 | 0.99 |
| $m_2 \oplus m_2$ | 0 | 1 | 0 |

As is shown, both $m_1$ and $m_2$ give little support for B. But after combination, the fusion result gives a full support for B. Obviously it is unreasonable.

(2)  Paradox caused by minor disturbance

Taking the example in (1) and making a minor adjustment, The BPA of rules and the combination result is shown in Table 2.

**Table 2.**  BPA of evidence and the combination result

| Evidence | $A$ | $B$ | $C$ |
|---|---|---|---|
| $m_1$ | 0.98 | 0.01 | 0.01 |
| $m_2$ | 0.01 | 0.01 | 0.98 |
| $m_2 \oplus m_2$ | 0.4975 | 0.005 | 0.4975 |

There are only minor adjustments compared with the previous example, but the result is completely different [7].

(3) Paradox caused by the same evidence

When all pieces of evidence are the same, the combination result should not change. However, the Dempster rule takes it for granted that there are conflicts among evidence [8]. So the fusion result changes. For example (Table 3):

**Table 3.** BPA of evidence and the combination result

| Evidence | A | B | C |
|---|---|---|---|
| $m_1$ | 0.5 | 0.3 | 0.2 |
| $m_2$ | 0.5 | 0.3 | 0.2 |
| $m_2 \oplus m_2$ | 0.6579 | 0.2368 | 0.1053 |

To solve the existing problems of D-S evidence theory, scholars have proposed various solutions. Some aimed at improving fusion rules. For example, Yanger [9] proposed to assign conflict information to unknown domains to solve the Zadeh Paradox, but it increased the uncertainty of the fusion result. Sun [10] further introduced the concept of evidence credibility. A new synthesis formula was proposed, which made the result of synthesis of evidence with different conflict degree more ideal. Some scholars were devoted to amending the sources of evidence. For example, Murphy [11] proposed to replace the original evidence by generating new evidence by averaging the different evidences to participate in the combination. Guan [12] proposed that the conflicting evidence should be combined after being additively synthesized to eliminate the conflict. Han Deqiang proposed to use variance of evidence continuously adjusting weight of evidence when recursively combining evidences; Lin, Deng, Song, Wang et al. [13–16] put forward a method to measure evidence conflicts and calculate evidence preprocessing by calculating distance between evidence. Others have synthesized the above two ideas. Firstly, the sources of evidence are preprocessed, and then the fusion rules are improved to complete the evidence fusion, including the evidence synthesis method based on the credibility of evidence proposed by Li [17]. Among them, the Evidential Reasoning Rule (ER) proposed by Yang [4] is the representative of such ideas. Next section introduces the fundamentals of ER rules.

## 3    Evidence Reasoning Rule

### 3.1    ER Rule

The ER rule is a new evidence combination rule proposed by Yang in 2013. It uses a new weighted belief distribution with reliability (WBDR) method which takes and importance and reliability into account in evidence pretreatment.

Firstly, Yang put forward the concept of the importance and reliability of evidence. He thought that on discount of evidence, the importance and the reliability should be separated. The importance of evidence reflects the degree of influence of the evidence on the decision-making result, and the reliability reflects the working status of evidence source. Evidence of high importance and reliable working conditions should have a greater impact on the outcome of the decision. The WBDR method is defined as follows.

Let the weights of importance and reliability of evidence $m_i$ be $\varpi_i$ and $r_i(\varpi_i, r_i \in [0, 1])$ respectively. And $m_i$ is discounted with WBDR as formula (4) shown:

$$\widehat{m}_{A,i} = \widehat{m}_i(A) = \begin{cases} c_i m_{A,i}, & A \subset U \\ 1 - c_i, & A = \Omega \end{cases} \tag{4}$$

Here $c_i = \varpi_i/(1 + \varpi_i - r_i)$. We should pay attention to that $1 - c_i$ is not assigned to the identification frame U, which means unknown domain, instead it is assigned to the frame power set $\Omega = 2^U$, which means unallocated reliability values influenced by weights limit of $m_i$. It can be reassigned to any subset of the framework, its role is reflected in the combination with other evidence. The evidence is then synthesized using the following rules:

$$\widehat{m}_1 \oplus \widehat{m}_2(A) = \begin{cases} \dfrac{\widehat{m}(A)}{\sum_{D \subset \Theta, D \neq \Phi} \widehat{m}(D)} \\ 0, A = \phi \end{cases} \tag{5}$$

$$\begin{cases} \widehat{m}(A) = \sum_{B \cap C = A} \widehat{m}_{B,1} \widehat{m}_{C,2} + \widehat{m}_{A,1} \widehat{m}_{\Omega,2} + \widehat{m}_{A,2} \widehat{m}_{\Omega,1} \\ \widehat{m}(\Omega) = \widehat{m}_{\Omega,1} \widehat{m}_{\Omega,2} = (1 - c_1)(1 - c_2) \end{cases} \tag{6}$$

It is proved that the ER rule satisfies the commutative law and the combined law and the Dempster's rule becomes a special case of the ER rule when the weight of all the evidences and the reliability weights are all 1. At present, the rule has been widely used in fault diagnosis, multi-attribute decision-making and other fields.

## 3.2   Analysis on ER Rule

The ER rule is an extension of the ER algorithm [18], from the Bayesian trust function to the general trust function. At its core lies the treatment of the weight of evidence sources. Similar to the evidence discount, the evidence is multiplied by the final weight proportionally, but the remaining reliability is assigned to subset of the power set in the evidence combination instead of being assigned to the global unknown domain. While defining the weight of evidence, although both the importance and reliability of evidence are taken into consideration, the two are not equivalently treated. Instead, the reliability weight is based on the importance weight to adjust the overall weight. For example, evidence of higher importance may further increase its weight if its reliability weight is high. On the other hand, when its reliability weight is low and at extreme case being zero, even its importance weight is high to 1, the conclusion of this evidence source should be not credible at all. But in ER rule, the final weight $c_i = \varpi_i/1 + \varpi_i$. $c_i$ can be up to 0.5 at most. It will still have some impact on the results. Therefore, a new method of weight calculation is proposed in reference [19], which makes the final weight coefficient $c_i' = \varpi_i r_i$, being more reasonable. However, it failed to consider the specific impact of evidence on the basis of importance and reliability, nor does it give a feasible method of calculating the weight of evidence and the weight of reliability.

## 4   Framework of Proposed Method

### 4.1   Weight of Importance

The importance of evidence reflects the objective nature of the evidence source [20, 21]. In the fusion of target recognition, when we consider a type of sensor being important, its performance should be stable with high accuracy in previous observation. Therefore, the importance of evidence source should come from its historical identification data. Under the condition of stable observation conditions and consistent recognition algorithm, the importance of the source of evidence can be measured by using the correct rate of historical recognition data. However, in D-S evidence theory, the existence of ambiguous and indefinite information is allowed. For example, an evidence source identifies the target A as A or B, and the correct information may be implicit in uncertain information.

Suppose the total number of observations in history is $M$ times. Each sensor recognition result may be any one of the power sets $\Omega = 2^U$. Assuming that the number of recognition results including one basic event is $M_1$ times, the number of results including two basic events is $M_2$ times, and so on, the number of results including all basic events, or no conclusion being reached, is $M_N$. Apparently $\sum_{i=1}^{N} M_i = M$. Of the $M_1$-times recognition results with the single-element subset, it is assumed that the number of correct recognitions is $C_1$ times. When number of basic events contained in the recognition result $i \geq 2$, the number of times that the real target category contained in recognition result is assumed as $C_i$ respectively. Sensor historical observation recognition accuracy is defined as:

$$\rho = \frac{\sum_{i=1}^{N} [\exp(-(i-1)) \cdot C_i]}{M} \tag{7}$$

Here, molecules represent the weighted accumulation of "correct" recognition from previous observations. When i = 1, the weight of $C_1$ is 1; as i increases, the number of uncertain fuzzy information increases and the correct information contained therein decreases, so the weight of $C_i$ also decreases and approaches 0. $\rho$ can characterize the importance of evidence. The higher $\rho$ is, the more important the evidence is.

The evidence $m_i$ is processed by $\rho$ in formula (8):

$$\tilde{m}_{B_a,i} = \tilde{m}_i(B_a) = \begin{cases} \rho_i m_{B_a,i}, B_a \subset U \\ 1 - \sum \rho_i m_{B_a,i}, B_a = \Omega \end{cases} \tag{8}$$

$1 - \sum \rho_i m_{B_a,i}$ represents uncertain, or even possibly wrong information and it is assigned to the frame power set $\Omega = 2^U$, which can be reallocated to any subset of the framework in subsequent evidence combinations. For the fusion result of this recognition, it should be put into the historical data to form feedback and correcting the accuracy $\rho$ of evidence source constantly.

## 4.2  Weight of Reliability

The reliability of the evidence depends on many factors, including the working state of the sensor, noise in the measurement, enemy interference, and identification algorithms [22]. We cannot directly use a particular indicator to prove the reliability of evidence, but the reliability of evidence is reflected in the recognition results, which can be interpreted as the degree of conflict between pieces of evidence. The theory of evidence follows essentially the principle of minority obedience. For a small number of evidence sources that obviously conflict with most of the evidence, they should be considered as not stable enough in measurement and less reliable, and their weight should be appropriately reduced, which is in favor of the convergence of the evidence combination and promptly draws the correct conclusion.

Firstly we give an analyst on conflict of evidence. Compared with the exact probability under the Bayesian Probability System, the BPA function itself allows uncertainties, unknown or even wrong information under the D-S theory framework. The conflicting evidence comes from the following points:

(1) Incomplete recognition framework. The elements in the recognition framework may not cover every possible situation, but this situation is beyond the scope of this paper.
(2) The work condition of the sensor. Including the working environment factors (such as weather), the enemy interference (such as releasing of electronic interference), its own error (measurement noise, system error, etc.), all those may result in the sensor to determine the deviation, causing the conflict between evidence.

Through the above analysis, the low reliability of the sensor will exacerbate the conflict between evidence. Essentially, the combination of evidence theory follows the principle of minority majority. Therefore, the conflict can be used to characterize the reliability of the evidence. For evidence of high conflict and low reliability, we can reduce its impact by reducing its weight in the combination.

Scholars proposed many ways to measure the degree of conflict between evidences, such as conflict index K in D-S Evidence theory [2], Jousselme distance [23] (referred to as J), KL Distance [24] (referred to as KL), cosine of angle distance [25] (referred to as Cos) and so on. The following gives several examples of evidence distance in different BPA (Table 4).

As is shown, K-L distance is not normalized, failing to directly reflect the relative conflict between evidence, besides its distance value depends on the value of $\alpha$. Therefore, it is not suitable for measuring the conflict of evidence. In Case 1, the two pieces of evidence are the same. The conflict index K = 0.5, indicating that there is still conflict between evidence; evidence of Case 2 is complete different, which is considered as full of conflict, but J = 0.7071, indicating that the conflict is not so much. Relatively, the method of calculating the cosine distance between the evidence is the

**Table 4.** The distance between evidence

| Case | BPA | K | J | K-L $\alpha = 0.001$ | Cos |
|------|-----|---|---|------|-----|
| 1 | $m_1(A_1) = m_1(A_2) = 0.5$ <br> $m_1(A_1) = m_2(A_2) = 0.5$ | 0.5 | 0 | 0 | 1 |
| 2 | $m_1(A_1) = m_1(A_2) = 0.5$ <br> $m_2(A_3) = m_2(A_4) = 0.5$ | 1 | 0.7071 | 5.5493 | 0 |
| 3 | $m_1(A_1) = m_1(A_2) = 0.5$ <br> $m_2(A_2) = m_2(A_3) = 0.5$ | 0.75 | 0.5 | 9.5991 | 0.3536 |
| 4 | $m_1(A_1A_2) = m_1(A_2A_3) = 0.5$ <br> $m_2(A_3) = m_2(A_2A_3) = 0.5$ | 0.25 | 0.5 | 10.9490 | 0 |

most accurate. But it is not suitable for cases where the focal element is not a single subset like Case 4. So we need to fix the angel distance.

The cosine of angle distance on evidence is calculated in formula (9):

$$\begin{cases} cos(m_i, m_j) = \dfrac{m_i \cdot m_j^T}{\|m_i\| \|m_j\|} \\ \|m\| = \sqrt{m \cdot m^T} \end{cases} \tag{9}$$

The two pieces of evidence are considered as two vectors. When the two pieces of evidence are closer, the smaller the angle between them is, the larger the corresponding cosine value is. Obviously, for case 4, the two pieces of evidence have a certain degree of support for basic event $A_1$, $A_2$, $A_3$, so they have a certain degree of similarity. However, when calculating the inner product $m_1 \cdot m_2^T$, the corresponding coordinate components are not zero at the same time, resulting in the conclusion of complete conflict between evidence.

Here we take the method of mapping the BPA of non-single-subset focal points to the basic events to correct the evidence. If the support of evidence for the x-element event collection $\{A_{n1}, A_{n2}, \ldots, A_{nx}\}$ is $m(A_{n1}A_{n2}\ldots A_{nx}) = p$, and p is assigned to $A_{n1}, A_{n2}, \ldots, A_{nx}$ according to the principle of equal distribution:

$$m_i'(A_j) = \sum_{B_s \cap A_j = A_j} \frac{m_i(B_s)}{x_s} \tag{10}$$

Where $x_s$ denotes the number of basic events contained in the focal element $B_s$.

In this way, the BPA of all non-single-subset focal points is mapped to the basic events, and a new set of evidence $m_i'$ that contains only the basic event focal points corresponding to the original evidence is obtained. Calculate the cosine distance of new evidence $m_i'$. Since the cosine function is a monotonically decreasing function on $[0, \pi/2]$, the larger the inter-evidence conflict, the smaller the angle cosine obtained. In order to get the conclusion that is consistent with intuition, here we make an inverse cosine transform and do the normalization to get the angle distance between the evidence:

$$\theta(m_i, m_j) = \theta_{ij} = \frac{2}{\pi} arccos \frac{m_i' \cdot m_j'^T}{\|m_i'\| \|m_j'\|} \tag{11}$$

Such a method maps inaccurate basic probability assignments to basic events and changes the original evidence space, but it reflects the degree to which evidence sources support basic events and justifies the measurement of evidence-based conflicts. Compared with method in reference [16], this method is not only simple and easy to implement, but also it corrects the situation in reference [15] that cosine distance cannot be applied to a non-single subset of focal elements.

Assuming that the total number of evidence sources is n, an angular distance information matrix is constructed:

$$\Theta = \begin{pmatrix} \theta_{11} & \theta_{12} & \cdots & \theta_{1n} \\ \theta_{21} & \theta_{22} & \cdots & \theta_{2n} \\ \vdots & & \ddots & \vdots \\ \theta_{n1} & \theta_{n2} & \cdots & \theta_{nn} \end{pmatrix} \tag{12}$$

The sum of the angle distance between evidence $m_i$ and all the other evidence is:

$$T_i = \sum_{j=1, j\neq i}^{n} \theta_{ij} \tag{13}$$

$T_i$ reflects the degree of conflict between all evidence and evidence $m_i$ in the whole observation. The larger $T_i$ is, the greater conflict between $m_i$ and the overall evidence it reflects, indicating that the lower the reliability of the sensor is, and its weight in the fusion should be lower. The reliability weight here can be defined as:

$$t_i = 1 - \frac{T_i}{\sum_{i=1}^{n} T_i} \tag{14}$$

Using the weight of reliability to correct the evidence $\tilde{m}_i$, the result is as follows:

$$\check{m}_{B_a,i} = \check{m}_i(B_a) = \begin{cases} t_i \tilde{m}_{B_a,i}, & B_a \subset U \\ 1 - \sum t_i \tilde{m}_{B_a,i}, & B_a = \Omega \end{cases} \tag{15}$$

When $B_a \subset U$, $\tilde{m}_{B_a,i}$ is further corrected using the reliability weight and the unreliable part of the evidence: $1 - \sum t_i \tilde{m}_{B_a,i}$ is still assigned to the power set of frame $\Omega = 2^U$.

## 4.3    Evidence Combination Rules

Drawing on the ER rule, the weighted evidence $\widetilde{m_i}$ (i = 1, 2, ..., n) after processing are combined to obtain the final fusion result. Among them, $c_i$ in ER rule is obtained by the following formula:

$$c_i = \sum t_i \widetilde{m}_{B_a,i} \tag{16}$$

The algorithm flow chart is shown in Fig. 1.

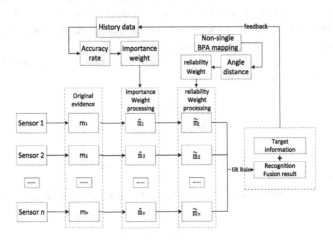

**Fig. 1.** Algorithm flow chart in this paper

# 5    Experimental Evaluation

Firstly we verify the effect of the ER rule on three paradoxes against the three examples in Sect. 2. Since we cannot measure the evidence conflict between two pieces of evidence, the evidence is only preprocessed with the importance weight and suppose the weight value be ρ. The results obtained are shown in the Table 5.

It can be seen from the results that the problems in the evidence theory of D-S can be well solved by preprocessing the evidence, indicating that the ER rule has good performance.

The following example of specific scenarios gives comparison with this method and methods in other paper. It is assumed that the targets in the same sea area are observed and identified independently by photoelectric camera ($m_1$), infrared camera ($m_2$), detection radar ($m_3$), SAR radar ($m_4$) and imaging spectrometer ($m_5$). The target type identification framework is U = {A, B, C}. The recognition results of each sensor or the BPA functions of 5 evidence sources are:

$m_1(A) = 0.5, m_1(B) = 0.2, m_1(C) = 0.3;$
$m_2(B) = 0.1, m_2(C) = 0.9;$
$m_3(A) = 0.55, m_3(B) = 0.1, m_3(A, C) = 0.35;$

**Table 5.** The fusion results using ER rule

| Case 1 | A | B | C | $\rho$ |
|---|---|---|---|---|
| $m_1$ | 0.99 | 0.01 | 0 | 0.8 |
| $m_2$ | 0 | 0.01 | 0.99 | 0.5 |
| $m_1 \oplus m_2$ | 0.7919 | 0.0101 | 0.1980 | – |
| Case 2 | A | B | C | $\rho$ |
| $m_1$ | 0.98 | 0.01 | 0.01 | 0.8 |
| $m_2$ | 0.01 | 0.01 | 0.98 | 0.5 |
| $m_1 \oplus m_2$ | 0.7815 | 0.0099 | 0.2086 | – |
| Case 3 | A | B | C | $\rho$ |
| $m_1$ | 0.5 | 0.3 | 0.2 | 0.8 |
| $m_2$ | 0.5 | 0.3 | 0.2 | 0.5 |
| $m_1 \oplus m_2$ | 0.5368 | 0.2853 | 0.1779 | – |

$m_4(A) = 0.6$, $m_4(B) = 0.1$, $m_4(A, B) = 0.3$;
$m_5(A) = 0.6$, $m_5(B) = 0.1$, $m_5(A, B, C) = 0.3$;

According to the experiments of target recognition of different sensors in reference [26–28], it is assumed that the historical accuracy rate of each sensor in ship recognition is: $\rho_1 = 0.85$; $\rho_2 = 0.95$; $\rho_3 = 0.80$; $\rho_4 = 0.85$; $\rho_5 = 0.65$.

The method of this paper, the classical Dempster's rule [2] and the Sun Quan's method, Han Deqiang's method, Murphy's method and Song Yafei's method in reference [4, 10, 11] and [15] are used and the results are shown as following. Among them, in Han Deqiang's method, the value of $\alpha$ is 2 according to reference [10].

It can be seen that the traditional Dempster's rule has no effect on the combination of evidence because evidence 2 has 0 support for target A and target C, The degree of support for target B is not high, but the final decision is B. Sun Quan's method draw the final conclusion as uncertain, indicating that it is not easy to eliminate the impact of evidence of conflict. The remaining five methods all conclude that the fusion result is A, which shows that these methods may not be affected by the evidence 2 of high conflict and get a consistent recognition result after fusion. However, the result of Han Deqiang's method is related to the order of fusion of evidences. In the observation, the sensors are independent and the order of fusion is random. We could not draw a consistent conclusion using Han's method. In addition, the result of Han's method is related to parameter $\alpha$, The parameter $\alpha$ is determined according to experience, with a certain subjectivity. The Murphy's method eliminates the effects of conflicting evidence by simple averages, and Song Yafei improved it by considering the credibility and the degree of falsehood of evidence, which converges faster. But in fact, they all used the conflicting among the same evidence and the conclusion is biased in favor of events with a larger probability of basic probabilities, even if the basic probabilities of the two events differ slightly, which may lead to irrational conclusions. The method proposed in this paper gives a way to measure the importance of evidence and the weight of reliability, and through the ER rule processing, the conclusion will be biased toward the final recognition result A when the third piece of evidence is added (Table 6).

**Table 6.** The fusion results of different methods

| Method | $m_1 \oplus m_2$ | $m_1 \oplus m_2 \oplus m_3$ | $m_1 \oplus m_2 \oplus m_3 \oplus m_4$ | $m_1 \oplus m_2 \oplus m_3 \oplus m_4 \oplus m_5$ | Fusion conclusion |
|---|---|---|---|---|---|
| Dempster's rule | $m(A) = 0$ <br> $m(B) = 0.0690$ <br> $m(C) = 0.9310$ | $m(A) = 0$ <br> $m(B) = 0.0207$ <br> $m(C) = 0.9793$ | $m(A) = 0$ <br> $m(B) = 1$ <br> $m(C) = 0$ | $m(A) = 0$ <br> $m(B) = 1$ <br> $m(C) = 0$ | **B** |
| Sun Quan's method | $m(A) = 0.0873$ <br> $m(B) = 0.0724$ <br> $m(C) = 0.4793$ <br> $m(X) = 0.3610$ | $m(A) = 0.1730$ <br> $m(B) = 0.0659$ <br> $m(C) = 0.2922$ <br> $m(AC) = 0.0596$ <br> $m(X) = 0.4093$ | $m(A) = 0.2339$ <br> $m(B) = 0.0727$ <br> $m(C) = 0.1708$ <br> $m(AC) = 0.0496$ <br> $m(AB) = 0.0425$ <br> $m(X) = 0.4305$ | $m(A) = 02656$ <br> $m(B) = 0.0711$ <br> $m(C) = 0.1417$ <br> $m(AC) = 0.0413$ <br> $m(AB) = 0.0354$ <br> $m(ABC) = 0.0354$ <br> $m(X) = 0.4095$ | – |
| Han Deqiang's method | $m(A) = 0.3732$ <br> $m(B) = 0.0895$ <br> $m(C) = 0.5373$ | $m(A) = 0.4543$ <br> $m(B) = 0.0384$ <br> $m(C) = 0.5073$ | $m(A) = 0.5802$ <br> $m(B) = 0.0216$ <br> $m(C) = 0.4080$ | $m(A) = 0.7143$ <br> $m(B) = 0.0087$ <br> $m(C) = 0.2770$ | **A** |
| Murphy's method | $m(A) = 0.1404$ <br> $m(B) = 0.0506$ <br> $m(C) = 0.8090$ | $m(A) = 0.4163$ <br> $m(B) = 0.0099$ <br> $m(C) = 0.5672$ <br> $m(AC) = 0.0066$ | $m(A) = 0.6253$ <br> $m(B) = 0.0677$ <br> $m(C) = 0.2808$ <br> $m(AC) = 0.0111$ <br> $m(AB) = 0.0151$ | $m(A) = 0.7427$ <br> $m(B) = 0.0455$ <br> $m(C) = 0.1877$ <br> $m(AC) = 0.0085$ <br> $m(AB) = 0.0093$ <br> $m(ABC) = 0.0063$ | **A** |
| Song Yafei's method | $m(A) = 0.1404$ <br> $m(B) = 0.0506$ <br> $m(c) = 0.8090$ | $m(A) = 0.4286$ <br> $m(B) = 0.0368$ <br> $m(C) = 0.5064$ <br> $m(AC) = 0.0272$ | $m(A) = 0.7189$ <br> $m(B) = 0.0380$ <br> $m(C) = 0.1787$ <br> $m(AC) = 0.0016$ <br> $m(AB) = 0.0028$ | $m(A) = 0.8018$ <br> $m(B) = 0.0658$ <br> $m(C) = 0.0899$ <br> $m(AC) = 0.0163$ <br> $m(AB) = 0.0199$ <br> $m(ABC) = 0.0063$ | **A** |
| Method in this paper | $m(A) = 0.2399$ <br> $m(B) = 0.1224$ <br> $m(C) = 0.4321$ <br> $m(\Omega) = 0.2056$ | $m(A) = 0.4143$ <br> $m(B) = 0.0807$ <br> $m(C) = 0.3341$ <br> $m(AC) = 0.0804$ <br> $m(\Omega) = 0.0905$ | $m(A) = 0.6907$ <br> $m(B) = 0.0762$ <br> $m(C) = 0.1341$ <br> $m(AC) = 0.0323$ <br> $m(AB) = 0.0304$ <br> $m(\Omega) = 0.0363$ | $m(A) = 0.7953$ <br> $m(B) = 0.0609$ <br> $m(C) = 0.0968$ <br> $m(AC) = 0.0215$ <br> $m(AB) = 0.0105$ <br> $m(ABC) = 0.0150$ | **A** |

It can be found that with the addition of evidence, the support of 5 methods to Event A is increasing, of which Song Yafei's method and the method proposed in this paper have the fastest convergence rate. However, Song Yafei's algorithm produced a new body of evidence in the fusion and added redundant information, involving the calculation of $2^N \times 2^N$ dimensional matrices when determining the weight of evidence, resulting in a huge increase in computation. As the number of focal cells increases, the complexity increases exponentially, and the algorithm complexity is $O(d2N)$ while the complexity of algorithm in this paper is $O(dN)$. With the increase of the number of focal elements, the computational complexity increases linearly, which is much lower than that of Song Yafei's method. Therefore, it is more suitable for engineering implementation.

# 6 Conclusion

On the application background of multi-sensor target recognition, this paper presents an objective calculation method of evidence importance and reliability weight in ER rule. The importance weights of evidence sources represent their objective property and are measured by history recognition accuracy, which is a variable regulated by constant feedback. The reliability weight of evidence is evaluated by the conflicting between pieces of evidence, which is measured by the mapped angle distance between evidence. The recognition results of each sensor are fused by ER rules. The simulation results show that the proposed method is applicable to a wide range of applications. It is not only applicable to the case with single-point focal cells but also to the case that the recognition results include non-single focal elements. In addition, the convergence speed of this method is fast and its computational complexity is relatively low, which makes it more suitable for engineering implementation.

# References

1. He, Y., Wang, G., Guan, X.: Information Fusion Theory with Application, 3rd edn. Electronic Industry Press, Beijing (2016)
2. Dempster, A.P.: Upper and lower probabilities induced by a multi-valued mapping. Ann. Math. Stat. **38**, 325–339 (1967)
3. Han, D., Yang, Y., Han, C.: Advances in D-S evidence theory and related discussions. Control Decis. **29**(1), 1–11 (2014)
4. Yang, J.-B., Xu, D.-L.: Evidential reasoning rule for evidence combination. Artif. Intell. **205**, 1–29 (2013)
5. Shafer, G.: A Mathematical Theory of Evidence. Princeton University Press, Princeton (1976)
6. Zadeh, L.: A simple view of the Dempster-Shafer theory of evidence and its implication for the rule of combination. AI Magaz. **7**(2), 85–90 (1986)
7. Li, J., Cheng, Y., Liang, Y.: Research of D-ST algorithm based on local conflict distribution strategy. Control Decis. **25**(10), 1485–1488 (2010)
8. Deng, Y., Wang, D., Li, Q.: A new method to analyze evidence conflict. Control Theory Appl. **28**(6), 839–844 (2011)
9. Yager, R.R.: On the D-S framework and new combination rules. Inf. Sci. **41**(2), 93–138 (1987)
10. Sun, Q., Ye, X., Gu, W.: A new combination rules of evidence theory. Acta Electronica Sinica **28**(8), 117–119 (2000)
11. Murphy, C.K.: Combining belief functions when evidence conflicts. Decis. Supp. Syst. **29**(1), 1–9 (2000)
12. Guan, X., Yi, X., Sun, X.: Efficient fusion approach for conflicting evidence. J. Tsinghua Univ. (Sci. Tech.) **49**(1), 138–141 (2009)
13. Lin, Y., Wang, C., Ma, C.: A new combination method for multisensor conflict information. J. Supercomput. **72**, 2874–2890 (2016)
14. Deng, Y., et al.: Combining belief functions based on distance of evidence. Decis. Support Syst. **38**(3), 489–493 (2004)
15. Song, Y.-f., Wang, X.-d., Lei, L.: Measurement of evidence conflict based on correlation coefficient. J. Commun. **35**(5), 95–100 (2014)

16. Wang, L., Mao, Q.-h., Mao, Y.-f.: Weighted evidence combination based on degree of credibility and certainty. J. Commun. **38**(1), 83–88 (2017)
17. Li, W., Guo, K.: Combination rules of D-S evidence theory and conflict problem. Syst. Eng. Theory Pract. **8**(30), 1422–1432 (2010)
18. Yang, J.B., Xu, D.L.: On the evidential reasoning algorithm for multiple attribute decision analysis under uncertainty. IEEE Trans. Syst. Man Cybern. Part A Syst. Hum. **32**(3), 289–304 (2002)
19. Ke, X., Ma, L., Li, Z.: Property research and approach modification of evidential reasoning rule. Inf. Control **45**(2), 165–170 (2016)
20. Li, X.-D., Wang, Q.-Q., Wang, F.-Y.: A method of conflictive evidence combination based on the Markov chain. Acta Automatica Sinica **41**(5), 915–926 (2015)
21. Liu, X., Deng, J.: Improved D-S method based on conflict evidence correction. J. Electron. Meas. Instrum. **31**(9), 1499–1506 (2017)
22. Jousselme, A.L., Grenier, D., Bosse, E.: A new distance between two bodies of evidence. Inf. Fusion **2**(1), 91–101 (2001)
23. Li, Y., Guo, Y., Yang, Y.: Identification and application of the evidence conflict based on K-L information distance. Syst. Eng. Theory Pract. **34**(8), 2071–2077 (2014)
24. Wang, X., Yang, F.: A kind of evidence combination rule in conflict. J. Missile Guidance **27**(5), 255–257 (2007)
25. Hao, Z.-w., Wu, Y., Zhang, J.-d.: Aerial target identification based on bp neural networks and improved combination evidence rule. Electron. Opt. Control **21**(12), 36–40 (2014)
26. Liu, S.: Research on infrared ship target recognition in the background of air and sea. Master's thesis of University of Electronic Science and Technology (2011)
27. Yong, S.: Research on ship recognition with image processing. Comput. Digit. Eng. **43**(7), 1207–1211 (2015)
28. Han, D.-q., Han, C.-z., Deng, Y.: Weighted combination of conflicting evidence based on evidence variance. Acta Electronica Sinica **39**(3), 153–157 (2011)

# Application of SVM and PSO Arithmetic in Deep Space Exploration Data Analysis

Mingxing Zhou[✉], Jianfeng Zhang, and Fangyong Lan

Panda Electronics Group Co., Ltd., Nanjing, China
mail-zmx@163.com

**Abstract.** A method of SVM optimized by using the PSO arithmetic is presented to solve nonlinear regression estimation problems in deep space exploration data analysis. This method is used to process the microwave brightness temperature (TB) data acquired by the CE-1 satellite. Firstly, the SVM regression model is established and some parameters of which are optimized by using the PSO arithmetic. Then, by training the TB data with the optimized SVM model, the relationship between the TB from four frequency channels and the lunar hour angle is established. Finally, the distribution maps of TB from four frequency channels on the entire lunar surface in certain short period are obtained. The error analysis indicates that the results of this paper can be used in the further study of lunar regolith depth. Furthermore, the abnormal data among the measured data can be found out and modified by using this method.

**Keywords:** SVM · PSO · TB data · CE-1 · Hour angle · Data analysis

## 1 Introduction

SVM (Support Vector Machine), developed by Vapnik [1], is gaining popularity due to many attractive features and promising empirical performance. Originally, SVM is developed for pattern recognition problems. Recently, SVM has been extended to solve nonlinear regression estimation, and represented splendiferous learning ability [2]. It can better solve nonlinear and small sample size problem.

In Chinese lunar exploration project, a microwave radiometer (MRM) with frequency channels of 3.0 GHz, 7.8 GHz, 19.35 GHz, and 37 GHz was loaded on CE-1 satellite. Its goal is to detect the thickness of lunar regolith from the lunar surface TB data obtained by the MRM. This work aroused many scientists' interest [3–5].

The existed map of TB distribution on the lunar surface were mostly projected by the TB data in a long period of a lunar day (29.53 earth days). However, the TB value at different time is extremely different even at a certain position, as well as at higher frequency channel, the more differences of TB value. After analyzing the 2C level TB data, it reveals that the distribution of TB obtained by using the data in a short period can be better to stand for the characters of lunar surface. In addition, the process of inverse the lunar regolith depth can be simplified. However, the TB data obtained by the CE-1's MRM could not cover all the period of a lunar day. Thus, the entire lunar surface TB distribution in a certain short period can not be obtained directly from the 2C level TB data. Aiming at this fact, this paper attempts using SVM and Particle

© Springer Nature Singapore Pte Ltd. 2019
Q. Yu (Ed.): SINC 2018, CCIS 972, pp. 229–235, 2019.
https://doi.org/10.1007/978-981-13-5937-8_23

swarm optimization (PSO) arithmetic [6] regress the 2C level TB to obtain the entire lunar surface TB distribution in a certain short period.

## 2   SVM for Regression Estimation

The mathematical description of the regression problem as: according to the given training set $T = \{(x_1, y_1), \cdots (x_l, y_l)\}$, where $x_i \in R^n$ is input, $y_i \in R$ is output, $i = 1, \ldots, l$ is the number of samples, seeking a function $f(x)$ in $R^n$ to infer the output $y$ that correspond to any input $x$ [7]. For linear situation, $f(x) = w \cdot x + b$ is used to fit the samples. For nonlinear situation, the input space is mapped to a high dimensional feature space by using nonlinear transformation $\phi(\cdot)$. Then, in this feature space, using linear function $f(x) = w \cdot \phi(x) + b$ fits samples. Thus, the nonlinear problem is transformed into linear problem. This problem is equivalent to the linear constrained quadratic programming optimization problem as following:

$$\min[\frac{1}{2}\|w\|^2 + C\sum_{i=1}^{l} (\xi_i + \xi_i^*)] \quad st. \begin{cases} y_i - ((w \cdot x_i) + b) \le \varepsilon + \xi_i^* \\ ((w \cdot x_i) + b - y_i) \le \varepsilon + \xi_i \\ \xi_i \xi_i^* \ge 0 \end{cases} \quad (1)$$

Where, minimizing $1/2\|w\|^2$ means minimizing VC dimension. $\varepsilon$ is fitting error. $\xi_i$ and $\xi_i^*$ are slack variables. $C$ is the penalty factor, $C > 0$. Thus, the optimization problem described above embodies the structural risk minimization principle. Using Lagrange multiplier method, the dual optimization problem is obtained [2]:

$$\min_{\alpha,\alpha^*} \frac{1}{2} \sum_{i=1}^{l} \sum_{j=1}^{l} (\alpha_i - \alpha_i^*)(\alpha_j - \alpha_j^*) K(x_i, x_j) + \varepsilon \sum_{i=1}^{l} (\alpha_i + \alpha_i^*) - \sum_{i=1}^{l} y_i(\alpha_i - \alpha_i^*)$$

$$st. \sum_{i=1}^{l} (\alpha_i - \alpha_i^*) = 0, 0 \le \alpha_i, \alpha_i^* \le C, i = 1, \cdots, l$$

$$(2)$$

Where $\alpha_i, \alpha_i^*$ are Lagrange multipliers; $K(x_i, x) = \exp\left(-\|x - x_i\|^2/\sigma^2\right)$ is kernel function. The regression function is obtained from the optimal solution of this problem:

$$f(x) = \sum_{i=1}^{l} (\alpha_i - \alpha_i^*) K(x_i, x) + b \quad (3)$$

## 3   Modeling for CE-1 TB Data Using SVM and PSO

### 3.1   Establishing the Regression Model by Using SVM and PSO

According to the information provided by the 2C level data, the corresponding time on the moon can be calculated. To describe this time information more accurate, the "hour angle" [8] is introduced in this paper. Thus, when the moon rotated a period, the hour angle at the observation site increased from 0° to 360°. The sunrise time is selected as the start time of a lunar day (hour angle is 0°) in this paper.

As mentioned above, the existing TB data could not cover all the period of a lunar day. Therefore, if the TB data is lacked in a certain location at a certain time, the TB value should be regressed by fitting the TB data at other times in this place. By calculating the hour angle information of all the data sample sites, it indicates that the sampling time mainly concentrates on the period near the noon (hour angle is 90°) and midnight (hour angle is 270°). To obtain minimum fitting error, selecting lunar noon or midnight to obtain the entire lunar surface TB distribution is more reasonable than selecting other time.

To obtain the entire lunar surface TB distribution in a certain short period, the appropriate projection gridding should be decided firstly. According to the resolution of the MRM, $360 \times 360$ is selected as the size of the projection gridding. Because SVM is suitable for resolve nonlinear and small sample size problems, it is used to predict the TB value at certain time in each gridding range of lunar surface. Some parameters such as $\varepsilon$, $C$ and $\sigma$ have very important influences on the training result of the regression model. In this paper, $\varepsilon$ is given value $10^{-3}$, the optimum value of $C$ and $\sigma$ are selected by using PSO arithmetic.

PSO derives from the research for the movement of organisms in a bird flocking or fish schooling [6]. When solving optimization problems, the solution of each problem is regard as a particle (point) in d-dimensional search space. Each particle moves in the search space with a velocity and is characterized by a value of fitness which indicates how well the particle is doing in the search process. The location of the particle at which it has attained the best fitness is denoted by "pbest". Similarly, "gbest" denotes the best location attained among all "pbest". To find optimal solution, each particle moves in the direction of its previously best position (pbest) and its best global position (gbest). For each particle $i$ and dimension $j$, the velocity and position of particles can be updated by the following equations:

$$
\begin{aligned}
v_{ij}^{t+1} &= w \cdot v_{ij}^t + c_1 r_1 \cdot \left( pbest_{ij}^t - p_{ij}^t \right) + c_2 r_2 (gbest_{ij}^t - p_{ij}^t) \\
p_{ij}^{t+1} &= p_{ij}^t + \beta \cdot v_{ij}^t
\end{aligned}
\tag{4}
$$

Where $t$ is the evolutionary generation. $v_{ij}$ is the velocity of particle $i$ on dimension $j$. $p_{ij}$ is the position of particle $i$ on dimension $j$. The inertia weight coefficient "w" is used to control the velocity updating. $r_1$ and $r_2$ are random numerical values in [0, 1]. $\beta$ is usually set to 1. $c_1$ and $c_2$ are positive "acceleration factor". In the process of optimizing the parameters of SVM model with PSO, the particles include $C$ and $\sigma$. The process is described as following:

Step 1:    Randomly generate "N" particles, and initialize their velocities.
Step 2:    Train SVM model with training set, and evaluate the fitness of each particle. In this paper, the $k$-fold cross validation is used to evaluate fitness.
Step 3:    Update pbest and gbest according to fitness.
Step 4:    Update the velocity and position of each particle according to formula (4).

*Step 5:*    Repeat step 2–4 until the variety of the optimal solution less than the set value, then, stop update and output the optimal $C$ and $\sigma$.

After above optimization processes finished, the SVM regression model should be retained with the optimal $C$ and $\sigma$ for each grid.

## 3.2    Errors Analysis

To ensure the accuracy of regression result, the parameters $\varepsilon$, $C$ and $\sigma$ are optimized by PSO in this paper. the regression accuracy of each pixel grid is decided by the quality of the measured TB data in the range of corresponding projection grid. Figure 1 shows the comparison of the measured TB values obtained from four frequency channels with the regression values at the Apollo 11 landing site. This is an example to explain the errors between the measured TB values and the regression results by the SVM model which optimized by PSO.

It should be noticed that the two TB values pointed by arrow are measured values of 3 GHz and 7.8 GHz at the hour angle 226°. According to the variation character of the TB [9], there should not be a jumping change between the TB values of the adjacent time. But, the two measured values pointed by arrows are obviously much less than the other measured values of the adjacent time. So, it can be judged that the two measured values pointed by arrows are abnormal values.

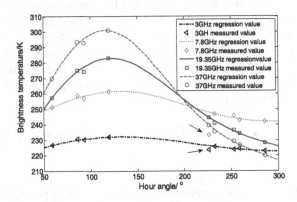

**Fig. 1.** The comparison of the real values of TB with the regression values.

Except for the two abnormal values, the errors between the measured values and regression values are small enough. The mean errors between the measured values and the regression values are 0.23 K, 0.66 K, 0.66 K and 0.72 K respectively at the frequency channel of 3 GHz, 7.8 GHz, 19.35 GHz and 37 GHz. In 3 GHz channel, the error is the least. It is less than the temperature resolution of the MRM. In the process of inversing the lunar regolith thickness, the TB data of 3 GHz are mainly used. So, in the future work, the TB distribution at certain time obtained by the method in this paper can be tried to estimate the distribution of the lunar regolith thickness. In addition, the error points of measured values can be found out and modified since the TB value in a localized region could not change abruptly.

## 4   The Distribution of the Microwave Brightness Temperature on the Moon

As described above, the lunar surface is divided into $360 \times 360$ grids to project the TB data on the global moon. Within the range of each grid, by using the optimized SVM regression model, the relationship between the TB of the 4 channels and the defined time angle is obtained. Thus, the TB of each grid at a specific time is obtained. After projection, the global TB distribution at a specific time is obtained. Figure 2 shows the distribution of TB from 37 GHz channels at lunar noon.

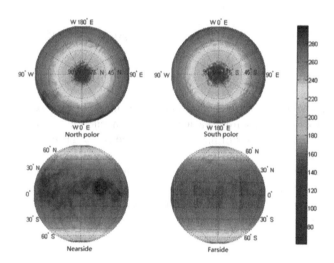

**Fig. 2.** TB distributions of 37 GHz on the entire lunar surface at noon

Figure 3 is the projection maps of the TB form 37 GHz channel, which ranged in the 45° south latitude to 45° north latitude on the lunar surface. (a) represents at the lunar noon (the hour angle range is $90 \pm 1°$) while (b) stands for at midnight of the moon (the hour angle range is $270 \pm 1°$). In the figure, the TB projection displays more details. The relationships between these details and the lunar topography, the iron and titanium contents of the lunar regolith, temperature and density need further study.

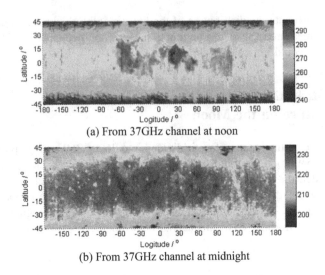

(a) From 37GHz channel at noon

(b) From 37GHz channel at midnight

**Fig. 3.** 37 GHz TB distributions ranged in N45°–S45°.

## 5 Conclusion

By using the SVM regression method and PSO, the entire lunar surface TB distribution map with $360 \times 360$ pixels from each frequency channel at certain short period is obtained. Some characteristics of the TB are revealed in the TB distribution map. The error analysis indicates that the regression errors are small enough. Therefore, the results of this paper can be used to inverse the lunar regolith depth in the future work. Furthermore, the abnormal data points included in the 2C level TB data can be found out in the TB projection maps and modified. This method can be widely applied to solve the regression problem in deep space exploration data analysis.

## References

1. Vapnik, V.: The Nature of Statistical Learning Theory. Information Science and Statistics. Springer, New York (1995). https://doi.org/10.1007/978-1-4757-3264-1
2. Du, S.-X., Wu, T.-J.: Support vector machines for regression. J. Syst. Simul. **15**(11), 1580–1663 (2003)
3. Zheng, Y.C., Bian, W., Su, Y., et al.: Brightness temperature distribution of the moon: result from Chinese Chang'E-1 Lunar Orbiter. In: Goldschmidt Conference 2009, 21–26 June 2009 (2009)
4. Fa, W., Jin, Y.: Analysis of microwave brightness temperature of lunar surface and inversion of regolith layer thickness: primary results of Chang-E 1 multi-channel radiometer observation. Sci. China Ser. F Inf. Sci. **53**(1), 168–181 (2010)
5. Chan, K.L., et al.: Lunar regolith thermal behavior revealed by Chang'E-1 microwave brightness temperature data. Earth Planet. Sci. Lett. **295**, 287–291 (2010)

6. Pedrycz, W., Park, B.J., Pizzi, N.J.: Identifying core sets of discriminatory features using particle swarm optimization. Expert Syst. Appl. **36**, 4610–4616 (2009)
7. Deng, N., Tian, Y.: New Method for Data Mining: Support Vector Machine, pp. 77–78. Science Press, Beijing (2006)
8. Xi, X., Wang, W., Gao, Y.: Fundamentals of Near-Earth Spacecraft Orbit, pp. 20–36. National Defense University Press, Changsha (2003)
9. Zhou, M.X., Zhou, J.J., Wang, F.: Analysis and simulation of microwave brightness temperature on lunar surface. In: 60th International Astronautical Congress (2009)

# Author Index

Printed in the United States
By Bookmasters